THE 2,548 BEST THINGS ANYBODY EVER SAID

The 2,548

BEST THINGS

ANYBODY

EVER SAID

Robert Byrne

GALAHAD BOOKS
NEW YORK

First Galahad Books edition published in 1996.

Galahad Books
A division of BBS Publishing Corporation
386 Park Avenue South
New York, NY 10016

Galahad Books is a registered trademark of BBS Publishing Corporation.

Published by arrangement with Simon and Schuster, Inc.

Library of Congress Catalog Card Number: 96-77430

ISBN: 0-88365-960-3

Printed in the United States of America.

CONTENTS

Book I

The 637 Best Things Anybody Ever Said

Book II

The Other 637 Best Things Anybody Ever Said

Book III

The Third—And Possibly the Best—
637 Best Things Anybody Ever Said

Book IV

The Fourth—And By Far the Most Recent—
637 Best Things Anybody Ever Said

THE 637
BEST THINGS

ANYBODY EVER SAID

Contents

Introduction

PART ONE

God, Life, Death, Murder, Stupidity, Narcissism, Birth, Youth, Sex, Love, Marriage, Horses, Greeks, Romans, Politics, Literature, Drink, Presidents, and a great deal more

PART TWO

Miscellaneous

Sources, References, and Notes

Index of Authors

Index of Subjects and Key Words

Introduction

Many of the best things ever said were, in fact, written. Aside from that, the title of this book is accurate.

The quotations are arranged with readers rather than the alphabet in mind. By readers I mean people who normally start at the front of a book and digest the pages consecutively; I don't mean those who intend to turn to a given subject heading in hopes of finding a smart remark. There are no subject headings.

The arrangement is intended to have a cumulative effect, with an occasional interactive juxtaposition. This is especially true in Part One, where the entries are grouped under loosely defined themes. In Part Two the sequence is governed by subjective criteria that even I don't fully understand.

Most collections of quotations strive for such things as comprehensiveness, balance, and fairness. Not this one.

No attempt is made to cite every major author, authority, and humorist.

No attempt is made to include a quote from every topic or from every epoch.

While it is undeniably interesting and perhaps even important to discover that Martin Luther (1483–1546) was the first to point out that it depends on whose ox is gored, no quotes were included merely to teach history or establish priorities.

The book is simply a compilation of the best things anybody ever said. The entries are characterized by their insight, surprise, wit, pith, or punch. Because surprise was one of the elements I sought, some great remarks were left out on the grounds of excessive familiarity. No sense giving you a tour of your own living room. If you do spot some old friends here, I can only hope that you will be glad to see them again.

Some quotations take on added point when their age is known. For that reason and as a sop to scholars I have included birth and death dates for historical figures. Where no dates are given, it can be assumed that the person is either still alive or only lately dead.

Some may wonder why there are 637 quotations instead of, say, 631 or 643. The reason is that I didn't want any padding and I didn't want to leave any good ones out. I didn't know that the best things anybody ever said amounted to 637 until after I had sifted through the world's literature, oral traditions, and wisecracks.

But who, after all, can say what is "best"? I can. So can you. What follows are my choices. Now it may be that you have said, heard, written, or read something that merits inclusion in a cream-of-the-crop collection like this but which is missing because for one reason or another you simply have never called it to my attention. Whose fault is that? I'm as close as your mailbox.

Robert Byrne

PART ONE

---◈---

God
Life
Death
Murder
Stupidity
Narcissism
Birth
Youth
Sex
Love
Marriage
Horses
Greeks
Romans
Politics
Literature
Drink
Presidents
and a great deal more

1

Why don't you get a haircut? You look like a chrysanthemum. *P. G. Wodehouse (1811–1975)*

2

How can I believe in God when just last week I got my tongue caught in the roller of an electric typewriter? *Woody Allen*

3

If I had been present at creation, I would have given some useful hints.

Alfonso the Wise (1221–1284)

4

The gods play games with men as balls.

Titus Maccius Plautus (254?–184 B.C.*)*

5

He was a wise man who invented God.

Plato (427?–348? B.C.*)*

6

Plato is a bore. *Nietzsche (1844–1900)*

7

It is the final proof of God's omnipotence that he need not exist in order to save us. *Peter De Vries*

8

Man is a god in ruins.

Ralph Waldo Emerson (1803–1882)

9

God has always been hard on the poor.

Jean Paul Marat (1743–1793)

1 0

Man is certainly stark mad. He cannot make a worm, and yet he will be making gods by dozens.

Montaigne (1553–1592)

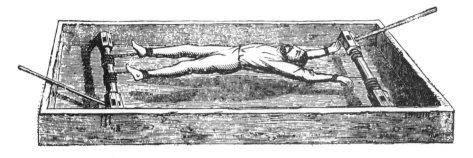

1 1

The good Lord never gives you more than you can handle. Unless you die of something.

Guindon cartoon caption

1 2

If I had been the Virgin Mary, I would have said "No." *Margaret "Stevie" Smith (1902–1971)*

1 3

Few people can be happy unless they hate some other person, nation, or creed.

Bertrand Russell (1872–1970)

1 4

Religions change; beer and wine remain.

Hervey Allen (1889–1949)

15

The chicken probably came before the egg because it is hard to imagine God wanting to sit on an egg.

Unknown

16

In England there are sixty different religions and only one sauce. *Francesco Caracciolo (1752–1799)*

17

Living with a saint is more grueling than being one.

Robert Neville

18

He was of the faith chiefly in the sense that the church he currently did not attend was Catholic.

Kingsley Amis

19

Everybody should believe in something; I believe I'll have another drink. *Unknown*

20

Under certain circumstances, profanity provides a relief denied even to prayer. *Mark Twain (1835–1910)*

21

The trouble with born-again Christians is that they are an even bigger pain the second time around.

Herb Caen

22

I'm astounded by people who want to "know" the universe when it's hard enough to find your way around Chinatown. *Woody Allen*

2 3

It is better to know some of the questions than all of the answers. *James Thurber (1894–1961)*

2 4

It is only possible to live happily ever after on a day to day basis. *Margaret Bonnano*

2 5

I have a new philosophy. I'm only going to dread one day at a time. *Charles Schulz*

2 6

I have a simple philosophy. Fill what's empty. Empty what's full. Scratch where it itches.

Alice Roosevelt Longworth (1884–1980)

2 7

I know the answer! The answer lies within the heart of all mankind! The answer is twelve? I think I'm in the wrong building. *Charles Schulz*

2 8

Life is like an overlong drama through which we sit being nagged by the vague memories of having read the reviews. *John Updike*

2 9

There is more to life than increasing its speed.
Mahatma Gandhi (1869–1948)

3 0

Life is like playing a violin in public and learning the instrument as one goes on.
Samuel Butler (1835–1902)

3 1

Life is what happens while you are making other plans. *John Lennon (1940–1980)*

3 2

Life is a God-damned, stinking, treacherous game and nine hundred and ninety-nine men out of a thousand are bastards.

Theodore Dreiser (1871–1945)
quoting an unnamed newspaper editor

3 3

There is no cure for birth and death save to enjoy the interval.   *George Santayana (1863–1952)*

3 4

Why is it that we rejoice at a birth and grieve at a funeral? It is because we are not the person involved.
Mark Twain (1835–1910)

3 5

The cost of living is going up and the chance of living is going down.   *Flip Wilson*

3 6

Is life worth living? That depends on the liver.
Unknown

3 7

Dying is one of the few things that can be done as easily lying down.   *Woody Allen*

38

I'm not afraid to die. I just don't want to be there
when it happens. *Woody Allen*

39

Perhaps there is no life after death . . . there's just
Los Angeles. *Rick Anderson*

40

Death is nature's way of saying "Howdy."

Unknown

41

The best way to get praise is to die. *Italian proverb*

42

There is no such thing as inner peace. There is only
nervousness and death. *Fran Liebowitz*

43

In the long run we are all dead.

John Maynard Keynes (1883–1946)

44

The patient is not likely to recover who makes the
doctor his heir. *Thomas Fuller (1608–1661)*

45

After I'm dead I'd rather have people ask why I have no monument than why I have one.

Cato the Elder (234–149 B.C.*)*

46

For three days after death hair and fingernails continue to grow but phone calls taper off.

Johnny Carson

47

I wonder if anybody ever reached the age of thirty-five in New England without wanting to kill himself.

Barrett Wendell (1855–1921)

48

I have had just about all I can take of myself.

S. N. Behrman (1893–1973) on reaching the age of 75

49

When you don't have any money, the problem is food. When you have money, it's sex. When you have both, it's health. If everything is simply jake, then you're frightened of death.

J. P. Donleavy

50

Most people would sooner die than think; in fact, they do so. *Bertrand Russell (1872–1970)*

51

Early one June morning in 1872 I murdered my father—an act which made a deep impression on me at the time. *Ambrose Bierce (1842–1914)*

52

One murder makes a villain, millions a hero.
Beilby Porteus (1731–1808)

53

If once a man indulges himself in murder, very soon he comes to think little of robbing; and from robbing he next comes to drinking and Sabbath-breaking, and from that to incivility and procrastination.
Thomas De Quincey (1785–1859)

54

A murderer is one who is presumed to be innocent until proven insane. *Unknown*

55

Either this man is dead or my watch has stopped.
Groucho Marx (1890–1977)

56

There is no money in poetry, but then there is no poetry in money, either. *Robert Graves*

5 7

This poem will never reach its destination.

Voltaire (1694–1778) on Rousseau's
Ode to Posterity

5 8

I hope that one or two immortal lyrics will come out of all this tumbling around.

Poet Louise Bogan (1898–1970) on her love affair with poet Theodore Roethke

5 9

I write poetry not for publication but merely to kill time. Airplanes are a good place to write poetry and then firmly throw it away. My collected works are mostly on the vomit bags of Pan American and TWA.

Charles McCabe

6 0

The writing of more than 75 poems in any fiscal year should be punishable by a fine of $500.

Ed Sanders

6 1

Show me a poet and I'll show you a shit.

A. J. Liebling (1904–1963)

6 2

The human mind treats a new idea the way the body treats a strange protein; it rejects it.

Biologist P. B. Medawar

6 3

The intelligent man finds almost everything ridiculous, the sensible man hardly anything.

Goethe (1749–1832)

6 4

The difference between genius and stupidity is that genius has its limits. *Unknown*

6 5

The only reason some people get lost in thought is because it's unfamiliar territory. *Paul Fix*

6 6

Only the mediocre are always at their best.

Jean Giraudoux (1882–1944)

6 7

I'm going to speak my mind because I have nothing to lose. *S. I. Hayakawa*

6 8

I live in the crowd of jollity, not so much to enjoy
company as to shun myself.

Samuel Johnson (1709–1784)

6 9

For every ten jokes, thou hast got an hundred
enemies.   *Laurence Sterne (1713–1768)*

7 0

Wit is educated insolence.   *Aristotle (384–322* B.C.*)*

7 1

Seriousness is the only refuge of the shallow.

Oscar Wilde (1854–1900)

7 2

He who laughs, lasts.

Mary Pettibone Poole (c. 1938)

7 3

Man: An animal [whose] . . . chief occupation is
extermination of other animals and his own species,
which, however, multiplies with such insistent rapidity
as to infest the whole habitable earth and Canada.

Ambrose Bierce (1842–1914)

74

Woman: An animal . . . having a rudimentary susceptibility to domestication . . . The species is the most widely distributed of all beasts of prey. . . . The woman is omnivorous and can be taught not to talk. *Ambrose Bierce (1842–1914)*

75

Cabbage: A . . . vegetable about as large and wise as a man's head. *Ambrose Bierce (1842–1914)*

76

Memorial Service: Farewell party for someone who has already left. *RB*

77

Eunuch: A man who has had his works cut out for him. *RB*

78

I hate definitions. *Benjamin Disraeli (1804–1881)*

79

The affair between Margot Asquith and Margot Asquith will live as one of the prettiest love stories in all literature. *Dorothy Parker (1893–1967) in a review of a book by Margot Asquith*

8 0

To love oneself is the beginning of a life-long romance.　*Oscar Wilde (1854–1900)*

81

Like all self-made men he worships his creator.

Unknown

82

Egotist: A person . . . more interested in himself than in me.

Ambrose Bierce (1842–1914)

83

A narcissist is someone better looking than you are.

Gore Vidal

84

Don't be humble. You're not that great.

Golda Meir (1898–1978)

85

Stop crime at its source! Support Planned Parenthood.

RB

86

When turkeys mate they think of swans.

Johnny Carson

8 7

Except during the nine months before he draws his first breath, no man manages his affairs as well as a tree does. *George Bernard Shaw* (*1856–1950*)

8 8

It is now quite lawful for a Catholic woman to avoid pregnancy by a resort to mathematics, though she is still forbidden to resort to physics or chemistry.

H. L. Mencken (*1880–1956*)

89

Somewhere on this globe, every ten seconds, there is a woman giving birth to a child. She must be found and stopped.   *Sam Levenson (1911–1980)*

90

To enter life by way of the vagina is as good a way as any.   *Henry Miller (1891–1980)*

91

I have an intense desire to return to the womb. Anybody's.   *Woody Allen*

92

To my embarrassment I was born in bed with a lady.
Wilson Mizner (1876–1933)

93

My obstetrician was so dumb that when I gave birth he forgot to cut the cord. For a year that kid followed me *everywhere*. It was like having a dog on a leash.
Joan Rivers

94

I knew I was an unwanted baby when I saw that my bath toys were a toaster and a radio.   *Joan Rivers*

95

A child is a curly, dimpled lunatic.
Ralph Waldo Emerson (1803–1882)

96

All children are essentially criminal.
Denis Diderot (1713–1784)

97

A vegetarian is a person who won't eat anything that can have children.   *David Brenner*

98

When I was a child what I wanted to be when I grew up was an invalid.   *Quentin Crisp*

99

Children of the poor should work for some part of the day when they reach the age of three.
John Locke (1632–1704) in 1697

100

Of all the animals, the boy is the most unmanageable.
Plato (427?–348? B.C.)

Plato is a bore.   *Nietzsche (1844–1900)*

101

Children are guilty of unpardonable rudeness when they spit in the face of a companion; neither are they excusable who spit from windows or on walls or furniture.   *St. John Baptist de La Salle (c. 1695)*

1 0 2

Thank God kids never mean well. *Lily Tomlin*

1 0 3

Mothers are fonder than fathers of their children because they are more certain they are their own.

Aristotle (384–322 B.C.)

1 0 4

There's nothing wrong with teenagers that reasoning with them won't aggravate. *Unknown*

1 0 5

Young people are more hopeful at a certain age than adults, but I suspect that's glandular. As for children, I keep as far from them as possible. I don't like the sight of them. The scale is all wrong. The heads tend to be too big for the bodies, and the hands and feet are a disaster. They keep falling into things. The nakedness of their bad character! We adults have learned how to disguise our terrible character, but children, well, they are like grotesque drawings of *us*. They should be neither seen nor heard, and no one must make another one. *Gore Vidal*

1 0 6

I tell you I can feel them! They're all around us! Young people! Getting closer and closer!

Hamilton cartoon caption

107

The reason husbands and wives do not understand each other is because they belong to different sexes.

Dorothy Dix (1870–1951)

108

There was a time when we expected nothing of children but obedience, as opposed to the present, when we expect everything of them but obedience.

Anatole Broyard

109

The reason grandparents and grandchildren get along so well is that they have a common enemy.

Sam Levenson (1911–1980)

110

I never met a kid I liked.   *W. C. Fields (1880–1946)*

111

It is a good thing for an uneducated man to read books of quotations.

Winston Churchill (1874–1965)

112

I hate quotations.

Ralph Waldo Emerson (1803–1882)

1 1 3

If men could get pregnant, abortion would be a sacrament. *Florynce Kennedy*

1 1 4

Ever since the young men have owned motorcycles, incest has been dying out. *Max Frisch*

1 1 5

Familiarity breeds attempt.

Goodman Ace (1899–1982)

116

Sex drive: A physical craving that begins in adolescence and ends at marriage.   *RB*

117

Sex is the most fun you can have without smiling.

Unknown

118

I would rather go to bed with Lillian Russell stark naked than Ulysses S. Grant in full military regalia.

Mark Twain (1835–1910)

119

Last time I tried to make love to my wife nothing was happening, so I said to her, "What's the matter, you can't think of anybody either?"   *Rodney Dangerfield*

120

If it weren't for pickpockets I'd have no sex life at all.

Rodney Dangerfield

121

I've tried several varieties of sex. The conventional position makes me claustrophobic and the others give me a stiff neck or lockjaw.

Tallulah Bankhead (1903–1968)

122

A woman occasionally is quite a serviceable substitute for masturbation.   *Karl Kraus*

1 2 3

Sex is nobody's business except the three people
involved. *Unknown*

1 2 4

What men desire is a virgin who is a whore.
Edward Dahlberg (1900–1977)

1 2 5

The orgasm has replaced the Cross as the focus of
longing and the image of fulfillment.
Malcolm Muggeridge

All this fuss about sleeping together. For physical
pleasure I'd sooner go to my dentist any day.
Evelyn Waugh (1903–1966)

What a man enjoys about a woman's clothes are his
fantasies of how she would look without them.
Brendan Francis

128

Women who miscalculate are called "mothers."

Abigail Van Buren

129

Nothing is so much to be shunned as sex relations.

St. Augustine (354–430)

130

I kissed my first girl and smoked my first cigarette on the same day. I haven't had time for tobacco since.

Arturo Toscanini (1867–1957)

131

The only really indecent people are the chaste.

J. K. Huysmans (1848–1907)

132

For the preservation of chastity, an empty and rumbling stomach and fevered lungs are indispensable.

St. Jerome (340?–420)

133

I hate women because they always know where things are. *James Thurber (1894–1961)*

134

Sex is the biggest nothing of all time. *Andy Warhol*

1 3 5

Love is the delightful interval between meeting a beautiful girl and discovering that she looks like a haddock.   *John Barrymore (1882–1942)*

1 3 6

Love is an ocean of emotions entirely surrounded by expenses.   *Lord Dewar*

1 3 7

Love is a grave mental disease.

Plato (427?–348? B.C.*)*

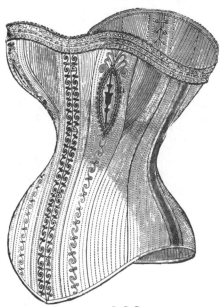

1 3 8

Whatever deceives seems to produce a magical enchantment.   *Plato (427?–348?* B.C.*)*

Plato is a bore.   *Nietzsche (1844–1900)*

1 3 9

The heaviest object in the world is the body of the woman you have ceased to love.

Marquis de Luc de Clapiers Vauvenargues
(1715–1747)

1 4 0

In expressing love we belong among the undeveloped countries. *Saul Bellow*

1 4 1

A man can be happy with any woman as long as he does not love her. *Oscar Wilde (1854–1900)*

1 4 2

Love will find a lay. *RB*

1 4 3

It takes a woman twenty years to make a man of her son, and another woman twenty minutes to make a fool of him. *Helen Rowland (1876–1950)*

1 4 4

It is better to have loved and lost than never to have lost at all. *Samuel Butler (1835–1902)*

1 4 5

I sold my memoirs of my love life to Parker Brothers and they are going to make a game out of it.

Woody Allen

146

The only solid and lasting peace between a man and his wife is doubtless a separation.

Lord Chesterfield (1694–1773)

147

Marriage: A master, a mistress and two slaves, making in all, two. *Ambrose Bierce (1842–1914)*

148

Marriage is not a word but a sentence. *Unknown*

149

Marriage is a great institution, but I'm not ready for an institution. *Mae West (1893–1980)*

150

If I ever marry it will be on a sudden impulse, as a man shoots himself. *H. L. Mencken (1880–1956)*

151

For the upper middle class, marriage is the only adventure left. *Unknown*

152

We want playmates we can own.

Jules Feiffer on marriage

153
It was so cold I almost got married.   *Shelley Winters*

154
At American weddings, the quality of the food is inversely proportional to the social position of the bride and groom.   *Calvin Trillin*

155
I was married once. Now I just lease.
From the movie Buddy, Buddy (*1981*)

1 5 6

I married beneath me. All women do.

Nancy, Lady Astor (1879–1964)

1 5 7

An archeologist is the best husband a woman can have;
the older she gets, the more interested he is in her.

Agatha Christie (1891–1976),
who was married to one

1 5 8

I tended to place my wife under a pedestal.

Woody Allen

1 5 9

My mother-in-law broke up my marriage. One day my
wife came home early from work and found us in bed
together.   *Lenny Bruce (1926–1966)*

1 6 0

Divorce is the sacrament of adultery.   *French proverb*

1 6 1

What scares me about divorce is that my children
might put me in a home for unwed mothers.

Teressa Skelton

162
Take my wife . . . please! *Henny Youngman*

163

A CURSE

May your soul be forever tormented by fire and your bones be dug up by dogs and dragged through the streets of Minneapolis. *Garrison Keillor*

1 6 4

My work is done, why wait?

Suicide note left by Kodak founder
George Eastman (1854–1932)

1 6 5

All right, then, I'll say it: Dante makes me sick.

Last words of Spanish playwright
Lope de Vega on being assured on his
deathbed that the end was very near.

1 6 6

I don't feel good.

Last words of Luther Burbank (1849–1926)

1 6 7

Don't let it end like this. Tell them I said something.

Last words of Pancho Villa (1877?–1923)

1 6 8

It is better to be a coward for a minute than dead for
the rest of your life.   *Irish proverb*

1 6 9

The reverse side also has a reverse side.

Japanese proverb

1 7 0

Tell the truth and run.   *Yugoslavian proverb*

1 7 1

Do not insult the mother alligator until after you have
crossed the river.   *Haitian proverb*

1 7 2

Too clever is dumb.   *German proverb*

1 7 3

The Irish ignore anything they can't drink or punch.
                                              Old saying

174

If God lived on earth, people would break his windows.

Jewish proverb

175

It is nothing, they are only thrashing my husband.

Portuguese proverb

176

When the cat and mouse agree, the grocer is ruined.

Persian proverb

177

I do not say a proverb is amiss when aptly and reasonably applied, but to be forever discharging them, right or wrong, hit or miss, renders conversation insipid and vulgar.   *Miguel Cervantes (1547–1616)*

178

Wise men make proverbs but fools repeat them.

Samuel Palmer (c. 1710)

179

Nobody has ever bet enough on the winning horse.

Overheard at a track by Richard Sasuly

180

One of the worst things that can happen in life is to win a bet on a horse at an early age.

Danny McGoorty (1901–1970)

181

Nobody ever committed suicide who had a good two-year-old in the barn. *Racetrack proverb*

182

It is morally wrong to allow suckers to keep their money. *"Canada Bill" Jones*

183

All life is six to five against.

Damon Runyon (1884–1946)

184

Much as he is opposed to lawbreaking, he is not bigoted about it. *Damon Runyon (1884–1946)*

185

You might as well fall flat on your face as lean over too far backward. *James Thurber (1894–1961)*

186

Alexander III of Macedonia is known as Alexander the Great because he killed more people of more different kinds than any other man of his time.

Will Cuppy (1884–1949)

187

Aristotle was famous for knowing everything. He taught that the brain exists merely to cool the blood and is not involved in the process of thinking. This is true only of certain persons.

Will Cuppy (1884–1949)

188

All Gaul is divided into three parts: igneous, metamorphic, and sedimentary.

Geologist Wilson Hinckley (1928–1972)

189

What a time! What a civilization!

Cicero (106–43 B.C.)

190

Oh, this age! How tasteless and ill-bred it is!

Catullus (87?–54? B.C.)

191

How little you know about the age you live in if you think that honey is sweeter than cash in hand.

Ovid (43? B.C.–A.D. 18)

192

It is sometimes expedient to forget who we are.

Publilius Syrus (c. 42 B.C.)

193

There is no glory in outstripping donkeys.

Martial (40–102)

194

The school of hard knocks is an accelerated curriculum. *Menander (342?–292? B.C.)*

195

There is nothing so absurd but some philosopher has said it.

Cicero (106–43 B.C.)

196

A man with his belly full of the classics is an enemy of the human race. *Henry Miller (1891–1980)*

197

Patriotism is the willingness to kill and be killed for trivial reasons. *Bertrand Russell (1872–1970)*

198

Democracy substitutes election by the incompetent many for appointment by the corrupt few.

George Bernard Shaw (1856–1950)

199

America has been discovered before, but it has always been hushed up. *Oscar Wilde (1854–1900)*

200

The 100% American is 99% an idiot.
George Bernard Shaw (1856–1950)

201

A government which robs Peter to pay Paul can always depend on the support of Paul.
George Bernard Shaw (1856–1950)

202

And that's the world in a nutshell—an appropriate receptacle. *Stan Dunn*

203

The remarkable thing about Shakespeare is that he really is very good, in spite of all the people who say he is very good. *Robert Graves*

204

Crude, immoral, vulgar, and senseless.
Tolstoy (1882–1910) on Shakespeare

205

I know not, sir, whether Bacon wrote the works of Shakespeare, but if he did not it seems to me that he missed the opportunity of his life.

James Barrie (1860–1937)

206

If Shakespeare had been in pro basketball he never would have had time to write his soliloquies. He would always have been on a plane between Phoenix and Kansas City. *Paul Westhead, basketball coach*

207

A team is a team is a team. Shakespeare said that many times. *Dan Devine, football coach*

208

A piano is a piano is a piano.—Gertrude Steinway

Unknown

209

A manuscript, like a foetus, is never improved by showing it to somebody before it is completed.

Unknown

2 1 0

Every journalist has a novel in him, which is an excellent place for it. *Russell Lynes*

2 1 1

Why authors write I do not know. As well ask why a hen lays an egg or a cow stands patiently while a farmer burglarizes her. *H. L. Mencken (1880–1956)*

2 1 2

Why do writers write? Because it isn't there.
Thomas Berger

2 1 3

Never let a domestic quarrel ruin a day's writing. If you can't start the next day fresh, get rid of your wife.
*One of Mario Puzo's rules for writing
a best-selling novel*

2 1 4

Every novel should have a beginning, a muddle, and an end. *Peter De Vries*

2 1 5

Boy meets girl; girl gets boy into pickle; boy gets pickle into girl.
Jack Woodford (1894–1971) on plotting

216

Writing is easy. All you do is stare at a blank sheet of paper until drops of blood form on your forehead.

Gene Fowler (1890–1960)

217

With a novelist, like a surgeon, you have to get a feeling that you've fallen into good hands—someone from whom you can accept the anesthetic with confidence. *Saul Bellow*

218

Sometimes when reading Goethe I have a paralyzing suspicion that he is trying to be funny.

Guy Davenport

219

The novelist, afraid his ideas may be foolish, slyly puts them in the mouth of some other fool and reserves the right to disavow them. *Diane Johnson*

220

He can compress the most words into the smallest idea of any man I ever met.

Abraham Lincoln (1809–1865)

221

If a writer has to rob his mother he will not hesitate; the *Ode On a Grecian Urn* is worth any number of old ladies. *William Faulkner (1897–1962)*

222

In literature as in love, we are astonished at what is chosen by others. *André Maurois (1885–1967)*

223

It is a delicious thing to write, to be no longer yourself but to move in an entire universe of your own creating. Today, for instance, as man and woman, both lover and mistress, I rode in a forest on an autumn afternoon under the yellow leaves, and I was also the horses, the leaves, the wind, the words my people uttered, even the red sun that made them almost close their love-drowned eyes. When I brood over these marvelous pleasures I have enjoyed, I would be tempted to offer God a prayer of thanks if I knew he could hear me. Praised may he be for not creating me a cotton merchant, a vaudevillian, or a wit.

Gustave Flaubert (1821–1880)

2 2 4

I'm a lousy writer; a helluva lot of people have got lousy taste.   *Grace Metalious (1924–1964)*

2 2 5

A custom loathsome to the eye, hateful to the nose, harmful to the brain, dangerous to the lungs, and in the black, stinking fumes thereof, nearest resembling the horrible Stygian smoke of the pit that is bottomless.   *King James (c. 1604) on smoking*

226

I can write better than anybody who can write faster, and I can write faster than anybody who can write better.   *A. J. Liebling (1904–1963)*

227

I used to be treated like an idiot, now I'm treated like an idiot savant.   *Martin Cruz Smith after his novel* Gorky Park *became a best-seller*

228

Income tax returns are the most imaginative fiction being written today.   *Herman Wouk*

229

Marry money.
Max Shulman's advice to aspiring authors

230

What is a writer but a shmuck with an Underwood?
Jack Warner (ascribed)

231

There's no thief like a bad book.   *Italian proverb*

232

A big book is a big bore.   *Callimachus (c. 260 B.C.)*

233

Never read a book that is not a year old.
Ralph Waldo Emerson (1803–1882)

234

The man who doesn't read good books has no advantage over the man who can't read them.
Mark Twain (1835–1910)

235

Any ordinary man can . . . surround himself with two thousand books . . . and thenceforward have at least one place in the world in which it is possible to be happy. *Augustine Birrell (1850–1933)*

236

I have always imagined that Paradise will be a kind of library. *Jorge Luis Borges*

237

Studying literature at Harvard is like learning about women at the Mayo Clinic. *Roy Blount, Jr.*

238

I wonder how so insupportable a thing as a bookseller was ever permitted to grow up in the Commonwealth. Many of our modern booksellers are but needless excrements, or rather vermin.
George Wither (1588–1667)

2 3 9

It takes the publishing industry so long to produce books it's no wonder so many are posthumous.

Teressa Skelton

2 4 0

In every fat book there is a thin book trying to get out. *Unknown*

2 4 1

No, I haven't read the New Testament, but I read the Old Testament, and I liked it very, very much.

One shepherd to another in a New Yorker *cartoon*

2 4 2

What an ugly beast is the ape, and how like us.

Cicero (106–43 B.C.*)*

2 4 3

Your life story would not make a good book. Don't even try.   *Fran Liebowitz*

2 4 4

Drunkenness is the ruin of reason. It is premature old age. It is temporary death.   *St. Basil (330?–379?)*

2 4 5

I drink no more than a sponge.

Rabelais (1494–1553)

2 4 6

They talk of my drinking but never my thirst.

Scottish proverb

2 4 7

A drinker has a hole under his nose that all his money runs into.   *Thomas Fuller (1608–1661)*

2 4 8

'Twas a woman who drove me to drink, and I never had the courtesy to thank her for it.

W. C. Fields (1880–1946)

249

An Irishman is the only man in the world who will step over the bodies of a dozen naked women to get to a bottle of stout. *Unknown*

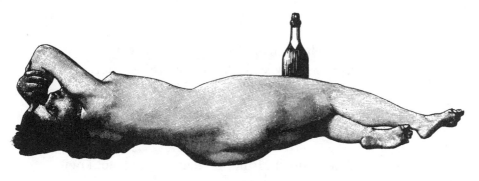

250

One more drink and I'll be under the host.
Dorothy Parker (1893–1967)

251

I drink to make other people more interesting.
George Jean Nathan (1882–1958)

252

Inflation has gone up over a dollar a quart.
W. C. Fields (1880–1946)

253

Even though a number of people have tried, no one has yet found a way to drink for a living.

Jean Kerr

254

I haven't touched a drop of alcohol since the invention of the funnel. *Malachy McCourt*

255

The less I behave like Whistler's mother the night before, the more I look like her the morning after.
Tallulah Bankhead (1903–1968)

256

One reason I don't drink is that I want to know when I am having a good time.
Nancy, Lady Astor (1879–1964)

257

I'd rather have a free bottle in front of me than a prefrontal lobotomy. *Unknown*

258

I hate to advocate drugs, alcohol, violence, or insanity to anyone, but they've always worked for me.
Hunter S. Thompson

259

If you drink, don't drive. Don't even putt.
Dean Martin

2 6 0

I tremble for my country when I reflect that God is just. *Thomas Jefferson (1743–1826)*

2 6 1

If you weren't such a great man you'd be a terrible bore. *Mrs. William Gladstone to her husband*

2 6 2

He speaks to me as if I were a public meeting.
Queen Victoria (1819–1901) on Gladstone

2 6 3

Harding was not a bad man, he was just a slob.
Alice Roosevelt Longworth (1884–1980)

2 6 4

The only man, woman, or child who ever wrote a simple declarative sentence with seven grammatical errors is dead.
e. e. cummings (1894–1962) on the death of Warren G. Harding, 1923

2 6 5

In 1932, lame duck President Herbert Hoover was so desperate to remain in the White House that he dressed up as Eleanor Roosevelt. When FDR discovered the hoax in 1936, the two men decided to stay together for the sake of the children. *Johnny Carson*

266

The Arabs are a backward people who eat nothing but camel dung. *Winston Churchill (1874–1965)*

267

Things have never been more like the way they are today in history.
> *Dwight David Eisenhower (1890–1969)*

268

John Foster Dulles.
> *Mort Sahl on being asked to say something funny*

269

Listen, there is no courage or any extra courage that I know of to find out the right thing to do. Now, it is not only necessary to do the right thing, but to do it in the right way and the only problem you have is what is the right thing to do and what is the right way to do it. That is the problem. But this economy of ours is not so simple that it obeys to the opinion of bias or the pronouncements of any particular individual, even to the President. This is an economy that is made up of 173 million people and it reflects their desires, they're ready to buy, they're to spend, it is a thing that is too complex and too big to be affected adversely or advantageously just by a few words or any particular—say, a little this and that, or even a panacea so alleged.
> *Dwight David Eisenhower (1890–1969) in response to the question: "Has government been lacking in courage and boldness in facing up to the recession?"*

270

Nixon is a shifty-eyed goddamn liar. . . . He's one of the few in the history of this country to run for high office talking out of both sides of his mouth at the same time and lying out of both sides.

Harry S Truman (1884–1972)

271

I don't give a shit about the Italian lira.

President Richard M. Nixon on being asked by H. R. Haldeman if he wanted to hear a report on the decline of the Italian lira.

272

I would have made a good Pope. *Richard M. Nixon*

273

How do you like that guy? Can't run six balls and he's President of the United States.

Pool hustler Johnny Irish on Nixon

274

Henry Kissinger may have wished I had presented him as a combination of Charles DeGaulle and Disraeli, but I didn't . . . out of respect for DeGaulle and Disraeli. I described him as a cowboy because that is how he described himself. If I were a cowboy I would be offended. *Oriana Fallaci*

2 7 5

Jerry Ford is a nice guy, but he played too much football with his helmet off.

Lyndon Baines Johnson (1908–1973)

2 7 6

I never trust a man unless I've got his pecker in my pocket. *Lyndon Baines Johnson (1908–1973)*

2 7 7

No.

President Jimmy Carter's daughter Amy when asked by a reporter if she had any message for the children of America.

2 7 8

Sometimes when I look at my children I say to myself, "Lillian, you should have stayed a virgin."

Lillian Carter, mother of Jimmy and Billy

2 7 9

"Who's Virginia?"

Rose Kennedy when asked why her daughter-in-law Joan lived in Boston while her son Ted lived in Virginia.

280

I see the world in very fluid, contradictory, emerging, interconnected terms, and with that kind of circuitry I just don't feel the need to say what is going to happen or will not happen.

California Governor Jerry Brown

281

Ronald Reagan is not a typical politician because he doesn't know how to lie, cheat, and steal. He's always had an agent for that. *Bob Hope*

282

Ronald Reagan is the Fred Astaire of foot-in-mouth disease. *Jeff Davis*

283

Never forget that the most powerful force on earth is love.

Nelson Rockefeller (1908–1979) to Henry Kissinger

284

Sure Reagan promised to take senility tests. But what if he forgets? *Lorna Kerr-Walker*

285

Ronald Reagan is the most ignorant president since Warren Harding. *Ralph Nader*

286

Ronald Reagan has held the two most demeaning jobs in the country—President of the United States and radio broadcaster for the Chicago Cubs.

George Will

287

Nancy Reagan fell down and broke her hair.

Johnny Carson

288

Well, I would—if they realized that we—again if—if we led them back to that stalemate only because that our retaliatory power, our seconds, or strike at them after our first strike, would be so destructive that they couldn't afford it, that would hold them off.

Ronald Reagan when asked if nuclear war could be limited to tactical weapons.

289

Nixon, Ford, Carter, Reagan—a Mount Rushmore of incompetence.   *David Steinberg*

290

When I was a boy I was told that anybody could become President; I'm beginning to believe it.

Clarence Darrow (1857–1938)

291

I'd rather entrust the government of the United States
to the first 400 people listed in the Boston telephone
directory than to the faculty of Harvard University.
William F. Buckley, Jr.

292

The only thing that saves us from the bureaucracy is
its inefficiency. *Eugene McCarthy*

293

We have a crisis of leadership in this country. Where
are the Washingtons, the Jeffersons, and the Jacksons?
I'll tell you where they are—they are playing professional football and basketball. *Unknown*

294

It is inaccurate to say I hate everything. I am strongly
in favor of common sense, common honesty, and common decency. This makes me forever ineligible for any
public office. *H. L. Mencken (1880–1956)*

295

What this country needs is more unemployed politicians. *Edward Langley*

296

All right, I will learn to read, but when I have learned,
I never, never shall. *British novelist David Garnett
at age 4, to his mother*

297

Henry James writes fiction as if it were a painful duty.
Oscar Wilde (1854–1900)

298

Henry James chews more than he bites off.
Mrs. Henry Adams (c. 1880)

299

Henry James was one of the nicest old ladies I ever
met. *William Faulkner (1897–1962)*

300

Henry James would have been vastly improved as a
novelist by a few whiffs of the Chicago stockyards.
H. L. Mencken (1880–1956)

301

Henry James created more convincing women than
Iris Murdoch put together. *Wilfred Sheed*

3 0 2

Go not in and out of court that thy name may not stink.   *The Wisdom of Anii* (*c. 900* B.C.)

3 0 3

A lawyer and a wagon-wheel must be well greased.
German proverb

3 0 4

Law is a bottomless pit.
John Arbuthnot (*1667–1735*) (*c. 1712*)

3 0 5

Lawyers, I suppose, were children once.
Charles Lamb (*1775–1834*)

3 0 6

When men are pure, laws are useless; when men are corrupt, laws are broken.
Benjamin Disraeli (*1804–1881*)

3 0 7

I became a policeman because I wanted to be in a business where the customer is always wrong.
Unnamed officer quoted by Arlene Heath

3 0 8

The mistakes are all there waiting to be made.
Chessmaster Savielly Grigorievitch Tartakower (*1887–1956*) *on the game's opening position*

309

Moral victories don't count.
Savielly Grigorievitch Tartakower (1887–1956)

310

The only reason I would take up jogging is so that I could hear heavy breathing again. *Erma Bombeck*

311

I don't jog. If I die I want to be sick. *Abe Lemons*

312

It was such a primitive country we didn't even see any joggers. *Hamilton cartoon caption*

313

Be careful about reading health books. You may die of a misprint. *Mark Twain (1835–1910)*

314

Old people shouldn't eat health foods. They need all the preservatives they can get. *Robert Orben*

315

A closed mouth gathers no feet. *Unknown*

PART TWO

Miscellaneous

316

Never eat more than you can lift. *Miss Piggy*

317

Punctuality is the thief of time.
                        Oscar Wilde (1856–1900)

318

Platitudes are the Sundays of stupidity. *Unknown*

319

It is unbecoming for young men to utter maxims.
                        Aristotle (384–322 B.C.)

320

They were such a progressive couple they tried to adopt a gay baby. *Unknown*

321

He who marries a widow will often have a dead man's head thrown in his dish. *Spanish proverb*

322

I don't know the key to success, but the key to failure is trying to please everybody. *Bill Cosby*

3 2 3

The brain is a wonderful organ; it starts working the moment you get up in the morning and does not stop until you get to the office.

Robert Frost (1874–1963)

3 2 4

I have never seen a greater monster or miracle than myself. *Montaigne (1533–1592)*

3 2 5

Until you walk a mile in another man's moccasins you can't imagine the smell. *RB*

3 2 6

I don't have a warm personal enemy left. They've all died off. I miss them terribly because they helped define me. *Claire Boothe Luce*

3 2 7

I'm lonesome. They are all dying. I have hardly a warm personal enemy left.

James McNeill Whistler (1834–1903)

3 2 8

Nothing is said that has not been said before.

Terence (185–159 B.C.)

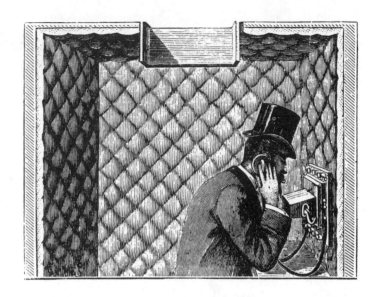

3 2 9

I'm in a phone booth at the corner of Walk and Don't
Walk. *Unknown*

3 3 0

How come they picked you to be an astronaut? You
got such a great sense of direction? *Jackie Mason*

3 3 1

Recipe (in its entirety) for boiled owl:
Take feathers off. Clean owl and put in cooking pot
with lots of water. Add salt to taste.

The Eskimo Cookbook (*1952*)

3 3 2

Do not make loon soup.

Valuable advice from The Eskimo Cookbook

333

Fall is my favorite season in Los Angeles, watching the birds change color and fall from the trees.

David Letterman

334

I met a guy once who was half Italian and half Chinese. His name was Video Pong. *Unknown*

335

My father never lived to see his dream come true of an all-Yiddish-speaking Canada. *David Steinberg*

336

That man has missed something who has never left a brothel at sunrise feeling like throwing himself into the river out of pure disgust.

Gustave Flaubert (1821 1880)

337

Gary Cooper and Greta Garbo may be the same person. Have you ever seen them together?

Ernst Lubitsch (1892–1947)

338

He had a God-given killer instinct.

Al Davis of the Oakland Raiders on George Blanda

339

I was gratified to be able to answer promptly. I said I don't know. *Mark Twain (1835–1910)*

340

Few people know how to be old.
La Rochefoucauld (1613–1680)

341

The enemy came. He was beaten. I am tired. Goodnight. *Message sent by Vicomte Turenne after the battle of Dunen, 1658*

342

Byrne's Law: In any electrical circuit, appliances and wiring will burn out to protect fuses. *RB*

343

McCabe's Law: Nobody *has* to do *anything.*
Charles McCabe

344

Parker's Law: Beauty is only skin deep, but ugly goes clear to the bone. *from* Murphy's Law

345

Chamberlain's Law: Everything tastes more or less like chicken. *from* The Official Rules

3 4 6

A man can wear a hat for years without being oppressed by its shabbiness.   *James Douglas*

3 4 7

Boozer's Revision: A bird in the hand is dead.
from The Official Rules

3 4 8

Any fool can make a rule.
Henry David Thoreau (1817–1862)

349

Happiness Is Seeing Lubbock, Texas, in the Rear-view Mirror. *Song title*

350

The important thing in acting is to be able to laugh and cry. If I have to cry, I think of my sex life. If I have to laugh, I think of my sex life. *Glenda Jackson*

351

There are more bores around than when I was a boy.
Fred Allen (1894–1956)

352

I've tried relaxing, but—I don't know—I feel more comfortable tense. *Hamilton cartoon caption*

353

I'm just a person trapped inside a woman's body.
Elaine Boosler

354

I happened to catch my reflection the other day when I was polishing my trophies, and, gee, it's easy to see why women are nuts about me. *Tom Ryan*

355

What to do in case of emergency:
1. Pick up your hat
2. Grab your coat
3. Leave your worries on the doorstep
4. Direct your feet to the sunny side of the street.

Unknown

356

Nolan Ryan is pitching much better now that he has his curve ball straightened out. *Joe Garagiola*

357

In many ways the saying "Know thyself" is lacking. Better to know other people.

Menander (342?–292? B.C.)

358

Only the shallow know themselves.

Oscar Wilde (1854–1900)

359

We all have the strength to endure the misfortunes of others. *La Rochefoucauld (1613–1680)*

360

There is no sweeter sound than the crumbling of one's fellow man. *Groucho Marx (1890–1977)*

3 6 1

It takes a great man to make a good listener.
Arthur Helps (1813–1875)

3 6 2

In this business you either sink or swim or you don't.
David Smith

3 6 3

I don't have a photograph, but you can have my footprints. They're upstairs in my socks.
Groucho Marx (1890–1977)

364

I've always been interested in people, but I've never liked them. *Somerset Maugham (1874–1965)*

365

Are you going to come quietly or do I have to use ear-plugs? *From* The Goon Show

366

One of the symptoms of an approaching nervous breakdown is the belief that one's work is terribly important. *Bertrand Russell (1872–1970)*

367

A little inaccuracy sometimes saves tons of explanation. *H. H. Munro (Saki) (1870–1916)*

368

It's really hard to be roommates with people if your suitcases are much better than theirs.

J. D. Salinger

369

Take most people, they're crazy about cars. I'd rather have a goddamn horse. A horse is at least *human*, for God's sake. *J. D. Salinger*

370

Three o'clock is always too late or too early for anything you want to do. *Jean-Paul Sartre (1905–1980)*

371

A reformer is a guy who rides through a sewer in a glass-bottomed boat.

*New York Mayor Jimmy Walker
(1881–1946) in 1928*

372

The doctor can bury his mistakes but an architect can only advise his client to plant vines.

Frank Lloyd Wright (1869–1959)

373

I wash everything on the gentle cycle. It's much more humane. *Unknown*

374

The breakfast of champions is not cereal, it's the opposition. *Nick Seitz*

375

There is nothing in the world so enjoyable as a thorough-going monomania.

Agnes Repplier (1858–1950)

376

Virtue is its own revenge.

E. Y. Harburg (1898–1981)

377

A good deed never goes unpunished. *Gore Vidal*

378

The curtain rises on a vast primitive wasteland, not
unlike certain parts of New Jersey. *Woody Allen*

379

Man is the only animal that laughs and has a state legislature. *Samuel Butler (1835–1902)*

380

Until a child is one year old it is incapable of sin.

The Talmud (c. 200)

381

I wish people who have trouble communicating would just shut up. *Tom Lehrer*

382

A man is as young as the woman he feels.

Variously ascribed

383

Toots Shor's restaurant is so crowded nobody goes there anymore. *Yogi Berra*

384

I don't care what is written about me so long as it isn't true. *Dorothy Parker (1893–1967)*

385

He can beat yourn with hisn and he can beat hisn with yourn. *Pro football coach "Bum" Phillips on the merits of coach Don Shula*

386

More than any time in history mankind faces a cross-roads. One path leads to despair and utter hopeless-ness, the other to total extinction. Let us pray that we have the wisdom to choose correctly. *Woody Allen*

387

It is dangerous to be sincere unless you are also stupid.
George Bernard Shaw (1856–1950)

388

You can't steal second base and keep one foot on first. *An unnamed 60-year-old junior executive*

389

When something good happens it's a miracle and you should wonder what God is saving up for you later.
Marshall Brickman

390

Cogito ergo spud. I think, therefore I yam.
Graffito

391

If you want an audience, start a fight.
Gaelic proverb

392

Everything hurts. *Michelangelo Antonioni*

I propose getting rid of conventional armaments and replacing them with reasonably priced hydrogen bombs that would be distributed equally throughout the world. *Idi Amin*

I like a woman with a head on her shoulders. I hate necks. *Steve Martin*

395

I don't know why people like the home run so much. A home run is over as soon as it starts . . . wham, bam, thank you, ma'am. The triple is the most exciting play of the game. A triple is like meeting a woman who excites you, spending the evening talking and getting more excited, then taking her home. It drags on and on. You're never sure how it's going to turn out.

Baseball player George Foster

396

Working on television is like being shot out of a cannon. They cram you all up with rehearsals, then someone lights a fuse and—BANG—there you are in someone's living room.

Tallulah Bankhead (1903–1968)

397

Talk is cheap because supply exceeds demand.

Unknown

398

Fifteen cents of every twenty-cent stamp goes for storage. *Louis Rukeyser*

399

The unique thing about Margaret Rutherford is that she can act with her chin alone. Among its many moods I especially cherish the chin commanding, the chin in doubt, and the chin at bay. *Kenneth Tynan*

400

Things are so bad on Broadway today an actor is lucky to be miscast.

George S. Kaufman (1889–1961)

401

The race may not be to the swift nor the victory to the strong, but that's how you bet.

Damon Runyon (1844–1946)

402

The Jewish position on abortion is that a foetus is a foetus until it gets out of medical school.   *Unknown*

403

I'm impressed with people from Chicago. Hollywood is hype, New York is talk, Chicago is work.

Actor-producer Michael Douglas

404

An empty taxi stopped, and Jack Warner got out.

Unknown

405

A liberated woman is one who has sex before marriage and a job after.   *Gloria Steinem*

406

If you haven't got anything nice to say about anybody, come sit next to me.

Alice Roosevelt Longworth (1884–1980)

407

I'll try anything once.

Alice Roosevelt Longworth (1884–1980) on giving birth at age 41.

408

Days off. *Spencer Tracy (1900–1967) when asked what he looks for in a script.*

409

We are drawn to our television sets each April the way we are drawn to the scene of an accident.

Vincent Canby on the Academy Awards

410

God sends meat and the devil sends cooks.

Thomas Deloney (1543–1600)

411

Husbands arc like fires. They go out if unattended.

Zsa Zsa Gabor (Miss Hungary of 1936)

412
Go, and never darken my towels again.
Groucho Marx (1895–1977)

413

California is the only state in the union where you can fall asleep under a rose bush in full bloom and freeze to death. *W. C. Fields (1880–1946)*

414

The difference between Los Angeles and yoghurt is that yoghurt has an active, living culture.

Unknown

415

We can see California coming, and we're scared.

James Brady

416

Many a man owes his success to his first wife and his second wife to his success. *Jim Backus*

417

Nature has given us two ears but only one mouth.

Benjamin Disraeli (1804–1881)

418

It is easier to stay out than get out.

Mark Twain (1835–1910)

419

A fat paunch never breeds fine thoughts.

St. Jerome (340?–420)

420

Absence makes the heart go yonder.   *RB*

421

Short, balding, Chinese gentleman seeks tall Negress with passion for leather and Brahms to attend openings.   *Classified ad in the* Berkeley Barb

422

Yard sale—Recently married couple is combining households. All duplicates will be sold, except children.
Classified ad in the San Jose Mercury News

423

It takes two to speak the truth—one to speak and another to hear.   *Henry David Thoreau (1817–1862)*

424

Only sick music makes money today.
Nietzsche (1844–1900) in 1888

425

I never know how much of what I say is true.

Bette Midler

426

I'm as pure as the driven slush.

Tallulah Bankhead (1903–1968)

427

I went around the world last year and you want to know something? It hates each other.

Edward J. Mannix

428

A great many people have come up to me and asked how I managed to get so much done and still look so dissipated. *Robert Benchley (1889–1945)*

429

I don't trust him. We're friends.

Bertolt Brecht (1898–1956)

430

A man can't be too careful in the choice of his enemies. *Oscar Wilde (1854–1900)*

431

Anyone can win, unless there happens to be a second entry. *George Ade (1866–1944)*

432

We have long passed the Victorian era, when asterisks were followed after a certain interval by a baby.

Somerset Maugham (1874–1965)

433

It was such a lovely day I thought it was a pity to get up. *Somerset Maugham (1874–1965)*

434

The biggest sin is sitting on your ass.

Florynce Kennedy

435

Laugh and the world laughs with you, snore and you sleep alone. *Anthony Burgess*

436

It was a blonde, a blonde to make a bishop kick a hole in a stained glass window.

Raymond Chandler (1888–1959)

437

I go to the theater to be entertained . . . I don't want to see rape, sodomy, and drug addiction. I can get all that at home. *Roger Law cartoon caption*

438

The higher the buildings, the lower the morals.

Noel Coward (1899–1973)

439

Nothing is illegal if a hundred businessmen decide to do it.   *Andrew Young*

440

I wish Frank Sinatra would just shut up and sing.

Lauren Bacall

441

England produces the best fat actors.

Jimmy Cannon (1910–1973)

442

If it weren't for Philo T. Farnsworth, inventor of television, we'd still be eating frozen radio dinners.

Johnny Carson

443

A luxury liner is just a bad play surrounded by water.

Clive James

444

The future isn't what it used to be. *Variously ascribed*

445

Some of us are becoming the men we wanted to marry.

Gloria Steinem

446

I haven't been wrong since 1961, when I thought I made a mistake. *Bob Hudson*

447

I may have my faults, but being wrong ain't one of them. *Jimmy Hoffa (1913–1975)*

448

He had a winning smile, but everything else was a loser. *George C. Scott at a Bob Hope roast*

449

He not only overflowed with learning, he stood in the slop. *Sydney Smith (1771–1845) on Macaulay*

450

Listening to the Fifth Symphony of Ralph Vaughan Williams is like staring at a cow for forty-five minutes. *Aaron Copland*

451

Forgive your enemies, but never forget their names.
John F. Kennedy (1917–1963)

452

There is no pleasure in having nothing to do; the fun is having lots to do and not doing it.
John W. Raper

453

Hope is the feeling you have that the feeling you have isn't permanent. *Jean Kerr*

454

I was probably the only revolutionary ever referred to as "cute." *Abbie Hoffman*

455

Success didn't spoil me; I've always been insufferable.
Fran Liebowitz

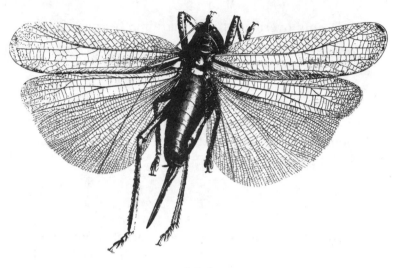

456

Men should stop fighting among themselves and start fighting insects. *Luther Burbank (1849–1926)*

457

They say you can't do it, but sometimes it doesn't always work. *Casey Stengel (1891–1975)*

458

Tumescence is the period between pubescence and senescence. *RB*

459

If this is coffee, please bring me some tea; but if this is tea, please bring me some coffee.

Abraham Lincoln (1809–1865)

460

Logic is in the eye of the logician.   *Gloria Steinem*

461

Everything is in a state of flux, including the status quo.   *RB*

462

The only people with a right to complain about what I do for a living are vegetarian nudists.

Ken Bates, one of California's
700 licensed fur trappers

463

I'm trying to arrange my life so that I don't even have to be present.   *Unknown*

464

To travel is to discover that everyone is wrong about other countries.   *Aldous Huxley (1894–1963)*

465

It can be great fun to have an affair with a bitch.

Louis Auchincloss

466

Never accept a drink from a urologist.

Erma Bombeck's father

467

In Rome I am weighed down by a lack of momentum, the inertia of a spent civilization. In New York I feel plugged into a strong alternating current of hope and despair. *Ted Morgan*

468

I'm six foot eleven. My birthday covers three days.
Darryl Dawkins

469

He who hesitates is not only lost, but miles from the next exit. *Unknown*

470

You can't measure time in days the way you can money in dollars because every day is different.

Jorge Luis Borges

471

Time is nature's way of keeping everything from happening at once. *Unknown*

472

If Today Was a Fish, I'd Throw It Back In. *Song title*

473

From the Gutter to You Ain't Up. *Song title*

474

I look at ordinary people in their suits, them with no scars, and I'm different. I don't fit with them. I'm where everybody's got scar tissue on their eyes and got noses like saddles. I go to conventions of old fighters like me and I see the scar tissue and all them flat noses and it's beautiful. Galento, may he rest in peace. Giardello, LaMotta, Carmen Basilio. What a sweetheart Basilio is. They talk like me, like they got rocks in their throats. Beautiful!

Willie Pastrano

475

Reality is a crutch for people who can't cope with drugs. *Lily Tomlin*

476

A cap of good acid costs five dollars and for that you can hear the Universal Symphony with God singing solo and the Holy Ghost on drums. *Hunter S. Thompson as quoted by William F. Buckley, Jr., who added: "Though one should be prepared to vomit rather frequently and disport with pink elephants and assorted grotesqueries while trying, often unsuccessfully, to make one's way to the toilet."*

477

The best way to lose weight is to get the flu and take a trip to Egypt. *Roz Lawrence*

478

Anyone who eats three meals a day should understand why cookbooks outsell sex books three to one.
L. M. Boyd

479

We don't know a millionth of one percent about anything. *Thomas Alva Edison (1847–1931)*

480

Something ignoble, loathsome, undignified attends all associations between people and has been transferred to all objects, dwellings, tools, even the landscape itself. *Bertolt Brecht (1898–1956) on America*

4 8 1

If I had known I was going to live this long I would
have taken better care of myself. *Unknown*

4 8 2

Is sloppiness in speech caused by ignorance or apathy?
I don't know and I don't care. *William Safire*

483

We had seen the light at the end of the tunnel, and it was out.   *John C. Clancy*

484

To err is human, to forgive supine.
S. J. Perelman (1904–1979)

485

What is true is what I can't help believing.
Oliver Wendell Holmes, Jr. (1841–1935)

486

I am the last of Britain's stately homos.
Quentin Crisp

487

I didn't want to be rich, I just wanted enough to get the couch reupholstered.   *Kate (Mrs. Zero) Mostel*

488

My father and he had one of those English friendships which begin by avoiding intimacies and eventually eliminate speech altogether.   *Jorge Luis Borges*

489

Shut up he explained.   *Ring Lardner (1885–1933)*

490

She had two complexions, A.M. and P.M.
Ring Lardner (1885–1933)

491

He writes so well he makes me feel like putting my quill back in my goose. *Fred Allen (1894–1956)*

492

If my film makes one more person miserable, I'll feel I've done my job. *Woody Allen*

493

The cloning of humans is on most of the lists of things to worry about from Science, along with behavior control, genetic engineering, transplanted heads, computer poetry and the unrestrained growth of plastic flowers. *Lewis Thomas*

494

No one can earn a million dollars honestly.
William Jennings Bryan (1860–1925)

495

There are very few Japanese Jews. As a result, there is no Japanese word for Alan King. *Johnny Carson*

496

From birth to age 18, a girl needs good parents, from
18 to 35 she needs good looks, from 35 to 55 she needs
a good personality, and from 55 on she needs cash.

Sophie Tucker (1884?–1966)

497

Outer space is no place for a person of breeding.

Lady Violet Bonham Carter (1887–1969)

498

Our national flower is the concrete cloverleaf.

Lewis Mumford

499

The only normal people are the ones you don't know very well.   *Joe Ancis*

500

You sofa-crevice fondler!   *Peter De Vries*

501

Cats are like Baptists. They raise hell but you can't catch them at it.   *Unknown*

502

So little time and so little to do.

Oscar Levant (1906–1972)

503

It's a rare person who wants to hear what he doesn't want to hear.   *Dick Cavett*

504

When I hear the word "culture" I reach for my gun.

Hans Johst (c. 1939)

505

He washed his legs today and can't do a thing with them. *Sportscaster Lon Simmons on seeing a base-ball player fall down twice in the first inning*

506

I like men to behave like men—strong and childish.
Françoise Sagan

507

A kleptomaniac is a person who helps himself because he can't help himself. *Henry Morgan*

508

A hypocrite is a person who—but who isn't?
Don Marquis (1878–1937)

509

Brain damage reading test:

People tell me one thing and out the other. I feel as much like I did yesterday as I did today. I never liked room temperature. My throat is closer than it seems. Likes and dislikes are among my favorites. No napkin is sanitary enough for me. I don't like any of my loved ones. *Daniel M. Wegner*

510

The two hardest things to handle in life are failure and success. *Unknown*

5 1 1

Progress might have been all right once but it has gone on too long.   *Ogden Nash (1902–1971)*

5 1 2

I consider exercise vulgar. It makes people smell.
Alec Yuill Thornton

5 1 3

There is no human problem which could not be solved if people would simply do as I advise. *Gore Vidal*

5 1 4

What's on your mind, if you will allow the overstatement? *Fred Allen (1894–1956)*

5 1 5

The young man who has not wept is a savage, and the old man who will not laugh is a fool.
George Santayana (1866–1952)

5 1 6

Though I am not naturally honest, I am so sometimes by chance. *Shakespeare (1564–1616)*

5 1 7

Early to rise and early to bed makes a male healthy, wealthy and dead. *James Thurber (1894–1961)*

5 1 8

I have no relish for the country; it is a kind of healthy grave. *Sydney Smith (1771–1845)*

5 1 9

A farm is an irregular patch of nettles, bound by short term notes, containing a fool and his wife who didn't know enough to stay in the city.
S. J. Perelman (1904–1979)

5 2 0

Everything has been figured out except how to live.
Jean-Paul Sartre (1905–1980)

5 2 1

Howard Hughes was able to afford the luxury of madness, like a man who not only thinks he is Napoleon but hires an army to prove it. *Ted Morgan*

5 2 2

When it is not necessary to make a decision, it is necessary not to make a decision.
Lord Falkland (1610?–1643)

5 2 3

This book fills a much-needed gap.
Moses Hadas (1900–1966) in a review

5 2 4

Thank you for sending me a copy of your book. I'll waste no time reading it.
Moses Hadas (1900–1966) in a letter

5 2 5

There are plenty of good five-cent cigars in the country. The trouble is they cost a quarter. What this country really needs is a good five-cent nickel.
Franklin P. Adams (1881–1960)

526

Being perfectly well-dressed gives a feeling of tranquility that religion is powerless to bestow.

Ralph Waldo Emerson (1803–1882),
quoting a friend

527

We are here and it is now. Further than that all human knowledge is moonshine.

H. L. Mencken (1880–1956)

528

There is no kind of dishonesty into which otherwise good people more easily and frequently fall than that of defrauding the government.

Benjamin Franklin (1706–1790)

529

Don't get the idea that I'm knocking the American system. *Al Capone (1899–1947)*

530

It wasn't raining when Noah built the ark.

Howard Ruff

531

The learned are seldom pretty fellows, and in many cases their appearance tends to discourage a love of study in the young. *H. L. Mencken (1880–1956)*

532

There is something going on now in Mexico that I happen to think is cruelty to animals. What I'm taking about, of course, is cat juggling. *Steve Martin*

5 3 3

Truth is beautiful, without doubt; but so are lies.

Ralph Waldo Emerson (1803–1882)

5 3 4

We will march forward to a better tomorrow so long as separate groups like the blacks, the Negroes, and the coloreds can come together to work out their differences.   *Steve Allen at a Redd Foxx roast*

5 3 5

Ninety-eight percent of the adults in this country are decent, hard-working, honest Americans. It's the other lousy two percent that get all the publicity. But then —we elected them.   *Lily Tomlin*

5 3 6

There are more of them than us.   *Herb Caen*

5 3 7

Suppose you were an idiot and suppose you were a member of Congress. But I repeat myself.

Mark Twain (1835–1910)

5 3 8

Never go to bed mad. Stay up and fight.

Phyllis Diller

539

When I go to the beauty parlor, I always use the emergency entrance. Sometimes I just go for an estimate.

Phyllis Diller

540

Orthodox medicine has not found an answer to your complaint. However, luckily for you, I happen to be a quack.   *Richter cartoon caption*

541

One of a hostess's duties is to act as a procuress.

Marcel Proust (1871–1922)

542

Here is a supplementary bulletin from the Office of Fluctuation Control, Bureau of Edible Condiments, Soluble and Indigestible Fats and Glutinous Derivatives, Washington, D.C. Correction of Directive 943456201, issued a while back, concerning the fixed price of groundhog meat. In the directive above named, the quotation on groundhog meat should read ground hogmeat.   *Bob and Ray*

543

I've known what it is to be hungry, but I always went right to a restaurant.   *Ring Lardner (1885–1933)*

What dreadful hot weather we have! It keeps me in a continual state of inelegance.

Jane Austen (1775–1817)

545

A single sentence will suffice for modern man: He fornicated and read the papers.

Albert Camus (1913–1960)

546

The rich are the scum of the earth in every country.

G. K. Chesterton (1874–1936)

547

One should never know too precisely whom one has married. *Nietzsche (1844–1900) on* Lohengrin

548

I never lecture, not because I am shy or a bad speaker, but simply because I detest the sort of people who go to lectures and don't want to meet them.

H. L. Mencken (1880–1956)

549

Bed is the poor man's opera.   *Italian proverb*

550

I'd rather be black than gay because when you're black you don't have to tell your mother.

Charles Pierce

551

Roses are red, violets are blue,
I'm a schizophrenic, and so am I.   *Frank Crow*

552

Lie Down and Roll Over and 159 Other Ways To Say I Love You.   *1981 book title*

553

I improve on misquotation.   *Cary Grant*

554

Partying is such sweet sorrow.   *RB*

555

Honest criticism is hard to take, particularly from a relative, a friend, an acquaintance, or a stranger.

Franklin P. Jones

556

If any cleric or monk speaks jocular words, such as provoke laughter, let him be anathema.

Ordinance, Second Council of Constance (1418)

557

Better that a girl has beauty than brains because boys see better than they think.   *Unknown*

558

I talk to myself because I like dealing with a better class of people.   *Jackie Mason*

559

It is better to have a permanent income than to be fascinating.   *Oscar Wilde (1854–1900)*

560

I did not sleep. I never do when I am over-happy, over-unhappy, or in bed with a strange man.

Edna O'Brien

5 6 1

Dostoyevsky was one of those neurotics who recover their health and even their serenity when disaster at last occurs.   *V. S. Pritchett*

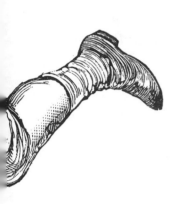 

5 6 2

Exit, pursued by a bear.

> *Stage direction in Shakespeare's*
> The Winter's Tale (*1611*)

5 6 3

¿Cómo frijoles? (Spanish for How have you bean?)

> *Unknown*

564

I don't make jokes. I just watch the government and report the facts. *Will Rogers (1879–1935)*

565

Even in civilized mankind faint traces of monogamous instinct can be perceived.

Bertrand Russell (1872–1970)

566

Things to do in Burbank:

     1. Go to the Safeway parking lot for the roller skating festival called Holiday on Tar.

Johnny Carson

567

I would rather be a coward than brave because people hurt you when you are brave.

E. M. Forster (1879–1970) as a small child

568

One day there will be only five kings left, hearts, spades, diamonds, clubs, and England.

King Farouk (1920–1965)
after his overthrow by Nasser

569

When ideas fail, words come in very handy.

Goethe (1749–1832)

5 7 0

Music with dinner is an insult both to the cook and the violinist. *G. K. Chesterton (1874–1936)*

5 7 1

The place of the father in the modern suburban family is a very small one, particularly if he plays golf.
Bertrand Russell (1872–1970)

5 7 2

Avarice is the sphincter of the heart.
Matthew Green (c. 1737)

5 7 3

It is easier to be gigantic than to be beautiful.
Nietzsche (1844–1900)

5 7 4

By the time we've made it, we've had it.
Malcolm Forbes

5 7 5

I only like two kinds of men: domestic and foreign.
Mae West (1893–1980)

5 7 6

Where but in Kenya can a man whose grandfather was a cannibal watch a really good game of polo?
Marina Sulzberger (1920–1976)

5 7 7

France was a long despotism tempered by epigrams.

Thomas Carlyle (1759–1881)

5 7 8

Never trust anyone over-dirty.   *RB*

579

There are more pleasant things to do than beat up people.

Muhammad Ali on the occasion of one of his retirements

580

Mirrors and copulation are abominable because they increase the numbers of men. *Jorge Luis Borges*

581

I don't worry about getting old. I'm old already. Only young people worry about getting old. When I was 65 I had cupid's eczema. I don't believe in dying. It's been done. I'm working on a new exit. Besides, I can't die now—I'm booked. *George Burns*

582

Men who never get carried away should be.

Malcolm Forbes

583

If you aren't fired with enthusiasm, you will be fired with enthusiasm. *Vince Lombardi (1913–1970)*

584

When I was kidnapped, my parents snapped into action. They rented out my room. *Woody Allen*

585

The best cure for hypochondria is to forget about your body and get interested in somebody else's.
Goodman Ace (1899–1982)

586

New invention: Snap-on acne for people who want to look younger. *Johnny Carson*

587

Love teaches even asses to dance. *French proverb*

588

Ammonia is beautiful. *Bumper sticker*

589

FECK OPUC. *Bumper sticker*

590

There is one fault that I must find
   With the twentieth century,
And I'll put it in a couple of words:
   Too adventury.
What I'd like would be some nice dull monotony
   If anyone's gotony. *Ogden Nash (1902–1971)*

591

If called by a panther
Don't anther. *Ogden Nash (1902–1971)*

592

First secure an independent income, then practice virtue. *Greek saying*

593

What we call real estate—the solid ground to build a house on—is the broad foundation on which nearly all of the guilt of the world rests.
                Nathaniel Hawthorne (1804–1864)

594

I have never liked working. To me a job is an invasion of privacy. *Danny McGoorty (1901–1970)*

595

Boy, the things I do for England.
               Prince Charles on sampling snake meat

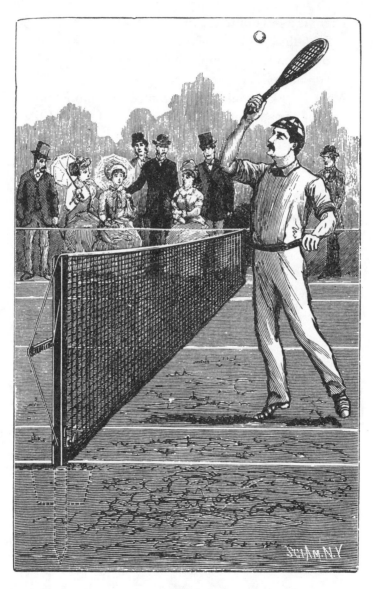

596

Victory goes to the player who makes the next-to-last mistake.

Savielly Grigorievitch Tartakower (1887–1956)

597

Of all noises, I think music is the least disagreeable.
Samuel Johnson (1709–1784)

598

One, two, three,
Buckle my shoe.   *Robert Benchley (1889–1945)*

599

It is rather to be chosen than great riches, unless I have omitted something from the quotation.
Robert Benchley (1889–1945)
in Maxims From the Chinese

600

There must be 500,000 rats in the United States; of course, I am only speaking from memory.
Bill Nye (1850–1896)

601

Newspapermen learn to call a murderer "an alleged murderer" and the King of England "the alleged King of England" to avoid libel suits.
Stephen Leacock (1869–1944)

602

Lord Ronald said nothing; he flung himself from the room, flung himself upon his horse and rode madly off in all directions.   *Stephen Leacock (1869–1944)*

603

I do not take a single newspaper, nor read one a month, and I feel myself infinitely the happier for it.
Thomas Jefferson (1743–1826)

604

Show me a hero and I will write you a tragedy.
F. Scott Fitzgerald (1896–1940)

605

We can't all be heroes because somebody has to sit on the curb and clap as they go by.
Will Rogers (1879–1935)

606

Some things have to be believed to be seen.
Ralph Hodgson on ESP

607

One of the most astounding cases of clairvoyance is that of the noted Greek psychic Achilles Loudos. Loudos realized that he had unusual powers by the age of ten, when he could lie in bed and, by concentrating, make his father's false teeth jump out of his mouth. *Woody Allen*

608

A cucumber should be well-sliced, dressed with pepper and vinegar, and then thrown out.
Samuel Johnson (1709–1784)

609
Middle age is when you've met so many people that every new person you meet reminds you of someone else. *Ogden Nash (1902–1971)*

610
Wagner's music is better than it sounds.
Bill Nye (1850–1896)

611

With those delicate features of his he would have made a pretty woman, and he probably never has.

Josefa Heifetz

612

I don't want any yes-men around me. I want everybody to tell me the truth even if it costs them their jobs. *Samuel Goldwyn (1882–1974)*

613

The advantage of the emotions is that they lead us astray. *Oscar Wilde (1854–1900)*

614

In the first place, God made idiots. That was for practice. Then he made school boards.

Mark Twain (1835–1910)

615

She wears her clothes as if they were thrown on with a pitchfork. *Jonathan Swift (1667–1745)*

616

A man is known by the company he avoids.

Unknown

617

Underneath this flabby exterior is an enormous lack of character. *Oscar Levant (1906–1972)*

618

Nobody roots for Goliath. *Wilt Chamberlain*

619

He went to Europe as a boy, where in Geneva his father arranged for a prostitute. He was so terrified by the experience that he didn't marry until he was 67 years old. *John Leonard on Borges*

620

Keep breathing. *Sophie Tucker (1884?–1966)*

621

If people don't want to come out to the ball park, nobody's going to stop them. *Yogi Berra*

622

Tradition is what you resort to when you don't have the time or the money to do it right.

Kurt Herbert Adler

623

It is impossible to imagine Goethe or Beethoven being good at billiards or golf.

H. L. Mencken (1880–1956)

624

All truths are half-truths.

Alfred North Whitehead (1861–1947)

625

To generalize is to be an idiot.

William Blake (1757–1827)

626

If you look like your passport photo, you're too ill to travel. *Will Kommen*

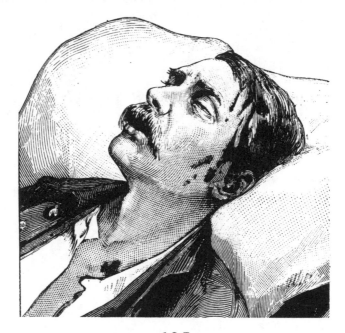

627

How can one conceive of a one-party system in a country that has over 200 varieties of cheese?

Charles de Gaulle (1890–1970)

628

When you have got an elephant by the hind legs and he is trying to run away, it is best to let him run.

Abraham Lincoln (1809–1865)

6 2 9

After three days, fish and guests stink.

John Lyly (1554?–1606)

6 3 0

I was born in Australia because my mother wanted me to be near her. *Unknown*

6 3 1

I will always cherish the initial misconceptions I had about you. *Unknown*

6 3 2

The majority of those who put together collections of verses or epigrams resemble those who eat cherries or oysters; they begin by choosing the best and end by eating everything. *Chamfort (1741–1794)*

6 3 3

If you were a member of Jesse James's band and people asked you what you were, you wouldn't say, "Well, I'm a desperado." You'd say something like, "I work in banks," or "I've done some railroad work." It took me a long time just to say "I'm a writer." It's really embarrassing. *Roy Blount, Jr.*

6 3 4

It takes about ten years to get used to how old you are. *Unknown*

6 3 5

After all is said and done, more is said than done.

Unknown

6 3 6

In the end, everything is a gag.

Charlie Chaplin (1889–1977)

6 3 7

Science has not yet found a cure for the pun.   *RB*

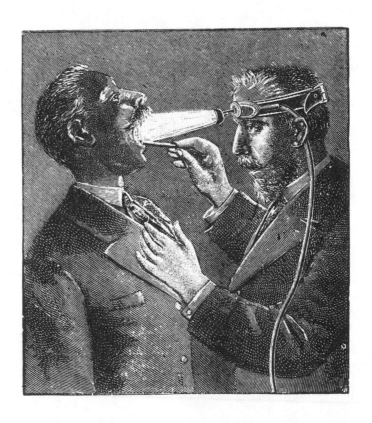

Sources, References, and Notes

Just because this is primarily a book of humor rather than scholarship doesn't mean that credit shouldn't be given where it is due. Unfortunately, my notebooks of "Remarks Worth Remembering" and my memory are spotty on documentation, as are most of the published collections of quotations I have turned to for help. If you know an author or source I failed to give, please write to me in care of the publisher (see copyright page). With help from readers there will be fewer partial and missing ascriptions in the next edition.

I would particularly like to hear from the professional writers of comedy and gags whose handiwork is no doubt credited here and elsewhere to their celebrity clients.

The principal secondary sources I consulted are listed in order of size, each with an identifying letter that will be referred to in the citations that follow.

A. *A New Dictionary of Quotations on Historical Principles*, Selected and edited by H. L. Mencken; Alfred A. Knopf, New York, 1952. (Approximately 37,000 entries)
B. *The Quotable Woman*, Compiled and edited by Elaine Partnow; Anchor Press/Doubleday, New York, 1978. (Approx. 21,000 entries)
C. *Familiar Quotations*, by John Bartlett; Little, Brown, Boston, 1955. (16,000 entries)
D. *The Crown Treasury of Relevant Quotations*, by Edward F. Murphy, Crown Publishers, New York, 1978. (8,000 entries)
E. *The Great Quotations*, Compiled by George Seldes; Lyle Stuart, New York, 1960. (7,000 entries)
F. *Peter's Quotations*, by Laurence J. Peter; William Morrow, New York, 1977. (6,000 entries)
G. *The Hamlyn Pocket Dictionary of Quotations*, Edited by Jonathan Hunt; The Hamlyn Publishing Group, London, 1979. (6,000 entries)
H. *The Penguin Dictionary of Modern Quotations*, J. M. and M. J. Cohen; Penguin Books, Harmondsworth, England, 1976. (5,500 entries)
I. *A Dictionary of Wit, Wisdom & Satire*, by Herbert V. Prochnow and Herbert V. Prochnow, Jr.; Harper & Row, New York, 1962. (5,000 entries)
J. *The Pocket Book of Quotations*, Edited by Henry Davidoff; Pocket Books, New York, 1952. (3,200 entries)

K. *The Book of Quotes*, by Barbara Rowes; E. P. Dutton, New York, 1979. (3,100 entries)

L. *The Quotable Quotations Book*, Compiled by Alec Lewis; Simon & Schuster, New York, 1980. (3,000 entries)

M. *The Viking Book of Aphorisms*, by W. H. Auden and Louis Kronenberger; Viking Press, New York, 1966. (3,000 entries)

N. *Popcorn in Paradise, The Wit and Wisdom of Hollywood*, Edited by John Robert Colombo; Holt, Rinehart and Winston, New York, 1980. (3,000 entries)

O. *Nobody Said It Better*, by Miriam Ringo; Rand McNally, Chicago, Ill., 1980. (2,700 entries)

P. *Proverbs and Epigrams*; Ottenheimer Publishers, Baltimore, Md., 1954. (2,500 entries)

Q. *Quotations of Wit and Wisdom*, John W. Gardner and Francesca Gardner Reese; W. W. Norton, New York, 1975. (1,200 entries)

R. *The Book of Insults*, Compiled by Nancy McPhee; St. Martin's Press, New York, 1978. (1,000 entries)

S. *The Writer's Quotation Book*, Edited by James Charlton; Pushcart Press, Yonkers, N.Y., 1980. (350 entries)

Quotation
Number

1. As given in R.

2. "Selections From the Allen Notebooks," in *Without Feathers*, 1975.

5. *Sisyphus.*

6. *Twilight of the Idols*, 1889.

7. *Mackeral Plaza*, 1958.

14. *Anthony Adverse*, 1933.

17. *Soldier, Sage, Saint*, 1978.

18. *One Fat Englishman*, 1963.

19. Possibly a corruption of something Thoreau said about fishing.

21. The *San Francisco Chronicle*, July 20, 1981.

24. *A Certain Slant of Light*, 1980.

25. A "Peanuts" comic strip.

26. As given in L.

27. From a "Peanuts" comic strip, January 1982.

28. *Coop*, 1978.

29. See 270.

30. As given in I.

32. *A Book About Myself*, 1922.

33. As given in M.

34. *The Tragedy of Pudd'nhead Wilson*, 1894.

35. Quoted in *On Being Funny*, by Eric Lax. 1975.

38. *Newsweek*, June 23, 1975.

39. *Seattle Times.*

41. As given in J.

42. *Metropolitan Life*, 1978.

47. *Barrett Wendell and His Letters*, 1924.

49. *The Ginger Man*, 1965.

51. First sentence of the short story *An Imperfect Conflagration*.

52. *Death, A Poem.*

53. *Murder Considered As One of the Fine Arts*, 1827.

54. As given in A. It has been suggested that some of the quotes ascribed to Anonymous in Mencken's great work were written by Mencken himself. This could be one of them.

55. *A Day at the Races*, 1936.

58. Quoted by Anatole Broyard in a *New York Times* book review, 1980.

59. *San Francisco Chronicle*, June 5, 1981.

60. *The Pushcart Prize V*, 1980.

65. Quoted in *Omni*.

70. *Rhetoric II*.

72. *A Glass Eye at the Keyhole*, 1938.

73–75. *The Devil's Dictionary*, 1906; all have been shortened.

82. *The Devil's Dictionary*, 1906.

83. As quoted in *The San Francisco Chronicle*, April 12, 1981.

84. As given in M.

88. *Notebooks*.

89. *You Don't Have to Be in Who's Who to Know What's What*, 1980.

90. As given in K.

95. *Nature*, 1841.

98. Quoted in *The San Francisco Chronicle*, November 11, 1979.

101. *The Rules of Christian Manners and Civility*, 1695.

105. *Conversations with Gore Vidal*, 1981.

107. As given in B.

108. *Books of the Times*, Vol. II, #7, p. 333.

110. As given in N.

111. *My Early Life*, 1930.

113. Quoted in "The Verbal Karate of Florynce Kennedy," by Gloria Steinem, *Ms.*, March 1973.

114. *Man in the Holocene*, 1980.

121. *Miss Tallulah Bankhead*, by Lee Israel, 1972.

122. *Karl Kraus*, by Harry Zohn, 1980.

124. *Reasons of the Heart*, 1965.

125. *The Most of Malcolm Muggeridge*, 1966.

126. *Vile Bodies*, 1930

129. *Soliloquies I.*

135. As given in Q.

140. As given in Q.

142. *The Picture of Dorian Gray*, 1891.

143. *Reflections of a Bachelor Girl*, 1903.

144. *The Way of All Flesh*, 1903.

147. See 82.

148. As given in A.

150. Quoted by Sara Mayfield in *The Constant Circle*, 1968.

153. Quoted by *The New York Times*, April 29, 1956.

156. Quoted in *Womanlist*, by Weiser and Arbeiter, 1981.

159. Quoted in *Funny People*, by Steve Allen, 1981.

161. TS to RB.

163. From *Happy to Be Here*, 1982. Mr. Keillor uses the third person.

164. Quoted in L. M. Boyd's syndicated newspaper column, *The Grab Bag*.

168. As given in A.
170. As given in E.
174. As given in Q.
175. As given in D.
177. *Don Quixote*, 1605.
179. Sasuly is the author of *Bookies and Bettors*, 1982.
180. Quoted by RB in *McGoorty, The Story of a Billiard Bum*, 1970.
182. Quoted by Charles McCabe in *The San Francisco Chronicle*, June 30, 1978.
186. *The Decline and Fall of Practically Everybody*, 1950.
187. See 186.
188. WH to RB.
196. *Tropic of Cancer*, 1934.
197. As given in I.
198. *Maxims for Revolution-aries*, 1903.
201. *Everybody's Political What's What.*
202. SD is a San Francisco disc jockey.
204. *Legend: Tolstoy's Letters*, 1978.
205. As given in O.
210. As given in Q.
211. In an interview.
217. Quoted by Herbert Mit-gang in *The New York Times Book Review*, July 1980.
218. Quoted by William Buckley in *The New York Times Book Review*, April 24, 1977.
219. *New York Times Book Review*, September 16, 1979.
222. As given in S.
223. From his *Journal*.
224. As given in E.
225. As given in E.
226. As recalled by Richard Sasuly (see 179).
230. Also ascribed to others.
238. Slightly shortened.
239. TS to RB.
243. See 42.
247. As given in A.
249. Unnamed "philosopher" quoted by Ron Butler in *San Francisco Examiner*, July 12, 1981.
250. *You Might As Well Live.*
253. *Poor Richard*, Act I, 1963.
254. Quoted in *Variety*.
255. See 150.
256. Quoted in *Reader's Digest*, November 1960.
257. Can anyone identify the creator of this, the greatest spoonerism of all time?
258. Quoted in *Life*, January 1981.
259. As given in K.
263. ARL was Teddy Roo-sevelt's daughter. For more see *Mrs. L: Conver-sations with Alice Roo-sevelt Longworth*, by Michael Teague, 1981.
269. Verbatim transcript, press conference.
270. Quoted by Leo Rosten in *Infinite Riches*, 1978.
271. From the White House tapes.
272. As given in K.
274. Quoted by Jack Ander-son, May 1979.
278. Quoted in *Life*, January 1981.
280. In Jeff Davis's column in the *San Francisco Examiner*, October 12, 1980.

284. Quoted by Herb Caen in his *San Francisco Chronicle* column, January 28, 1981.

285. Quoted in *The Pacific Sun*, March 21, 1981.

288. See 269.

290. As given in H.

294. Quoted in *Life*, August 5, 1946.

295. From a letter quoted by Charles McCabe in his *San Francisco Chronicle* column, October 24, 1980.

297. *The Decay of Lying*, 1891.

298. Quoted by Peter De Vries in *The New York Times Book Review*, December 6, 1981.

299. As given in R.

300. *The Smart Set*, November 1920, p. 140.

301. *The Good Word*, 1978.

307. Attorney AH to RB.

311. Quoted by Herb Caen in *The San Francisco Chronicle*, June 1980. AL is the former basketball coach at the University of Texas.

314. RO is a professional gag writer who markets his work to a wide variety of celebrities and politicians, enabling them to feign wit where none exists.

315. Needlepoint sampler recalled by Debi McFarland for RB.

316. *Miss Piggy's Guide to Life*, 1981, by Henry Beard.

317. *The Picture of Dorian Gray*, 1891.

318. As given in Q.

319. *Rhetoric*, c. 322 B.C.

322. As given in K.

323. As given in K.

326. On *The Dick Cavett Show*, July 21, 1981.

327. As given in R.

336. From his *Letters*.

339. *Life on the Mississippi*, 1883.

343. CM is a *San Francisco Chronicle* columnist.

344. *Murphy's Law*, by Arthur Block, 1977.

345. *The Official Rules*, Paul Dickson, 1978.

346. *Down Shoe Lane*.

347. See 345.

348. *Journal*, February 3, 1860.

350. See 164.

361. *Brevia*.

362. As recalled by Charles Champlin.

363. *A Night at the Opera*, 1935.

364. Quoted in *The Observer*, August 28, 1949.

365. *The Goon Show*, with Peter Sellers, Spike Milligan, and others, ran on BBC radio from 1951 to 1958.

366. As given in H.

367. *The Comments of Moung Ka*.

368, 369. *The Catcher in the Rye*, 1951.

370. *Nausea*, January 1932.

372. *New York Times Magazine*, 1953.

374. *Best Sports Stories*, 1978.

378. "A Guide to Some of the Lesser Ballets," in *Without Feathers*, 1975.

379. As given in I.

381. In concert at the Hungry i in San Francisco, July 1965.

384. Ascribed to Katharine Hepburn in N.

387. As given in R.

388. *Who's Nobody in America*, by Fulwiler and Evans, 1981.

390. Reported by Herb Caen in *The San Francisco Chronicle*, April 24, 1980.

392. As given in N.

395. In various newspapers, 1978.

396. Quoted in Terence O'Flaherty's column, *The San Francisco Chronicle*, March 18, 1980.

397. Rewritten to conform to current postal rates.

404. Also said of other people.

405. *Newsweek*, March 28, 1960.

406, 407. See 263.

412. *Duck Soup*, 1933.

416. As given in N.

418. See 34.

424. *The Case of Wagner*.

425. *A View From a Broad*, 1980.

427. As given in N.

428. *Chips Off the Old Benchley*, 1949.

432. *The Constant Wife*, 1926.

433. *Our Betters*, 1923.

434. See 113.

435. *Inside Mr. Enderby*, 1968.

436. *Farewell, My Lovely*, 1940.

437. 1962.

440. In an interview with Barbara Walters.

441. JC was a writer for the *New York Post*.

443. *Unreliable Memoirs*, 1981.

444. The author probably is Paul Valéry (1871–1945) and not Arthur C. Clarke.

446. BH to RB.

447. As given in Q.

450. As recalled by Andre Previn and quoted by Herb Caen, *San Francisco Chronicle*, February 1982.

451. The line "Forgive your enemies, but do not forget them," appears in the 1927 silent movie *Napoleon*, written and directed by Abel Gance.

453. *Finishing Touches*, Act III, 1973.

454. *Soon To Be a Major Motion Picture*, 1980.

456. As given in E.

457. Quoted in *A Thinking Man's Guide to Baseball*, 1967, by Leonard Koppet.

464. Quoted by Anatole Broyard in *The New York Times Book Review*, June 7, 1981.

465. *The Cat and the King*, 1981.

466. From an article on parental advice by Anthony Brown, distributed by *The Los Angeles Times* Syndicate.

467. *Rowing Toward Eden*, 1981.

469. As quoted by *The PG&E Progress*, January 1981.

474. Quoted by Dave Kindred in *The Washington Post*.

477. RL to RB.

478. In his syndicated newspaper column.

483. In an article on the death of *Scanlon's Magazine, Harper's*, April 1981.

485. In a letter to Sir Frederick Pollock.

488. In the story "Tlon, Uqbar, Orbis Tertius."

489. *The Young Immigrants*, 1920.

493. *The Medusa and the Snail*, 1979.

497. *Consenting Adults*, 1981.

504. And not his countryman, Hermann Goering.

507. See 270.

508. See 270.

509. A slightly different version appears in Herb Caen's column in the *San Francisco Chronicle*, May 1978. Mr. Wegner can be found at Trinity University in San Antonio, Texas.

512. Quoted by Merla Zellerbach in *The San Francisco Chronicle*, December 31, 1980.

515. *Dialogues in Limbo*, 1925.

516. *The Winter's Tale.*

521. *New York Times Book Review*, May 8, 1979.

523, 524. MH was a professor of Greek and Latin at Columbia.

530. *How to Prosper in the Coming Bad Years*, 1979.

534. Quoted in *Funny People*, by Steve Allen, 1981.

536. *San Francisco Chronicle*, February 9, 1981.

538. *Household Hints*, 1966.

541. As given in M.

542. *Write If You Get Work*, 1975.

543. As given in F.

544. From a letter dated 1796.

545. *The Fall*, 1957.

546. *The Flying Inn*, 1912.

548. In a letter to Charles Green Shaw.

549. Quoted by Aldous Huxley in *Heaven and Hell*, 1956.

550. *San Francisco Chronicle*, January 21, 1982.

551. Quoted by Herb Caen, *The San Francisco Chronicle*, February 14, 1982.

552. By Erskine & Moran, 1981.

553. As given in N.

555. Quoted in *The Wall Street Journal.*

559. *The Model Millionaire*, 1887.

560. *The Love Nest*, 1963.

561. *The Mythmakers*, 1979.

569. *Faust*, 1808.

570. *The Last Word.*

571. *Why I Am Not a Christian*, 1950.

574. *The Capitalist Handbook.*

576. From her *Letters.*

577. *The History of the French Revolution*, 1837.

579. June 26, 1979.

580. See 488.

581. Compiled from various interviews.

583. As given in K.

585. See 583.

586. *The Tonight Show*, February 7, 1979.

588. See 180.

590. From a poem titled "Put Back Those Whiskers, I Know You," in *Good Intentions*, 1942.
591. *Many Long Years Ago*, 1945.
592. Quoted by George Bernard Shaw in the preface to *Androcles and the Lion*, 1912.
593. *The House of the Seven Gables*, 1851.
598. *My Ten Years in a Quandary*, 1936.
599. See 598.
600. Quoted by Leacock in *Humor: Its Theory and Technique*, 1935.
601. *Too Much College*, 1941.
602. "Gertrude the Governess," in *Nonsense Novels*, 1914.
605. As given in F.
606. As given in F.
607. "Selections From the Allen Notebooks," in *Without Feathers*, 1975.

609. *Versus*, 1949.
611. JH to RB about a television talk-show host, 1970.
612. As given in K.
613. See 140.
614. See 34.
615. *Polite Conversation*, 1738.
619. *New York Times Book Review*.
620. As given in B.
622. Before his retirement in 1981, KHA was in charge of the San Francisco Opera Company.
624. *Dialogues*, 1954.
626. As given in F.
628. To C. A. Dana, April 1865.
629. *Euphues*, 1579.
633. As quoted by Allison Silver in *The New York Times Book Review*, February 28, 1982.
636. As given in K.

Principal Sources of Artwork

Harter's Picture Archives for Collage and Illustration, edited by Jim Harter and containing over 300 nineteenth-century cuts.
Music, A Pictorial Archive of Woodcuts & Engravings, selected by Jim Harter and containing 841 illustrations.
Men, A Pictorial Archive from Nineteenth-Century Sources, selected by Jim Harter and containing 412 illustrations.
Women, A Pictorial Archive from Nineteenth-Century Sources, selected by Jim Harter and containing 391 illustrations.
Picture Sourcebook for Collage and Decoupage, edited by Edmund V. Gillon, Jr., and containing over 300 illustrations.

The above five titles are published by Dover Publications.

Index of Authors

Ace, Goodman,
115, 585
Adams, Franklin
P., 525
Adams, Mrs.
Henry, 298
Ade, George, 431
Adler, Kurt Her-
bert, 622
Alfonso the Wise,
3
Ali, Muhammad,
579
Allen, Fred, 351,
491, 514
Allen, Hervey, 14
Allen, Steve, 534
Allen, Woody, 2,
22, 37, 38, 91,
145, 158, 378,
386, 492, 584,
607
Amin, Idi, 393
Amis, Kingsley, 18
Ancis, Joe, 499
Anderson, Rick,
39
Antonioni,
Michelangelo,
392
Arbuthnot, John,
304
Aristotle, 70, 103,
319
Astor, Nancy, 156,
256
Auchincloss,
Louis, 465
Augustine, Saint,
129
Austen, Jane, 544

Bacall, Lauren,
440
Backus, Jim, 416
Bankhead, Tallu-
lah, 121, 255,
396, 426
Barrie, James, 205
Barrymore, John,
135
Basil, Saint, 244
Bates, Ken, 462
Behrman, S. N., 48
Bellow, Saul, 140,
217
Benchley, Robert,
428, 598, 599
Berger, Thomas,
212
Berra, Yogi, 383,
621
Bierce, Ambrose,
51, 73, 74, 75,
82, 147
Birrell, Augustine,
235
Blake, William,
625
Blount, Roy, Jr.,
237, 633
Bob and Ray, 542
Bogan, Louise, 58
Bombeck, Erma,
310
Bombeck (Erma's
father), 466
Bonnano, Mar-
garet, 24
Boosler, Elaine,
353
Borges, Jorge Luis,
236, 470, 488,
580

Boyd, L. M., 478
Brady, James, 415
Brecht, Bertolt,
429, 480
Brenner, David, 97
Brickman, Mar-
shall, 389
Brown, Jerry, 280
Broyard, Anatole,
108
Bruce, Lenny, 159
Bryan, William
Jennings, 494
Buckley, William
F., Jr., 291
Burbank, Luther,
166, 456
Burgess, Anthony,
435
Burns, George,
581
Butler, Samuel,
30, 144, 379
Byrne, Robert, 76,
77, 85, 116,
142, 325, 342,
420, 458, 461,
554, 578, 637
Caen, Herb, 21,
536
Callimachus, 232
Camus, Albert,
545
Canby, Vincent,
409
Cannon, Jimmy,
441
Capone, Al, 529
Caracciolo,
Francesco, 16
Carlyle, Thomas,
577

Carson, Johnny, 46, 86, 265, 287, 442, 495, 566, 586

Carter, Amy, 277

Carter, Lillian, 278

Carter, Lady Violet Bonham, 497

Cato the Elder, 45

Catullus, 190

Cavett, Dick, 503

Cervantes, Miguel, 177

Chamberlain, Wilt, 618

Chamfort, Sébastien, 632

Chandler, Raymond, 436

Chaplin, Charlie, 636

Charles, Prince, 595

Chesterfield, Lord, 146

Chesterton, G. K., 546, 570

Christie, Agatha, 157

Churchill, Winston, 111, 266

Cicero, 189, 195, 242

Clancy, John C., 483

Copland, Aaron, 450

Cosby, Bill, 322

Coward, Noel, 438

Crisp, Quentin, 98, 486

Crow, Frank, 551

cummings, e.e., 264

Cuppy, Will, 186, 187

Dahlberg, Edward, 124

Dangerfield, Rodney, 119, 120

Darrow, Clarence, 290

Davenport, Guy, 215

Davis, Al, 338

Davis, Jeff, 282

Dawkins, Darryl, 468

De Gaulle, Charles, 627

Deloney, Thomas, 410

De Quincey, Thomas, 53

De Vega, Lope, 165

Devine, Dan, 207

De Vries, Peter, 7, 214, 500

Dewar, Lord, 136

Diderot, Denis, 96

Diller, Phyllis, 538, 539

Disraeli, Benjamin, 78, 306, 417

Dix, Dorothy, 107

Donleavy, J. P., 49

Douglas, James, 346

Douglas, Michael, 403

Dreiser, Theodore, 32

Dunn, Stan, 202

Eastman, George, 164

Edison, Thomas Alva, 479

Eisenhower, Dwight David, 267, 269

Emerson, Ralph Waldo, 8, 95, 112, 233, 526, 533

Falkland, Lord, 522

Fallaci, Oriana, 274

Farouk, King, 568

Faulkner, William, 221, 299

Feiffer, Jules, 152

Fields, W. C., 110, 248, 252, 413

Fitzgerald, F. Scott, 604

Fix, Paul, 65

Flaubert, Gustave, 223, 336

Forbes, Malcolm, 574, 582

Forster, E. M., 567

Foster, George, 395

Fowler, Gene, 216

Francis, Brendan, 127

Franklin, Benjamin, 528

Frisch, Max, 114

Frost, Robert, 323

Fuller, Thomas, 44, 247

Gabor, Zsa Zsa, 411

Gandhi, Mahatma, 29

Garagiola, Joe, 356

Garnett, David, 296

Giraudoux, Jean, 66

Gladstone, Mrs. William, 261

Goethe, Johann von, 63, 569

Goldwyn, Samuel, 612

Grant, Cary, 553

Graves, Robert, 56, 203

Green, Matthew,
572
Guindon, 11
Hadas, Moses,
523, 524
Hamilton, William,
106, 312, 352
Harburg, E. Y.,
376
Hawthorne,
Nathaniel, 593
Hayakawa, S. I.,
67
Heifetz, Josefa,
611
Helps, Arthur, 361
Hinckley, Wilson,
188
Hodgson, Ralph,
606
Hoffa, Jimmy, 447
Hoffman, Abbie,
454
Holmes, Oliver
Wendell, Jr.,
485
Hope, Bob, 281
Hudson, Bob, 446
Huxley, Aldous,
464
Huysmans, J. K.,
131
Irish, Johnny, 273
Jackson, Glenda,
350
James, Clive, 443
James, King, 225
Jefferson, Thomas,
260, 603
Jerome, Saint,
132, 419
John Baptist de La
Salle, Saint,
101
Johnson, Diane,
219
Johnson, Lyndon
Baines, 275,
276

Johnson, Samuel,
68, 597, 608
Johst, Hans, 504
Jones, Bill, 182
Jones, Franklin P.,
555
Kaufman, George
S., 400
Keillor, Garrison,
163
Kennedy, Flo-
rynce, 113, 434
Kennedy, John F.,
451
Kennedy, Rose,
279
Kerr, Jean, 253,
453
Kerr-Walker,
Lorna, 284
Keynes, John May-
nard, 43
Kommen, Will,
626
Kraus, Karl, 122
Lamb, Charles,
305
Langley, Edward,
295
Lardner, Ring,
489, 490, 543
La Rochefoucauld,
340, 359
Law, Roger, 437
Lawrence, Roz,
477
Leacock, Stephen,
601, 602
Lehrer, Tom, 381
Lemons, Abe, 311
Lennon, John, 31
Leonard, John,
619
Letterman, David,
333
Levant, Oscar,
502, 617
Levenson, Sam,
89, 109

Liebling, A. J., 61,
226
Liebowitz, Fran,
42, 243, 455
Lincoln, Abraham,
220, 459, 628
Locke, John, 99
Lombardi, Vince,
583
Longworth, Alice
Roosevelt, 26,
263, 406, 407
Lubitsch, Ernst,
337
Luce, Claire
Boothe, 326
Lyly, John, 629
Lynes, Russell,
210
Mannix, Edward
J., 427
Marat, Jean Paul,
9
Marquis, Don, 508
Martial, 193
Martin, Dean, 259
Martin, Steve, 394,
532
Marx, Groucho,
55, 360, 363,
412
Mason, Jackie,
330, 558
Maugham, Somer-
set, 364, 432,
433
Maurois, André,
222
McCabe, Charles,
59, 343
McCarthy, Eugene,
292
McCourt, Malachy,
254
McGoorty, Danny,
180, 594
Medawar, P. B., 62
Meir, Golda, 84
Menander, 194,
357

Mencken, H. L., 88, 150, 211, 294, 300, 527, 531, 548, 623
Metalious, Grace, 224
Midler, Bette, 425
Miller, Henry, 90, 196
Miss Piggy, 316
Mizner, Wilson, 92
Montaigne, Michel de, 10, 324
Morgan, Henry, 507
Morgan, Ted, 467, 521
Mostel, Kate, 487
Muggeridge, Malcolm, 125
Mumford, Lewis, 498
Munro, H. H., 367
Nader, Ralph, 285
Nash, Ogden, 511, 590, 591, 609
Nathan, George Jean, 251
Neville, Robert, 17
Nietzsche, Friedrich, 6, 424, 547, 573
Nixon, Richard M., 271, 272
Nye, Bill, 600, 610
O'Brien, Edna, 560
Orben, Robert, 314
Ovid, 191
Palmer, Samuel, 178
Parker, Dorothy, 79, 250, 384
Pastrano, Willie, 474
Perelman, S. J., 484, 519

Phillips, "Bum," 385
Pierce, Charles, 550
Plato, 5, 100, 137, 138
Plautus, Titus Maccius, 4
Poole, Mary Pettibone, 72
Porteus, Beilby, 52
Pritchett, V. S., 561
Proust, Marcel, 541
Puzo, Mario, 213
Rabelais, François, 245
Raper, John W., 452
Reagan, Ronald, 288
Repplier, Agnes, 375
Richter, Charles, 540
Rivers, Joan, 93, 94
Rockefeller, Nelson, 283
Rogers, Will, 564, 605
Rowland, Helen, 143
Ruff, Howard, 530
Rukeyser, Louis, 398
Runyon, Damon, 183, 184, 401
Russell, Bertrand, 13, 50, 197, 366, 565, 571
Ryan, Tom, 354
Safire, William, 482
Sagan, Françoise, 506
Sahl, Mort, 268

Salinger, J. D, 368, 369
Sanders, Ed, 60
Santayana, George, 33, 515
Sartre, Jean-Paul, 370, 520
Schulz, Charles, 25, 27
Scott, George C., 448
Seitz, Nick, 374
Shakespeare, William, 516, 562
Shaw, George Bernard, 87, 198, 200, 201, 387
Sheed, Wilfred, 301
Shulman, Max, 229
Simmons, Lon, 505
Skelton, Teressa, 161, 239
Smith, David, 362
Smith, Martin Cruz, 227
Smith, Stevie, 12
Smith, Sydney, 449, 518
Steinberg, David, 289, 335
Steinem, Gloria, 405, 445, 460
"Steinway, Gertrude," 208
Stengel, Casey, 457
Sterne, Laurence, 69
Sulzberger, Marina, 576
Swift, Jonathan, 615
Syrus, Publilius, 192

Tartakower,
  Savielly Grig-
  orievitch, 308,
  309, 596
Terence, 328
Thomas, Lewis,
  493
Thompson, Hunter
  S., 258, 476
Thoreau, Henry
  David, 348,
  423
Thornton, Alec
  Yuill, 512
Thurber, James,
  23, 133, 185,
  517
Tolstoy, Leo, 204
Tomlin, Lily, 475,
  535
Toscanini, Arturo,
  130
Tracy, Spencer,
  408
Trillin, Calvin, 154
Truman, Harry S,
  270
Tucker, Sophie,
  496, 620

Turenne, Vicomte,
  341
Twain, Mark, 20,
  34, 118, 234,
  313, 339, 418,
  537, 614
Tynan, Kenneth,
  399
Updike, John, 28
Van Buren, Abi-
  gail, 128
Vauvenargues,
  Marquis de,
  139
Victoria, Queen,
  262
Vidal, Gore, 83,
  105, 377, 513
Villa, Pancho, 167
Voltaire, 57
Walker, Jimmy,
  371
Warhol, Andy, 134
Warner, Jack, 230
Waugh, Evelyn,
  126
Wegner, Daniel M.,
  509
Wendell, Barrett,
  47

West, Mae, 149,
  575
Westhead, Paul,
  206
Whistler, James
  McNeill, 327
Whitehead, Alfred
  North, 624
Wilde, Oscar, 71,
  80, 141, 199,
  297, 317, 358,
  430, 559, 613
Will, George, 286
Wilson, Flip, 35
Winters, Shelley,
  153
Wither, George,
  238
Wodehouse, P. G.,
  1
Woodford, Jack,
  215
Wouk, Herman,
  228
Wright, Frank
  Lloyd, 372
Young, Andrew,
  439
Youngman, Henny,
  162

Index of Subjects and Key Words

Abortion, 113
Absence, 420
Academics, 531
Academy Awards, 409
Acne, 586
Actors, 441
Aging, 634
Alexander, 186
Alligator, 171
America, 198–200, 480, 529, 588
Answers, 27
Ape, 242
Architect, 372
Aristotle, 187
Astronaut, 330
Audience, 391
Australia, 630
Autobiography, 243
Avarice, 572
Baby, 320
Beauty, 539, 557, 573
Bed, 549
Beethoven, Ludwig van, 623
Belief, 19
Betting, 401
Bible, 241
Billiards, 623
Bird, 347
Birth, 79–93, 407
Birth control, 88, 128
Birthday, 468
Bitch, 465
Blacks, 534
Blonde, 436
Books, 231–243, 523, 524

Bores, 351
Borges, Jorge Luis, 619
Boxing, 474, 579
Boy, 100
Brahms, Johannes, 421
Brain damage, 509
Breathing, 620
Broadway, 400
Brothel, 336
Burbank, California, 566
Businessmen, 439
Cabbage, 75
California, 413, 416
Canada, 73, 335
Cars, 369
Cats, 173, 501, 532
Caution, 388
Censorship, 432
Champions, 374
Cheese, 627
Chicago, Illinois, 403
Chicken, 345
Children, 94–110, 380, 422
Christians, 21
Chrysanthemum, 1
Chutzpah, 513
Classics, 196
Clever, 172
Cloverleaf, 498
Coffee, 459
Communicating, 381
Complexion, 490
Cooks, 410
Copulation, 580

Country, 517
Cowardice, 168, 567
Crime, 85
Criticism, 406, 555
Crossroads, 386
Cucumber, 608
Culture, 504
Curve ball, 356
Dante, 165
Death, 37–49, 55, 76, 166, 167
Decision, 522
Definitions, 78
Democracy, 198
Dentist, 126
Diet, 477
Dirty, 578
Dishonesty, 528
Dissipation, 428
Divorce, 103, 160, 161
Donkeys, 193
Drink, 19, 244–259
Drugs, 476
Earplugs, 365
Egypt, 477
Elephant, 628
Emergency, 355
Emotions, 613
Enemy, 326, 327, 341, 430, 451
England, 595
Enthusiasm, 583
Err, 484
Eschatology, 33–50
ESP, 606, 607
Eunuch, 77
Exercise, 512

Failure, 322, 510
Faith, 18
Fall, 333
Farm, 519
Fat, 419, 477
Fatherhood, 571
Feet, 315
Feminism, 405, 445
Film, 491
Fish, 472
Flab, 617
Flux, 461
Foetus, 209, 402
Food, 316
Footprints, 363
Foresight, 418, 530, 628
France, 577
Friendship, 429, 488
Frijoles, 563
Fur trapping, 462
Fuses, 342
Future, 444
Gag, 636
Garbo, Greta, 337
Gaul, 188
Gay, 550
Generalize, 625
God, 2–11, 15, 174, 389
Goethe, Johann von, 218, 623
Golf, 623
Goliath, 618
Good deed, 377
Government, 201, 260–295, 379, 528, 564
Guests, 629
Gutter, 473
Haircut, 1
Happiness, 349
Hard knocks, 194
Hat, 346
Hate, 13, 427
H-bombs, 393

Health, 313–314, 517, 626
Hero, 604, 605
Hesitate, 470
Hogmeat, 542
Holy Ghost, 476
Honesty, 516, 612
Hope, 453
Horses, 179–181
Hughes, Howard, 521
Hunger, 543
Husbands, 175, 411
Hypochondria, 585
Hypocrite, 508
Inaccuracy, 367
Incest, 114
Inelegance, 544
Inflation, 252, 525
Insects, 456
Intelligence, 62–67, 323
James, Henry, 297–301
James, Jesse, 633
Japanese, 495
Jogging, 310–312, 512
Kidnapped, 584
Killer instinct, 338
Kings, 568
Kleptomaniac, 507
Laughter, 68–72, 556
Law, lawyers, 302, 306
Lawbreaking, 184
Laziness, 433–434, 452
Learning, 449
Lectures, 548
Legs, 505
Lies, 533
Life, 28–36, 87, 463, 479, 496, 502, 520, 574, 620

Listener, 361
Literature, 222, 237
Logic, 460
Lohengrin, 549
Loon soup, 332
Lord Ronald, 602
Los Angeles, California, 414
Love, 80, 86, 135–145, 175, 552, 587
Lubbock, Texas, 349
Luck, 389
Man, 73
Manuscript, 209
Marriage, 107, 146–159, 175, 411, 416, 538, 547
Medicine, 540
Men, 506
Middle age, 609
Mind, 514
Minneapolis, Minnesota, 163
Misconceptions, 631
Mistakes, 308
Moccasins, 325
Modern man, 545
Monogamy, 565
Monomania, 375
Monotony, 590
Mothers, 128
Mouth, 417
Murder, 51–54, 601
Music, 424, 472, 473, 570, 597, 610
Narcissism, 79–84, 446, 354
Necks, 394
Neurosis, 561
New Jersey, 378

Newspaper, 603
New York City,
    467
Normality, 499
Old age, 340, 481,
    581
OPUC, 589
Outer space, 497
Owl, 331
Pain, 392
Panther, 591
Paranoia, 536
Partying, 554
Passport, 626
Patriotism, 197
People, 364
Philosophy, 24, 26,
    183, 195, 527
Phone booth, 329
Pickle, 215
Pitchfork, 615
Platitudes, 318
Pleasure, 452
Poetry, 56–61
Politicians,
    260–295, 535,
    537
Politics, 627
Polo, 576
Pong, Video, 334
Postage, 398
Presidents,
    260–293
Profanity, 22
Progress, 511
Proverbs, 177,
    178, 319
Pun, 637
Punctuality, 317
Purity, 426
Quotations, 23,
    111, 112, 177,
    178, 319, 328,
    553, 557, 599,
    632
Rats, 600

Real estate, 593
Reality, 475
Redundancy, 328
Reformer, 371
Religion, 14, 16,
    526
Rich, 487
Rome, 189–91,
    467
Rule, 348
Rutherford, Mar-
    garet, 399
Saint, 16
Savage, 515
Schizophrenia, 551
School boards, 614
Science, 493
Sex, 114–134,
    382, 458, 465,
    478, 541, 575,
    611
Sex life, 350
Shakespeare,
    William,
    203–207
Shallow, 358
Shoe, 598
Shula, Don, 385
Silence, 315, 381,
    489
Sin, 380
Sinatra, Frank,
    440
Sincerity, 387
Sloppiness, 482
Slush, 426
Smile, 448
Smoking, 225
Snore, 435
Sofa crevice, 500
Speed, 29
Sphincter, 572
Stockyards, 300
Success, 455
Suckers, 182
Suicide, 164

Suitcases, 368
Talk, 397
Team, 207
Television, 396
Tense, 352
Theater, 437, 443
Think, 50
Three o'clock, 370
Time, 47, 470
Toots Shor's, 383
Towels, 412
Tradition, 622
Travel, 427, 464
Triple, 395
Trophies, 354
Trust, 429
Truth, 170, 384,
    423, 425, 485,
    533, 624
Tumescence, 458
Tunnel, 483
Turkeys, 86
Ugly, 345
Universe, 22
Urologist, 466
Vaughan Williams,
    Ralph, 450
Virgin Mary, 12
Virtue, 376, 592
Wagner, Richard,
    610
Warner, Jack, 404
Wealth, 494, 546
Widow, 321
Wife, 416
Windows, 174
Winning, 385,
    431, 596
Woman, 74
Words, 569
Working, 594
World, 202
Writing, 209–230,
    633
Wrong, 446, 447
Yam, 390

THE OTHER
637
BEST THINGS
ANYBODY EVER SAID

To
Tom Stewart,
who has kept so much egg off my face

Contents

Introduction

PART ONE

Theology, Self-love, Self-abuse, Love, Sex,
Wedlock, Kids, Drink, Death, Comedy, Men and
Women, War, Money, Work, and a great deal more

PART TWO

Advice, Health, Food, Life Itself, America,
Psychoses, Books, Writers, Music, Show Business,
Animals, Doctors, Presidents, Politics, Sports,
and much else

PART THREE

Miscellaneous

Sources, References, and Notes

Index of Authors

Index of Subjects and Key Words

Introduction

My first collection of mostly humorous quotations was published in 1982 and was titled *The 637 Best Things Anybody Ever Said*, which might make you think that the sequel deals with the second best. Not true. These—the quotes in the book you are now holding—are in fact the 637 best things anybody ever said. In titling the first collection, I lied.

Most books of this sort are too full of chaff. For every quote you can use in conversation without being thrown down the stairs as an intolerable bore there are pages of the pompous, the banal, and the so what? The aim here is to present nothing but kernels of wheat. Open the book anywhere; if you don't find a gem that makes you smile at least inwardly, you should ask your doctor if you are clinically dead.

Quotes are generally grouped by subject. Subjects follow each other sometimes at random and sometimes in a way to encourage reading pages consecutively, never according to the alphabet. In Part One, it struck me as logical to arrange Love, Sex, Wedlock, Kids, Drink, Death, and Comedy in that order.

It has often been noted by researchers into pith that the wags of the world are funniest when they are cynical rather than sentimental. That, and not any presumed sourness on my part, explains the preponderance of negative remarks. The number of anti-marriage quotes, for example, doesn't necessarily mean that I personally am against it. In truth, I like marriage, though I happen to be free of it at the moment.

Many thanks to the readers of *The 637 Best Things Anybody Ever Said*, which last I heard was still in print in both hardcover and paperback, who sent me their favorite lines. Their specific contributions are acknowledged in the Sources, References, and Notes.

A word about ascriptions. "Unknown" is used when I have been unable to discover the source. Readers may be better informed. "Anonymous" is used when I am convinced that the source not only is unknown but is going to stay unknown.

Birth and death dates are given only for historical figures.

The significance of the number 637 and other odds and ends are discussed in the Introduction to the earlier volume.

Robert Byrne

PART ONE

Theology
Self-love
Self-abuse
Love
Sex
Wedlock
Kids
Drink
Death
Comedy
Men and Women
War
Money
Work
and a great deal more

1

My theology, briefly, is that the universe was dictated but not signed. *Christopher Morley (1890–1957)*

2

God made everything out of nothing, but the nothingness shows through. *Paul Valéry (1871–1945)*

3

God was satisfied with his own work, and that is fatal.
Samuel Butler (1835–1902)

4

God is not dead but alive and well and working on a much less ambitious project. *Graffito*

5

Why attack God? He may be as miserable as we are.
Erik Satie (1866–1925)

6

Every day people are straying away from the church and going back to God. *Lenny Bruce (1923–1966)*

7

Religion is what keeps the poor from murdering the rich. *Napoleon (1769–1821)*

8

What if there had been room at the inn?

Linda Festa on the
origins of Christianity

9

Christ died for our sins. Dare we make his martyrdom meaningless by not committing them? *Jules Feiffer*

1 0

Catholicism has changed tremendously in recent years. Now when Communion is served there is also a salad bar. *Bill Marr*

1 1

Faith is believing what you know ain't so.

"A schoolboy" quoted by
Mark Twain (1835–1910)

1 2

Faith is under the left nipple.

Martin Luther (1483–1546)

1 3

Because I'm Jewish, a lot of people ask why I killed Christ. What can I say? It was an accident. It was one of those parties that got out of hand. I killed him because he wouldn't become a doctor.

Lenny Bruce (1923–1966)

14

Your chances of getting hit by lightning go up if you stand under a tree, shake your fist at the sky, and say, "Storms suck!" *Johnny Carson*

15

Trust in Allah, but tie your camel. *Arabian proverb*

16

The last time I saw him he was walking down Lover's Lane holding his own hand. *Fred Allen (1894–1956)*

17

The nice thing about egotists is that they don't talk about other people. *Lucille S. Harper*

18

It is far more impressive when others discover your good qualities without your help.

Miss Manners (Judith Martin)

19

In an age when the fashion is to be in love with yourself, confessing to be in love with somebody else is an admission of unfaithfulness to one's beloved.

Russell Baker

20

If only it was as easy to banish hunger by rubbing the belly as it is to masturbate.

Diogenes the Cynic (412? to 323 B.C.*)*

21

Self-abuse is the most certain road to the grave.

Dr. George M. Calhoun in 1855

22

Many mothers are wholly ignorant of the almost universal prevalence of secret vice, or self-abuse, among the young. Why hesitate to say firmly and without quibble that personal abuse lies at the root of much of the feebleness, paleness, nervousness, and good-for-nothingness of the entire community?

Dr. J. H. Kellogg (1852–1943)

23

Masturbation! The amazing availability of it!
James Joyce (1882–1941)

24

Philosophy is to the real world as masturbation is to sex. *Karl Marx (1818–1883)*

25

I was the best I ever had. *Woody Allen*

26

The good thing about masturbation is that you don't have to dress up for it. *Truman Capote*

27

My brain is my second favorite organ. *Woody Allen*

28

Love is not the dying moan of a distant violin—it's the triumphant twang of a bedspring.
S. J. Perelman (1904–1979)

29

Love is what you've been through with somebody.
James Thurber (1894–1961)

3 0

Love is the delusion that one woman differs from another. *H. L. Mencken (1880–1956)*

3 1

Love is being stupid together.
Paul Valéry (1871–1945)

3 2

Love is an obsessive delusion that is cured by marriage.
Dr. Karl Bowman (1888–1973)

3 3

Love is the only game that is not called on account of darkness. *M. Hirschfield*

3 4

The greatest love is a mother's, then a dog's, then a sweetheart's. *Polish proverb*

3 5

If I love you, what business is it of yours?
Johann von Goethe (1749–1832)

3 6

A man in love mistakes a pimple for a dimple.
Japanese proverb

37

A lover without indiscretion is no lover at all.
Thomas Hardy (1840–1928)

38

The most important thing in a relationship between a man and a woman is that one of them be good at taking orders. *Linda Festa*

39

In a great romance, each person basically plays a part that the other really likes. *Elizabeth Ashley*

40

I love Mickey Mouse more than any woman I've ever known. *Walt Disney (1901–1966)*

41

I like young girls. Their stories are shorter.
Tom McGuane

42

The most romantic thing any woman ever said to me in bed was "Are you sure you're not a cop?"
Larry Brown

43

Someday we'll look back on this moment and plow into a parked car. *Evan Davis*

44

Sex is dirty only when it's done right.   *Woody Allen*

45

For flavor, instant sex will never supersede the stuff you have to peel and cook.   *Quentin Crisp*

46

Why won't you let me kiss you goodnight? Is it something I said?   *Tom Ryan*

47

Give a man a free hand and he'll run it all over you.

Mae West (1892–1980)

48

I've been in more laps than a napkin.

Mae West (1892–1980)

49

I used to be Snow White, but I drifted.

Mae West (1892–1980)

50

He who hesitates is a damned fool.

Mae West (1892–1980)

51

I wasn't kissing her, I was whispering in her mouth.

Chico Marx (1891–1961)

52

Contraceptives should be used on every conceivable occasion. *From* The Last Goon Show of All

53

Bisexuality immediately doubles your chances for a date on Saturday night. *Woody Allen*

54

What do hookers do on their nights off, type?

Elayne Boosler

55

I have perfumed my bed with myrrh, aloes, and cinnamon. Come, let us take our fill of love until the morning. *Proverbs 7: 17–18*

56

All the men on my staff can type. *Bella Abzug*

57

A is for Apple. *Hester Prynne*

58

The perfect lover is one who turns into a pizza at 4:00 A.M. *Charles Pierce*

59

If God had meant us to have group sex, he'd have given us more organs. *Malcolm Bradbury*

60

It's been so long since I made love I can't even remember who gets tied up. *Joan Rivers*

61

Ouch! That felt good! *Karen Elizabeth Gordon*

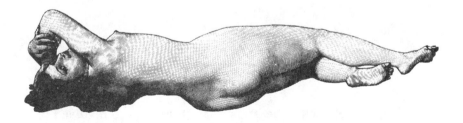

62

I never expected to see the day when girls would get sunburned in the places they do today.
Will Rogers (1879–1935)

63

The first time we slept together she drove a recreational vehicle into the bedroom. *Richard Lewis*

64

A man can sleep around, no questions asked, but if a woman makes nineteen or twenty mistakes she's a tramp. *Joan Rivers*

65

What do you give a man who has everything? Penicillin. *Jerry Lester*

66

Some men are so macho they'll get you pregnant just to kill a rabbit. *Maureen Murphy*

67

Chaste makes waste. *Unknown*

68

The trouble with incest is that it gets you involved with relatives. *George S. Kaufman (1889–1961)*

69

After we made love he took a piece of chalk and made an outline of my body. *Joan Rivers*

7 0

It's easy to make a friend. What's hard is to make a stranger. *Unknown*

7 1

The reason people sweat is so they won't catch fire when making love. *Don Rose*

7 2

He's such a hick he doesn't even have a trapeze in his bedroom. *Unknown*

7 3

The trouble with group sex is that you never know where to put your elbows. *Martin Cruz Smith*

7 4

If you want to read about love and marriage you've got to buy two separate books. *Alan King*

7 5

'Tis more blessed to give than receive; for example, wedding presents. *H. L. Mencken (1880–1956)*

7 6

Men have a much better time of it than women; for one thing they marry later; for another thing they die earlier. *H. L. Mencken (1880–1956)*

7 7

Monogamy is the Western custom of one wife and hardly any mistresses.

H. H. Munro (Saki) (1870–1916)

7 8

Marriage is based on the theory that when a man discovers a brand of beer exactly to his taste he should at once throw up his job and go to work in the brewery. *George Jean Nathan (1882–1958)*

7 9

A wife lasts only for the length of the marriage, but an ex-wife is there *for the rest of your life.*

Jim Samuels

8 0

A man in love is incomplete until he is married. Then he is finished. *Zsa Zsa Gabor*

8 1

A husband is what is left of the lover after the nerve has been extracted. *Helen Rowland (1876–1950)*

8 2

When a girl marries she exchanges the attentions of many men for the inattention of one.

Helen Rowland (1876–1950)

83

One man's folly is another man's wife.

Helen Rowland (1876–1950)

84

The most happy marriage I can imagine to myself would be the union of a deaf man to a blind woman.

Samuel Taylor Coleridge (1772–1834)

85

The trouble with some women is that they get all excited about nothing—and then marry him. *Cher*

86

Trust your husband, adore your husband, and get as much as you can in your own name.

Advice to Joan Rivers from her mother

87

Honesty has ruined more marriages than infidelity.

Charles McCabe (1915–1983)

88

Bachelors should be heavily taxed. It is not fair that some men should be happier than others.

Oscar Wilde (1854–1900)

89

I believe in the institution of marriage and I intend to keep trying until I get it right. *Richard Pryor*

90

I was a fifty-four-year-old virgin, but I'm all right now. *Unknown*

91

Eighty percent of married men cheat in America. The rest cheat in Europe. *Jackie Mason*

9 2

A man can have two, maybe three love affairs while he's married. After that it's cheating.   *Yves Montand*

9 3

Marriage has driven more than one man to sex.
Peter De Vries

9 4

It destroys one's nerves to be amiable every day to the same human being.
Benjamin Disraeli (1804–1881)

9 5

If you are looking for a kindly, well-to-do older gentleman who is no longer interested in sex, take out an ad in *The Wall Street Journal.*
Abigail Van Buren

9 6

Divorce is a game played by lawyers.   *Cary Grant*

9 7

She cried, and the judge wiped her tears with my checkbook.   *Tommy Manville (1894–1967)*

9 8

I can't mate in captivity.
Gloria Steinem on why she has never married

99

It wasn't exactly a divorce—I was traded.

Tim Conway

100

You don't know anything about a woman until you meet her in court. *Norman Mailer*

101

I'm very old-fashioned. I believe that people should marry for life, like pigeons and Catholics.

Woody Allen

102

Marriage is like a bank account. You put it in, you take it out, you lose interest. *Professor Irwin Corey*

103

I hate babies. They're so human.

H. H. Munro (Saki) (1870–1916)

104

The baby was so ugly they had to hang a pork chop around its neck to get the dog to play with it.

Unknown

105

My mother didn't breast-feed me. She said she liked me as a friend. *Rodney Dangerfield*

1 0 6

It is no wonder that people are so horrible when they start life as children. *Kingsley Amis*

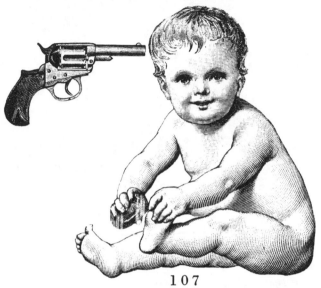

1 0 7

I was toilet-trained at gunpoint. *Billy Braver*

1 0 8

Life does not begin at the moment of conception or the moment of birth. It begins when the kids leave home and the dog dies. *Unknown*

1 0 9

One father is more than a hundred schoolmasters.
George Herbert (1593–1633)

1 1 0

An ounce of mother is worth a ton of priest.
Spanish proverb

111

Happy is the child whose father died rich. *Proverb*

112

Reinhart was never his mother's favorite—and he was an only child. *Thomas Berger*

113

Nature makes boys and girls lovely to look upon so they can be tolerated until they acquire some sense.
William Lyon Phelps (1865–1943)

114

The first half of our lives is ruined by our parents and the second half by our children.
Clarence Darrow (1857–1938)

115

Literature is mostly about having sex and not much about having children. Life is the other way around.
David Lodge

116

If you have never been hated by your child, you have never been a parent. *Bette Davis*

117

How to Raise Your I.Q. by Eating Gifted Children
Book title by Lewis B. Frumkes (1983)

118

Never raise your hand to your children—it leaves your midsection unprotected. *Robert Orben*

119

Blessed are the young, for they shall inherit the national debt. *Herbert Hoover (1874–1964)*

120

The denunciation of the young is a necessary part of the hygiene of older people, and greatly assists in the circulation of the blood.
Logan Pearsall Smith (1865–1946)

121

One of the disadvantages of having children is that they eventually get old enough to give you presents they make at school. *Robert Byrne*

122

Never have children, only grandchildren. *Gore Vidal*

123

No matter how old a mother is, she watches her middle-aged children for signs of improvement.
Florida Scott-Maxwell

124

Youth is such a wonderful thing. What a crime to waste it on children.
George Bernard Shaw (1856–1950)

125

Having children is like having a bowling alley installed in your brain. *Martin Mull*

126

If you think education is expensive, try ignorance. *Derek Bok*

127

I'm for bringing back the birch, but only for consenting adults. *Gore Vidal*

128

Education is the process of casting false pearls before real swine. *Irwin Edman (1896–1954)*

129

Good teaching is one-fourth preparation and three-fourths theatre. *Gail Godwin*

130

University politics are vicious precisely because the stakes are so small. *Henry Kissinger*

131

Political history is far too criminal a subject to be a fit thing to teach children.

W. H. Auden (1907–1973)

132

I think the world is run by C students. *Al McGuire*

133

Smartness runs in my family. When I went to school I was so smart my teacher was in my class for five years. *George Burns*

134

I was thrown out of college for cheating on the metaphysics exam; I looked into the soul of the boy next to me. *Woody Allen*

135

You can't expect a boy to be vicious till he's been to a good school   *H. H. Munro (Saki) (1870–1916)*

136

Beware of the man who does not drink.   *Proverb*

137

Water, taken in moderation, cannot hurt anybody.
Mark Twain (1835–1910)

1 3 8

A productive drunk is the bane of moralists.

Unknown

1 3 9

Come quickly, I am tasting stars!
*Dom Pérignon (1638–1715) at the
moment of his discovery of champagne*

1 4 0

The worst thing about some men is that when they are not drunk they are sober.
William Butler Yeats (1865–1939)

1 4 1

An Irishman is not drunk as long as he still has a blade of grass to hang onto. *Unknown*

1 4 2

Alcohol is the anesthesia by which we endure the operation of life. *George Bernard Shaw (1856–1950)*

143

To drink is a Christian diversion, unknown to the
Turk or the Persian. *William Congreve (1670–1729)*

144

To one large turkey add one gallon of vermouth and a demijohn of Angostura bitters. Shake.

Recipe for turkey cocktail from
F. Scott Fitzgerald (1896–1940)

145

An alcoholic is someone you don't like who drinks as much as you do. *Dylan Thomas (1914–1953)*

146

I can't die until the government finds a safe place to bury my liver. *Phil Harris*

147

My uncle was the town drunk—and we lived in Chicago. *George Gobel*

148

I've never been drunk, but often I've been overserved.

George Gobel

149

Somebody left the cork out of my lunch.

W. C. Fields (1880–1946)

150

I have to think hard to name an interesting man who does not drink. *Richard Burton*

151

I always wake up at the crack of ice.

Joe E. Lewis (1902–1971)

152

The graveyards are full of indispensable men.

Charles de Gaulle (1890–1970)

153

There are more dead people than living, and their numbers are increasing. *Eugène Ionesco*

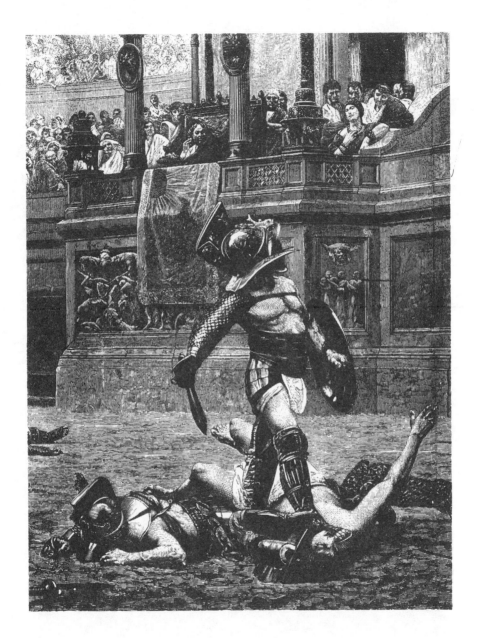

1 5 4

Defeat is worse than death because you have to live
with defeat. *Bill Musselman*

155

The executioner is, I hear, very expert, and my neck is very slender. *Anne Boleyn (1507?–1536)*

156

I didn't know he was dead; I thought he was British.

Unknown

157

I believe in sex and death—two experiences that come once in a lifetime. *Woody Allen*

158

There are worse things in life than death. Have you ever spent an evening with an insurance salesman?

Woody Allen

159

Go away. I'm all right.

Last words of H. G. Wells (1886–1946)

160

You can pretend to be serious; you can't pretend to be witty. *Sacha Guitry (1885–1957)*

161

Everybody likes a kidder, but nobody lends him money. *Arthur Miller*

162

One doesn't have a sense of humor. It has you.

Larry Gelbart

163

The aim of a joke is not to degrade the human being but to remind him that he is already degraded.

George Orwell (1903–1950)

164

If you don't count some of Jehovah's injunctions, there are no humorists in the Bible.   *Mordecai Richler*

165

Dying is easy. Comedy is difficult.

Actor Edmond Gwenn (1875–1959) on his deathbed

166

Humorists always sit at the children's table.

Woody Allen

167

I don't care where I sit as long as I get fed.

Calvin Trillin

168

What is comedy? Comedy is the art of making people laugh without making them puke.   *Steve Martin*

169

Until Eve arrived, this was a man's world.

Richard Armour

170

Whatever women do they must do twice as well as men to be thought half as good. Luckily, this is not difficult. *Charlotte Whitton (1896–1975)*

171

Don't accept rides from strange men, and remember that all men are strange. *Robin Morgan*

172

There are only two kinds of men—the dead and the deadly. *Helen Rowland (1876–1950)*

173

Men are creatures with two legs and eight hands.
Jayne Mansfield (1932–1967)

174

I refuse to consign the whole male sex to the nursery. I insist on believing that some men are my equals.
Brigid Brophy

175

Being a woman is a terribly difficult trade, since it consists principally of dealing with men.
Joseph Conrad (1857–1924)

176

Being a woman is of special interest only to aspiring male transsexuals. To actual women it is simply a good excuse not to play football. *Fran Lebowitz*

177

My advice to the women's clubs of America is raise more hell and fewer dahlias.

William Allen White (1868–1944)

178

A lady is one who never shows her underwear un-intentionally. *Lillian Day*

179

Anyone who says he can see through women is missing a lot. *Groucho Marx (1895–1977)*

180

The most popular labor-saving device today is still a husband with money. *Joey Adams*

181

A gentleman never strikes a lady with his hat on.

Fred Allen (1894–1956)

182

I've never struck a woman in my life, not even my own mother. *W. C. Fields (1880–1946)*

183

If you become a star, *you* don't change, everyone else does.   *Kirk Douglas*

184

I'm not a real movie star—I've still got the same wife I started out with twenty-eight years ago.
Will Rogers (1879–1935)

185

Fame lost its appeal for me when I went into a public restroom and an autograph seeker handed me a pen and paper under the stall door.   *Marlo Thomas*

186

If I had done everything I'm credited with, I'd be speaking to you from a laboratory jar at Harvard.
Frank Sinatra

187

AS USUAL, YOUR INFORMATION STINKS.
Telegram to Time *magazine from Frank Sinatra*

188

As an anti-American, I thank you for your rotten article devoted to my person.
Letter to Time *magazine from Prince Sihanouk*

189

I am a deeply superficial person. *Andy Warhol*

190

I have bursts of being a lady, but it doesn't last long.
Shelley Winters

191

Working with Julie Andrews is like getting hit over the head with a valentine. *Christopher Plummer*

192

I should have been a country-western singer. After all, I'm older than most western countries.
George Burns

193

Never face facts; if you do you'll never get up in the morning. *Marlo Thomas*

194

Nothing succeeds like the appearance of success.
Christopher Lasch

195

She's the kind of girl who climbed the ladder of success wrong by wrong. *Mae West (1892–1980)*

196

Nothing fails like success. *Gerald Nachman*

197

Anyone seen on a bus after the age of thirty has been a failure in life. *Loelia, Duchess of Westminster*

198

To err is human
And stupid.

Robert Byrne

199

You may already be a loser.
Form letter received by Rodney Dangerfield

200

How should they answer?
*Abigail Van Buren in reply to the question
"Why do Jews always answer a question
with a question?"*

201

If you live in New York, even if you're Catholic, you're Jewish. *Lenny Bruce (1923–1966)*

2 0 2

Jews always know two things: suffering and where to find great Chinese food.

From the movie My Favorite Year, *1982*

2 0 3

The goys have proven the following theorem. . . .

Physicist John von Neumann (1903–1957)
at the start of a classroom lecture

2 0 4

I want to be the white man's brother, not his brother-in-law. *Martin Luther King, Jr. (1929–1968)*

2 0 5

I have just enough white in me to make my honesty questionable. *Will Rogers (1879–1935)*

2 0 6

I never believed in Santa Claus because I knew no white dude would come into my neighborhood after dark. *Dick Gregory*

2 0 7

Work is of two kinds: first, altering the position of matter at or near the earth's surface relative to other matter; second, telling other people to do so.

Bertrand Russell (1872–1970)

208

All jobs should be open to everybody, unless they actually require a penis or a vagina.

Florynce Kennedy

209

It is impossible to enjoy idling unless there is plenty of work to do. *Jerome K. Jerome (1859–1927)*

210

Anybody who works is a fool. I don't work, I merely inflict myself on the public.   *Robert Morley*

211

Hard work never killed anybody, but why take a chance?

Charlie McCarthy (Edgar Bergen, 1903–1978)

212

If you have a job without aggravations, you don't have a job.   *Malcolm Forbes*

213

People who work sitting down get paid more than people who work standing up.

Ogden Nash (1902–1971)

214

Work is much more fun than fun.

Noel Coward (1899–1973)

215

The trouble with the rat race is that even if you win you're still a rat.   *Lily Tomlin*

216

Money is good for bribing yourself through the inconveniences of life. *Gottfried Reinhardt*

217

A billion here, a billion there—pretty soon it adds up to real money.
Senator Everett Dirksen (1896–1969)

218

I have enough money to last me the rest of my life, unless I buy something. *Jackie Mason*

219

The rich have a passion for bargains as lively as it is pointless. *Françoise Sagan*

220

Whoever said money can't buy happiness didn't know where to shop. *Unknown*

221

Behind every great fortune there is a crime.
Honoré de Balzac (1799–1850)

222

The richer your friends, the more they will cost you.
Elisabeth Marbury (1856–1933)

2 2 3

Money is always there, but the pockets change.

Gertrude Stein (1874–1946)

2 2 4

There must be more to life than having everything.

Maurice Sendak

2 2 5

If women didn't exist, all the money in the world would have no meaning.

Aristotle Onassis (1906–1975)

2 2 6

Better to be nouveau than never to have been riche at all. *Unknown*

2 2 7

Save a little money each month and at the end of the year you'll be surprised at how little you have.

Ernest Haskins

2 2 8

My problem lies in reconciling my gross habits with my net income. *Errol Flynn (1909–1959)*

2 2 9

Any man who has $10,000 left when he dies is a failure. *Errol Flynn (1909–1959)*

230

The wages of sin are unreported.   *Unknown*

231

I'm living so far beyond my income that we may almost be said to be living apart.

e e cummings (1894–1962)

232

To get back on your feet, miss two car payments.

Unknown

233

When I first arrived in this country I had only fifteen cents in my pocket and a willingness to compromise.

Weber cartoon caption

234

Fashion is a form of ugliness so intolerable that we have to alter it every six months.

Oscar Wilde (1856–1900)

235

Every generation laughs at the old fashions but religiously follows the new.

Henry David Thoreau (1817–1862)

236

If you look good and dress well, you don't need a purpose in life. *Fashion consultant Robert Pante*

237

I base my fashion taste on what doesn't itch.
Gilda Radner

238

War is a series of catastrophes that results in a victory. *Georges Clemenceau (1841–1929)*

239

You can no more win a war than you can win an earthquake. *Jeannette Rankin (1880–1973)*

240

I'd like to see the government get out of war altogether and leave the whole field to private industry.

Joseph Heller

241

The object of war is not to die for your country but to make the other bastard die for his.

General George Patton (1885–1945)

242

Name me an emperor who was ever struck by a cannonball. *Charles V (1500–1558)*

243

While you're saving your face you're losing your ass.
President Lyndon Johnson (1908–1973)

244

You can't say civilization don't advance . . . in every war they kill you a new way.
Will Rogers (1879–1935)

245

I have already given two cousins to the war and I stand ready to sacrifice my wife's brother.
Artemus Ward (1834–1867)

246

Join the army, see the world, meet interesting people, and kill them. *Unknown*

247

Being in the army is like being in the Boy Scouts, except that the Boy Scouts have adult supervision.
Blake Clark

248

The Israelis are the Doberman pinschers of the Middle East. They treat the Arabs like postmen.
Franklyn Ajaye

PART TWO

Advice
Health
Food
Life Itself
America
Psychoses
Books
Writers
Music
Show Business
Animals
Doctors
Presidents
Politics
Sports
and much else

249

Start slow and taper off. *Walt Stack*

250

Never get into fights with ugly people because they have nothing to lose. *Unknown*

251

Never miss a good chance to shut up.
Scott Beach's grandfather

252

The best way to keep one's word is not to give it.
Napoleon (1769–1821)

253

It's all right letting yourself go as long as you can let yourself back. *Mick Jagger*

254

Sometimes a scream is better than a thesis.
Ralph Waldo Emerson (1803–1882)

255

Aaeeeyaaayaaayaayaa . . .
Johnny Weissmuller (1904–1984)

256

When walking through a melon patch, don't adjust your sandals. *Chinese proverb*

257

Sometimes a fool makes a good suggestion.
Nicolas Boileau (1636–1711)

258

Good advice is one of those insults that ought to be forgiven. *Unknown*

259

It's no longer a question of staying healthy. It's a question of finding a sickness you like. *Jackie Mason*

260

I've just learned about his illness. Let's hope it's nothing trivial. *Variously ascribed*

261

I don't deserve this award, but I have arthritis and I don't deserve that either. *Jack Benny (1894–1974)*

2 6 2

As for me, except for an occasional heart attack, I feel as young as I ever did.

Robert Benchley (1889–1945)

2 6 3

I get my exercise acting as a pallbearer to my friends who exercise. *Chauncey Depew (1834–1928)*

2 6 4

Avoid running at all times.

Satchel Paige (1906?–1982)

2 6 5

It is more profitable for your congressman to support the tobacco industry than your life. *Jackie Mason*

2 6 6

Smoking is one of the leading causes of statistics.

Fletcher Knebel

2 6 7

Quit worrying about your health. It'll go away.

Robert Orben

2 6 8

Health nuts are going to feel stupid someday, lying in hospitals dying of nothing. *Redd Foxx*

269
To eat is human
To digest divine.
Mark Twain (1835–1910)

270
There is no sincerer love than the love of food.
George Bernard Shaw (1856–1950)

271
The most dangerous food is wedding cake.
American proverb

272
Roumanian-Yiddish cooking has killed more Jews than
Hitler. *Zero Mostel (1915–1977)*

273
I believe that eating pork makes people stupid.
David Steinberg

274
Eat, drink, and be merry, for tomorrow we may diet.
Unknown

275

When men reach their sixties and retire, they go to pieces. Women go right on cooking. *Gail Sheehy*

276

I've been on a diet for two weeks and all I've lost is two weeks. *Totie Fields (1931–1978)*

277

I'm on a seafood diet. I see food and I eat it.

Variously ascribed

278

Eat as much as you like—just don't swallow it.

Harry Secombe's diet

279

Recipe for chili from Allan Shivers,
former governor of Texas:

    Put a pot of chili on the stove to simmer.

    Let it simmer. Meanwhile, broil a good steak.

    Eat the steak. Let the chili simmer. Ignore it.

280

The two biggest sellers in any bookstore are the cookbooks and the diet books. The cookbooks tell you how to prepare the food and the diet books tell you how not to eat any of it. *Andy Rooney*

281

It's so beautifully arranged on the plate—you know someone's fingers have been all over it.

Julia Child on nouvelle cuisine

282

A gourmet who thinks of calories is like a tart who looks at her watch. *James Beard*

283

Where do you go to get anorexia? *Shelley Winters*

284

Nachman's Rule: When it comes to foreign food, the less authentic the better. *Gerald Nachman*

285

I eat merely to put food out of my mind.

N. F. Simpson

286

Isn't there any other part of the matzo you can eat?
*Marilyn Monroe (1926–1962) on being
served matzo ball soup three meals in a row*

287

A gourmet restaurant in Cincinnati is one where you
leave the tray on the table after you eat.   *Unknown*

288

When compelled to cook, I produce a meal that would
make a sword swallower gag.   *Russell Baker*

289

Poets have been mysteriously silent on the subject of
cheese.   *G. K. Chesterton (1874–1936)*

290

I don't even butter my bread. I consider that cooking.

Katherine Cebrian

291

Life is too short to stuff a mushroom.   *Storm Jameson*

292

The most remarkable thing about my mother is that for thirty years she served the family nothing but leftovers. The original meal has never been found.

Calvin Trillin

293

I'm in favor of liberalized immigration because of the effect it would have on restaurants. I'd let just about everybody in except the English.

Calvin Trillin

294

No man is lonely while eating spaghetti.

Robert Morley

295

I prefer my oysters fried;
That way I know my oysters died.

Roy G. Blount, Jr.

296

The trouble with life in the fast lane is that you get
to the other end in an awful hurry. *John Jensen*

297

It is not true that life is one damn thing after another
—it is one damn thing over and over.
Edna St. Vincent Millay (1892–1950)

298

Life is thirst. *Leonard Michaels*

299

The less things change, the more they remain the same. *Sicilian proverb*

300

There are days when it takes all you've got just to keep up with the losers. *Robert Orben*

301

If you can see the light at the end of the tunnel you are looking the wrong way. *Barry Commoner*

302

I have found little that is good about human beings. In my experience most of them are trash.
Sigmund Freud (1856–1939)

303

The brotherhood of man is not a mere poet's dream; it is a most depressing and humiliating reality.
Oscar Wilde (1854–1900)

304

We're all in this alone. *Lily Tomlin*

3 0 5

Our ignorance of history makes us libel our own times. People have always been like this.

Gustave Flaubert (1821–1880)

3 0 6

The British tourist is always happy abroad so long as the natives are waiters. *Robert Morley*

3 0 7

You can't judge Egypt by *Aïda*. *Ronald Firbank*

3 0 8

France is a country where the money falls apart and you can't tear the toilet paper. *Billy Wilder*

3 0 9

In Marseilles they make half the toilet soap we consume in America, but the Marseillaise only have a vague theoretical idea of its use, which they have obtained from books of travel.

Mark Twain (1835–1910)

310

Gaiety is the most outstanding feature of the Soviet Union. *Joseph Stalin (1879–1953)*

311

In Italy, for thirty years under the Borgias, they had warfare, terror, murder, and bloodshed, but they produced Michelangelo, Leonardo da Vinci, and the Renaissance. In Switzerland, they had brotherly love, they had five hundred years of democracy and peace —and what did they produce? The cuckoo clock.
From the movie The Third Man, *1949*

312

Canada is so square even the female impersonators are women. *From the movie* Outrageous, *1983*

313

Most Texans think Hanukkah is some sort of duck call.
Richard Lewis

314

Historians have now definitely established that Juan Cabrillo, discoverer of California, was not looking for Kansas, thus setting a precedent that continues to this day. *Wayne Shannon*

315

The big cities of America are becoming Third World countries. *Nora Ephron*

316

New York now leads the world's great cities in the number of people around whom you shouldn't make a sudden move. *David Letterman*

317

It isn't necessary to have relatives in Kansas City in order to be unhappy. *Groucho Marx (1895–1977)*

318

Isn't it nice that people who prefer Los Angeles to San Francisco live there? *Herb Caen*

319

San Francisco is like granola: Take away the fruits and the nuts, and all you have are the flakes.

Unknown

320

In San Francisco, Halloween is redundant.

Will Durst

321

Detroit is Cleveland without the glitter. *Unknown*

322

When I saw a sign on the freeway that said, "Los Angeles 445 miles," I said to myself, "I've got to get out of this lane." *Franklyn Ajaye*

323
Traffic signals in New York are just rough guidelines.
David Letterman

324

I have an existential map. It has "You are here"
written all over it. *Steven Wright*

325

I hate small towns because once you've seen the
cannon in the park there's nothing else to do.
Lenny Bruce (1923–1966)

326

Schizophrenia beats dining alone. *Unknown*

327

When we talk to God, we're praying. When God talks
to us, we're schizophrenic. *Lily Tomlin*

328

When dealing with the insane, the best method is to
pretend to be sane. *Hermann Hesse (1877–1962)*

329

I don't really trust a sane person.
Pro football lineman Lyle Alzado

330

Sometimes when you look in his eyes you get the
feeling that someone else is driving. *David Letterman*

3 3 1

I'm going to give my psychoanalyst one more year, then I'm going to Lourdes. *Woody Allen*

3 3 2

When a book and a head collide and there is a hollow sound, is it always from the book?
Georg Christoph Lichtenberg (1742–1799)

3 3 3

I've given up reading books. I find it takes my mind off myself. *Oscar Levant (1906–1972)*

3 3 4

Where do I find the time for not reading so many books? *Karl Kraus (1874–1936)*

3 3 5

A person who publishes a book appears willfully in public with his pants down.
Edna St. Vincent Millay (1892–1950)

3 3 6

The reason why so few good books are written is that so few people who can write know anything.
Walter Bagehot (1826–1877)

337

The newspaper is the natural enemy of the book, as the whore is of the decent woman.

The Goncourt Brothers, 1858

338

Manuscript: Something submitted in haste and returned at leisure. *Oliver Herford (1863–1935)*

339

Your manuscript is both good and original, but the part that is good is not original and the part that is original is not good. *Samuel Johnson (1709–1784)*

340

Autobiography is an unrivaled vehicle for telling the truth about other people.

Philip Guedalla (1889–1944)

341

A well-written life is almost as rare as a well-spent one. *Thomas Carlyle (1795–1881)*

342

I have read your book and much like it.

Moses Hadas (1900–1966)

343

A novel is a piece of prose of a certain length with something wrong with it. *Unknown*

344

There are two kinds of books: those that no one reads and those that no one ought to read.
H. L. Mencken (1880–1956)

345

The covers of this book are too far apart.
Ambrose Bierce (1842–1914?)

346

[He] took me into his library and showed me his books, of which he had a complete set.
Ring Lardner (1885–1933)

347

The man who reads nothing at all is better educated than the man who reads nothing but newspapers.
Thomas Jefferson (1743–1826)

348

Journalism largely consists in saying "Lord Jones is dead" to people who never knew Lord Jones was alive. *G. K. Chesterton (1874–1936)*

349

There is so much to be said in favor of modern journalism. By giving us the opinions of the uneducated it keeps us in touch with ignorance of the community.

Oscar Wilde (1854–1900)

350

Small Earthquake in Chile;
Not Many Killed

Headline suggested for The Times
of London by Claud Cockburn

351

Writers have two main problems. One is writer's block, when the words won't come at all, and the other is logorrhea, when the words come so fast that they can hardly get to the wastebasket in time.

Cecilia Bartholomew

352

All of us learn to write in the second grade. Most of us go on to greater things.

Basketball coach Bobby Knight

353

When writers refer to themselves as "we" and to the reader as "you," it's two against one. *Judith Rascoe*

3 5 4

Most writers regard the truth as their most valuable possession, and therefore are most economical in its use. *Mark Twain* (*1835–1910*)

3 5 5

Writing is turning one's worst moments into money.
J. P. Donleavy

3 5 6

Writing is the only profession in which one can make no money without being ridiculous.
Jules Renard (*1864–1910*)

3 5 7

Writers should be read, but neither seen nor heard.
Daphne Du Maurier

3 5 8

If you can't annoy somebody, there is little point in writing. *Kingsley Amis*

3 5 9

Unprovided with original learning, unformed in the habits of thinking, unskilled in the arts of composition, I resolved to write a book.
Edward Gibbon (*1737–1794*)

360

Everywhere I go I'm asked if I think the university stifles writers. My opinion is that they don't stifle enough of them. There's many a bestseller that could have been prevented by a good teacher.

Flannery O'Connor (1925–1964)

361

Great Moments in Literature: In 1936, Ernest Hemingway, while trout fishing, caught a carp and decided not to write about it. *Guindon cartoon caption*

362

All writing is garbage.

French playwright Antonin Artaud (1896–1948)

363

Novelists who go to psychiatrists are paying for what they should be paid for. *Unknown*

364

Every author, however modest, keeps a most outrageous vanity chained like a madman in the padded cell of his breast. *Logan Pearsall Smith (1865–1946)*

365

The trouble with our younger writers is that they are all in their sixties.

W. Somerset Maugham (1874–1965)

366
Authors are easy to get on with—if you like children.

Michael Joseph (1897–1958)

367
I write fiction because it's a way of making statements I can disown, and I write plays because dialogue is the most respectable way of contradicting myself.

Tom Stoppard

3 6 8

An essayist is a lucky person who has found a way to discourse without being interrupted. *Charles Poore*

3 6 9

Writers aren't exactly people . . . they're a whole lot of people trying to be one person.
F. Scott Fitzgerald (1896–1940)

3 7 0

An author's first duty is to let down his country.
Brendan Behan (1923–1964)

3 7 1

Asking a working writer what he thinks about critics is like asking a lamp-post how it feels about dogs.
Christopher Hampton

3 7 2

I can't read ten pages of Steinbeck without throwing up. *James Gould Cozzens (1903–1978)*

3 7 3

A poem is never finished, only abandoned.
Paul Valéry (1871–1945)

3 7 4

Immature poets imitate; mature poets steal.
T. S. Eliot (1888–1965)

3 7 5

Good swiping is an art in itself. *Jules Feiffer*

376

Finishing a book is just like you took a child out in the back yard and shot it.   *Truman Capote*

377

Dear Contributor: Thank you for not sending us anything lately. It suits our present needs.
> *Note from publisher received by Snoopy*
> *in comic strip "Peanuts" (Charles Schulz)*

378

You call this a script? Give me a couple of 5,000-dollar-a-week writers and I'll write it myself.
> *Movie producer Joe Pasternak*

379

I do most of my writing sitting down. That's where I shine.   *Robert Benchley (1889–1945)*

380

When in doubt, have two guys come through the door with guns.   *Raymond Chandler (1888–1959)*

381

Too many pieces of music finish too long after the end.   *Igor Stravinsky (1882–1971)*

382

My music is best understood by children and animals.
Igor Stravinsky (1882–1971)

383

You want something by Bach? Which one, Johann
Sebastian or Jacques Offen? *Victor Borge*

384

Even Bach comes down to the basic suck, blow, suck, suck, blow. *Mouth organist Larry Adler*

385

Classical music is the kind we keep thinking will turn into a tune. *Kin Hubbard (1868–1930)*

386

Opera in English is, in the main, just about as sensible as baseball in Italian. *H. L. Mencken (1880–1956)*

387

I tried to resist his overtures, but he plied me with symphonies, quartettes, chamber music, and cantatas.
S. J. Perelman (1904–1979)

388

Anything that is too stupid to be spoken is sung.

Voltaire (1694–1778)

389

Massenet
Never wrote a Mass in A.
It'd have been just too bad
If he had.

Anthony Butts

390

No statue has ever been put up to a critic.

Jean Sibelius (1865–1957)

391

Music played at weddings always reminds me of the music played for soldiers before they go into battle.

Heinrich Heine (1797–1856)

392

I don't know anything about music. In my line you don't have to. *Elvis Presley (1935–1977)*

393

Hell is full of musical amateurs.

George Bernard Shaw (1856–1950)

394

No sane man will dance.   *Cicero* (*106–43* B.C.)

395

Rock and roll is the hamburger that ate the world.
Peter York

396
Use an accordion, go to jail! That's the law!

Bumper sticker

397
You can make a killing as a playwright in America,
but you can't make a living.

Sherwood Anderson (1876–1941)

398

All playwrights should be dead for three hundred years. *Joseph L. Mankiewicz*

399

Actresses will happen in the best regulated families.
Oliver Herford (1863–1935)

400

My tears stuck in their little ducts, refusing to be jerked. *Peter Stack in a movie review*

401

His performance is so wooden you want to spray him with Liquid Pledge. *John Stark in a movie review*

402

Working in the theater has a lot in common with unemployment. *Arthur Gingold*

403

Only in show business could a guy with a C-minus average be considered an intellectual.
Mort Sahl on himself

404

I don't want to see the uncut version of anything.
Jean Kerr

405

It's always easier to see a show you don't like the second time because you know it ends.

Walter Slezak (1902–1983)

406

Hell is a half-filled auditorium.

Robert Frost (1874–1963)

407

A critic is a man who knows the way but can't drive the car. *Kenneth Tynan (1927–1980)*

408

Hollywood is a place where they place you under contract instead of under observation.

Walter Winchell (1897–1972)

409

The Hollywood tradition I like best is called "sucking up to the stars." *Johnny Carson*

410

"Hello," he lied.

Don Carpenter quoting a Hollywood agent

411

An associate producer is the only guy in Hollywood who will associate with a producer.

Fred Allen (1894–1956)

412

The dead actor requested in his will that his body be cremated and ten percent of his ashes thrown in his agent's face.   *Unknown*

413

It was like passing the scene of a highway accident and being relieved to learn that nobody had been seriously injured.

> *Martin Cruz Smith on being asked how he liked the movie version of his novel* Gorky Park

414

If you want to make it in show business, get the hell out of Oregon.

> *Advice from Sophie Tucker (1884–1966) to a young Johnnie Ray*

415

Television has proved that people will look at anything rather than each other.   *Ann Landers*

416

Television is more interesting than people. If it were not, we would have people standing in the corners of our rooms.   *Alan Corenk*

417

Television is a medium because anything well done is
rare.

Either Fred Allen (1894–1956)
or Ernie Kovacs (1919–1962)

418

Your picture tube is okay, but your cabinet has Dutch
elm disease. *TV repairman in a Ziggy cartoon*

419

I'm So Miserable Without You
It's Almost Like Having You Here
Stephen Bishop song title

420

She Got the Gold Mine, I Got the Shaft
Jerry Reed song title

421

When My Love Comes Back from the Ladies Room
Will I Be Too Old to Care?
Lewis Grizzard song title

422

I Don't Know Whether to Kill Myself or Go Bowling
Song title by Unknown

423

Why won't you lemme feelya, Cecilia?
I got two winnin' hands I wanna dealya.

Lyrics by Robert Byrne

424

They Tore Out My Heart and Stomped That Sucker
Flat   *Book title by Lewis Grizzard*

425

[Americans] are a race of convicts and ought to be
thankful for anything we allow them short of hanging.

Samuel Johnson (1709–1784)

426

America is a large friendly dog in a small room. Every
time it wags its tail it knocks over a chair.

Arnold Toynbee (1889–1975)

427

The United States is like the guy at the party who gives
cocaine to everybody and still nobody likes him.

Jim Samuels

428

On Thanksgiving Day all over America, families sit
down to dinner at the same moment—halftime.

Unknown

429

In America there are two classes of travel—first and
with children.   *Robert Benchley (1889–1945)*

430

Animals have these advantages over man: they never hear the clock strike, they die without any idea of death, they have no theologians to instruct them, their last moments are not disturbed by unwelcome and unpleasant ceremonies, their funerals cost them nothing, and no one starts lawsuits over their wills.

Voltaire (1694–1778)

431

A boy can learn a lot from a dog: obedience, loyalty, and the importance of turning around three times before lying down. *Robert Benchley (1889–1945)*

432

Man is the only animal that can remain on friendly terms with the victims he intends to eat until he eats them. *Samuel Butler (1835–1902)*

433

Fox hunting is the unspeakable in pursuit of the inedible. *Oscar Wilde (1856–1900)*

434

If you are a police dog, where's your badge?
The question James Thurber (1894–1961)
used to drive his German shepherd crazy

435

I loathe people who keep dogs. They are cowards who haven't got the guts to bite people themselves.
August Strindberg (1849–1912)

436

We tolerate shapes in human beings that would horrify us if we saw them in a horse.
W. R. Inge (1860–1954)

437

People on horses look better than they are, people in cars look worse. *Marya Mannes*

438

You're a good example of why some animals eat their young. *Jim Samuels to a heckler*

439

Cats are intended to teach us that not everything in nature has a function. *Garrison Keillor*

440

Groundhog Day has been observed only once in Los Angeles because when the groundhog came out of its hole, it was killed by a mud slide. *Johnny Carson*

441

Is that a beard, or are you eating a muskrat?

Dr. Gonzo

442

To err is human
To purr feline.

Robert Byrne

443

It isn't easy being green. *Kermit the Frog.*

444

Never go to a doctor whose office plants have died.

Erma Bombeck

445

Three out of four doctors recommend another doctor.

Graffito

446

I suppose one has a greater sense of intellectual degradation after an interview with a doctor than from any human experience. *Alice James (1848–1892)*

447

A young doctor means a new graveyard.

German proverb

448

I'm going to Boston to see my doctor. He's a very sick man. *Fred Allen (1894–1956)*

449

People who take cold baths never have rheumatism, but they have cold baths. *Unknown*

450

His ideas of first-aid stopped short of squirting soda water. *P. G. Wodehouse (1881–1975)*

451

Before undergoing a surgical operation, arrange your temporal affairs. You may live.

Ambrose Bierce (1842–1914?)

452

Psychoanalysis is that mental illness for which it regards itself a therapy. *Karl Kraus (1874–1936)*

453

Show me a sane man and I will cure him for you.

C. G. Jung (1875–1861)

454

Psychiatry is the care of the id by the odd.   *Unknown*

455

After twelve years of therapy my psychiatrist said something that brought tears to my eyes. He said, *"No hablo inglés."   Ronnie Shakes*

456

Doctors and lawyers must go to school for years and years, often with little sleep and with great sacrifice to their first wives.   *Roy G. Blount, Jr.*

457

I never did give anybody hell. I just told the truth and they thought it was hell.

Harry S Truman (1884–1972)

458

I can think of nothing more boring for the American people than to have to sit in their living rooms for a whole half hour looking at my face on their television screens.   *Dwight David Eisenhower (1890–1969)*

459

Do you realize the responsibility I carry? I'm the only person standing between Nixon and the White House.
John F. Kennedy (1917–1963), in 1960

460

I'm not sure I've even got the brains to be President.
Barry Goldwater in 1964

461

I would not like to be a political leader in Russia. They never know when they're being taped.
Richard Nixon

462

I love America. You always hurt the one you love.
David Frye impersonating Nixon

463

The thought of being President frightens me and I do not think I want the job.   *Ronald Reagan in 1973*

464

God! The country that produced George Washington has got this collection of crumb-bums!
Barbara Tuchman on the 1980
presidential candidates

465

Reagan won because he ran against Jimmy Carter. Had he run unopposed he would have lost. *Mort Sahl*

466

Ronald Reagan is a triumph of the embalmer's art.
Gore Vidal

467

Ronald Reagan's platform seems to be: Hey, I'm a big good-looking guy and I need a lot of sleep.
Roy G. Blount, Jr.

468

Walter Mondale has all the charisma of a speed bump.
Will Durst

469

You've got to be careful quoting Ronald Reagan, because when you quote him accurately it's called mudslinging. *Walter Mondale*

470

Women are being considered as candidates for Vice President of the United States because it is the worst job in America. It's amazing that men will take it. A job with real power is First Lady. I'd be willing to run for that. As far as the men who are running for President are concerned, they aren't even people I would date. *Nora Ephron*

471

The man with the best job in the country is the Vice President. All he has to do is get up every morning and say, "How's the President?"

Will Rogers (1879–1935)

472

The vice-presidency ain't worth a pitcher of warm spit.

Vice President John Nance Garner (1868–1967)

473

If it were not for the government, we would have nothing to laugh at in France.

Sébastian Chamfort (1740–1794)

474

Every decent man is ashamed of the government he lives under.   *H. L. Mencken (1880–1956)*

475

It has been said that democracy is the worst form of government except all the others that have been tried.

Winston Churchill (1874–1965)

476

Democracy substitutes election by the incompetent many for appointment by the corrupt few.

George Bernard Shaw (1856–1950)

477

Get all the fools on your side and you can be elected to anything. *Frank Dane*

478

If voting changed anything, they'd make it illegal.
                                            Unknown

479

Vote early and vote often. *Al Capone (1899–1947)*

480

Ninety percent of the politicians give the other ten percent a bad reputation. *Henry Kissinger*

481

Politics is applesauce. *Will Rogers (1879–1935)*

482

I might have gone to West Point, but I was too proud to speak to a congressman. *Will Rogers (1879–1935)*

483

An ambassador is an honest man sent abroad to lie for his country. *Sir Henry Wotton (1568–1639)*

484

A statesman is a politician who has been dead ten or fifteen years. *Harry S Truman (1884–1972)*

485

Right in the middle of Prague, Wenceslaus Square, there's this guy throwing up. And this other guy comes along, takes a look at him, shakes his head, and says, "I know just what you mean." *Milan Kundera*

486

When you go into court you are putting your fate into the hands of twelve people who weren't smart enough to get out of jury duty. *Norm Crosby*

487

Getting kicked out of the American Bar Association is like getting kicked out of the Book-of-the-Month Club.
Melvin Belli on the occasion of his getting kicked out of the American Bar Association

488

Laws are like sausages. It's better not to see them being made. *Otto von Bismarck (1815–1898)*

489

I always turn to the sports pages first, which record people's accomplishments. The front page has nothing but man's failures.

Chief Justice Earl Warren (1891–1974)

490

I was not successful as a ballplayer, as it was a game of skill. *Casey Stengel (1891–1975)*

491

It matters not whether you win or lose; what matters is whether *I* win or lose. *Darrin Weinberg*

492

I'm glad we don't have to play in the shade.

Golfer Bobby Jones (1902–1971) on being told that it was 105 degrees in the shade

493

Very few blacks will take up golf until the requirement for plaid pants is dropped. *Franklyn Ajaye*

494

San Francisco has always been my favorite booing city. I don't mean the people boo louder or longer, but there is a very special intimacy. When they boo you, you know they mean *you*. Music, that's what it is to me. One time in Kezar Stadium they gave me a standing boo.

Pro football coach George Halas (1895–1983)

495

Most weightlifters are biceptual.   *John Rostoni*

496

I never met a man I didn't want to fight.

Pro football lineman Lyle Alzado

PART THREE

Miscellaneous

497

If politicians and scientists were lazier, how much happier we should all be.

Evelyn Waugh (1903–1966)

498

If we see the light at the end of the tunnel
It's the light of an oncoming train.

Robert Lowell (1917–1977)

499

Ninety percent of everything is crap.

Theodore Sturgeon

500

You've always made the mistake of being yourself.

Eugène Ionesco

501

There is such a build-up of crud in my oven there is only room to bake a single cupcake. *Phyllis Diller*

502

Cleaning your house while your kids are still growing is like shoveling the walk before it stops snowing.

Phyllis Diller

503

There is no need to do any housework at all. After the first four years the dirt doesn't get any worse.

Quentin Crisp

504

All phone calls are obscene.   *Karen Elizabeth Gordon*

5 0 5

Coincidences are spiritual puns.

G. K. Chesterton (1874–1936)

5 0 6

If I had to live my life again, I'd make the same mistakes, only sooner.

Tallulah Bankhead (1903–1968)

5 0 7

Last night I dreamed I ate a ten-pound marshmallow, and when I woke up the pillow was gone.

Tommy Cooper

5 0 8

It's better to be wanted for murder than not to be wanted at all. *Marty Winch*

5 0 9

I have a hundred times wished that one could resign life as an officer resigns a commission.

Robert Burns (1759–1796)

5 1 0

If you tell the truth you don't have to remember anything. *Mark Twain (1835–1910)*

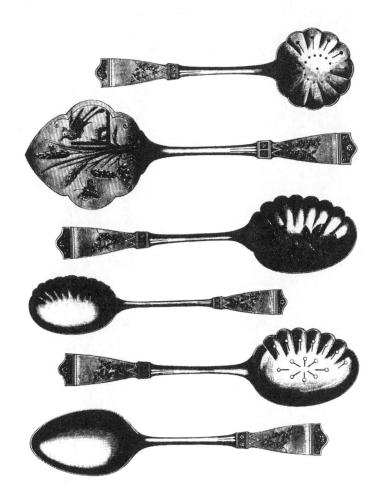

511

The more he talked of his honor the faster we counted our spoons. *Ralph Waldo Emerson (1803–1882)*

512

The truth is the safest lie. *Anonymous*

5 1 3

No one can have a higher opinion of him than I have,
and I think he's a dirty little beast.

W. S. Gilbert (1836–1911)

5 1 4

The future is much like the present, only longer.

Don Quisenberry

5 1 5

Advertising is the rattling of a stick inside a swill
bucket. *George Orwell (1903–1950)*

5 1 6

Winter is nature's way of saying, "Up yours."

Robert Byrne

5 1 7

I like winter because I can stay indoors without feeling guilty. *Teressa Skelton*

5 1 8

Weather forecast for tonight: dark. *George Carlin*

5 1 9

If I were two-faced, would I be wearing this one?

Abraham Lincoln (1809–1865)

520

A person can take only so much comforting.

Calvin Trillin

521

I have a rock garden. Last week three of them died.

Richard Diran

522

Nice guys finish last, but we get to sleep in.

Evan Davis

523

Illegal aliens have always been a problem in the United States. Ask any Indian.   *Robert Orben*

524

Few things are harder to put up with than a good example.   *Mark Twain (1835–1910)*

525

I just got wonderful news from my real estate agent in Florida. They found land on my property.

Milton Berle

526

Immigration is the sincerest form of flattery.

Jack Paar

527

The art of living is more like wrestling than dancing.
Marcus Aurelius (121–180)

528

We must believe in luck. For how else can we explain
the success of those we don't like?
Jean Cocteau (1889–1963)

529

Hell is other people.   *Jean Paul Sartre (1905–1980)*

530

Some people are always late, like the late King George V.   *Spike Milligan*

531

It is easier to get forgiveness than permission.
*Stewart's Law of Retroaction
in* Murphy's Law, Book Two

532

The popularity of a bad man is as treacherous as he is himself.   *Pliny the Younger (c. 62–c. 113)*

533

The hatred of relatives is the most violent.
Tacitus (c. 55–c. 117)

534

Every man sees in his relatives a series of grotesque caricatures of himself.   *H. L. Mencken (1880–1956)*

535

The first Rotarian was the first man to call John the Baptist "Jack."   *H. L. Mencken (1880–1956)*

536

H. L. Mencken suffers from the hallucination that he is H. L. Mencken. There is no cure for a disease of that magnitude. *Maxwell Bodenheim (1893–1954)*

537

Even if you're on the right track, you'll get run over if you just sit there. *Will Rogers (1879–1935)*

538

I prefer rogues to imbeciles because they sometimes take a rest.

Alexandre Dumas the Younger (1824–1895)

539

A wedding cake left out in the rain.

Stephen Spender commenting on the face of W. H. Auden (1907–1973)

540

Is this the party to whom I am speaking?

Lily Tomlin as Ernestine the operator

541

Let others praise ancient times; I am glad I was born in these. *Ovid (43* B.C.–A.D. *18)*

542

Happiness is good health and a bad memory.

Ingrid Bergman (1917–1982)

543

Never keep up with the Joneses. Drag them down to your level. *Quentin Crisp*

544

People who think they know everything are very irritating to those of us who do. *Unknown*

545

I want a house that has got over all its troubles; I don't want to spend the rest of my life bringing up a young and inexperienced house.

Jerome K. Jerome (1859–1927)

546

There is something about a closet that makes a skeleton restless.   *Unknown*

547

By dint of railing at idiots you run the risk of becoming idiotic yourself.

Gustave Flaubert (1821–1880)

548

There is no gravity. The earth sucks.   *Graffito*

549

When the going gets tough, the smart get lost.

Robert Byrne

550

Miss Erickson looked more peculiar than ever this morning. Is her spiritualism getting worse?

Noel Coward (1889–1973)

551

I shot an arrow into the air, and it stuck.

Graffito in Los Angeles

552

There's so much pollution in the air now that if it weren't for our lungs there'd be no place to put it all.

Robert Orben

553

I don't know how old I am because the goat ate the Bible that had my birth certificate in it. The goat lived to be twenty-seven.

Satchel Paige (1906?–1982)

554

Nothing ever goes away.   *Barry Commoner*

555

There's nothing wrong with you that reincarnation won't cure.   *Jack E. Leonard (1911–1973) to Ed Sullivan (1902–1974)*

556

A lie is an abomination unto the Lord and a very present help in time of trouble.

Adlai Stevenson (1900–1965)

557

During a carnival men put masks over their masks.

Xavier Forneret, 1838

5 5 8

One hundred thousand lemmings can't be wrong.

Graffito

5 5 9

He was the world's only armless sculptor. He put the chisel in his mouth and his wife hit him on the back of the head with a mallet. *Fred Allen (1894–1956)*

5 6 0

Modern art is what happens when painters stop looking at girls and persuade themselves that they have a better idea. *John Ciardi*

5 6 1

Either this wallpaper goes or I do.

Almost certainly not the last words of
Oscar Wilde (1856–1900)

5 6 2

A life spent making mistakes is not only more honorable but more useful than a life spent doing nothing.
George Bernard Shaw (1856–1950)

5 6 3

Friends may come and go, but enemies accumulate.

Thomas Jones

564

When down in the mouth, remember Jonah. He came out all right. *Thomas Edison (1847–1931)*

565

Retirement at sixty-five is ridiculous. When I was sixty-five I still had pimples. *George Burns*

566

Old age is the only disease you don't look forward to being cured of. *From the movie* Citizen Kane, *1941*

567

Start every day off with a smile and get it over with.
W. C. Fields (1880–1946)

568

I took a course in speed reading and was able to read *War and Peace* in twenty minutes. It's about Russia.
Woody Allen

569

When your IQ rises to 28, sell.
Professor Irwin Corey to a heckler

570

Some people are like popular songs that you only sing for a short time. *La Rochefoucauld (1613–1680)*

571

George the Third
Ought never to have occurred.
One can only wonder
At so grotesque a blunder.
Edmund Clerihew (1875–1956)

572

There are two kinds of pedestrians . . . the quick and the dead.
Lord Thomas Robert Dewar (1864–1930)

573

I used to work in a fire hydrant factory. You couldn't park anywhere near the place. *Steven Wright*

574

I don't have any trouble parking. I drive a forklift.
Jim Samuels

575

God help those who do not help themselves.
Wilson Mizner (1876–1933)

576

There is only one good substitute for the endearments of a sister, and that is the endearments of some other fellow's sister. *Josh Billings (1818–1885)*

577

When smashing monuments, save the pedestals—they
always come in handy. *Stanislaw Lem*

578

Great men are not always idiots.

Karen Elizabeth Gordon

579

Few great men could pass Personnel.

Paul Goodman (1911–1972)

580

Fanaticism consists of redoubling your effort when you have forgotten your aim.

George Santayana (1863–1952)

581

Mountains appear more lofty the nearer they are approached, but great men resemble them not in this particular.

Lady Marguerite Blessington (1789–1849)

582

There's a great woman behind every idiot.

John Lennon (1941–1980) on Yoko Ono

583

Nothing is more conducive to peace of mind than not having any opinions at all.

Georg Christoph Lichtenberg (1742–1799)

584

The mome rath isn't born that could outgrabe me.

Nicol Williamson

585

If you live to the age of a hundred you have it made because very few people die past the age of a hundred.

George Burns

586

Never accept an invitation from a stranger unless he gives you candy. *Linda Festa*

587

You can choose your friends, but you only have one mother. *Max Shulman*

588

One is not superior merely because one sees the world as odious. *Chateaubriand (1768–1848)*

589

If it weren't for the last minute, nothing would get done. *Unknown*

590

If I were a grave-digger or even a hangman, there are some people I could work for with a great deal of enjoyment. *Douglas Jerrold (1803–1857)*

591

It is easier to forgive an enemy than to forgive a friend. *William Blake (1757–1827)*

592

You are no bigger than the things that annoy you.

Jerry Bundsen

593

It is unpleasant to go alone, even to be drowned.

Russian proverb

594

Stay with me; I want to be alone.   *Joey Adams*

595

They made love only during total eclipses of the sun because they wouldn't take off their clothes unless it was dark in the entire world.   *Unknown*

596

We are what we pretend to be.   *Kurt Vonnegut, Jr.*

597

Thank you, but I have other plans.
Response to "Have a nice day"
suggested by Paul Fussell

598

WARNING TO ALL PERSONNEL
Firings will continue until morale improves.
Unknown

599

Do we really deserve top billing?
Fred Allen (1894–1956) to Henry Morgan at a
meeting of the National Conference of
Christians and Jews

600

Psychics will lead dogs to your body.
Alleged fortune cookie message

601

I don't worry about crime in the streets; it's the sidewalks I stay off of.   *Johnson Letellier*

602

Carney's Law: There's at least a 50-50 chance that someone will print the name Craney incorrectly.
Jim Canrey

603

Bad spellers of the world, untie!   *Graffito*

604

Complete this sentence:
  I never met a man I didn't like
    a. to cheat.
    b. at first.
    c. to avoid.
    d. better than you.   *Robert Byrne*

605

Fix this sentence:
  He put the horse before the cart.   *Stephen Price*

606

I am firm. You are obstinate. He is a pig-headed fool.
                            Katharine Whitehorn

607

Dr. Livingstone I Presume
                Full name of Dr. Presume

                                    Unknown

608

A language is a dialect with an army and navy.
                    Max Weinreich (1894–1969)

609

I can't seem to bring myself to say, "Well, I guess I'll
be toddling along." It isn't that I can't toddle. It's that
I can't guess I'll toddle.
                    Robert Benchley (1889–1945)

610

Hamlet as performed at the Brooklyn Shakespeare Festival:

"To be, or what?"

Steven Pearl

611

Smoking is, as far as I'm concerned, the entire point of being an adult. *Fran Lebowitz*

612

There is only one word for aid that is genuinely without strings, and that word is blackmail.

Colm Brogan

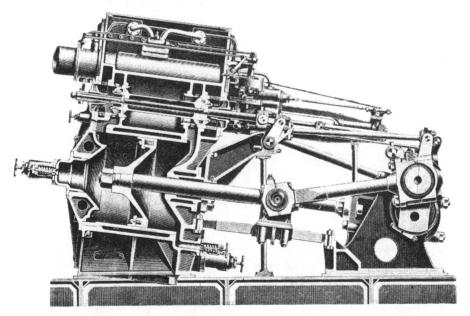

613

A steam engine has always got character. It's the most human of all man-made machines.

Reverend William Vere Awdrey

614

Al didn't smile for forty years. You've got to admire a man like that.

From the television series
"Mary Hartman, Mary Hartman"

615

All professions are conspiracies against the laity.

George Bernard Shaw (1856–1950)

616

Very few people do anything creative after the age of thirty-five. The reason is that very few people do anything creative before the age of thirty-five.

Joel Hildebrand (1881–1983)

617

There is no they, only us. *Bumper sticker*

618

I was in a beauty contest once. I not only came in last, I was hit in the mouth by Miss Congeniality.

Phyllis Diller

619

You can get more with a kind word and a gun than you can with a kind word alone. *Johnny Carson*

620

I think it would be a good idea.
Mahatma Gandhi (1869–1948) when asked
what he thought of Western civilization

621

Remember that a kick in the ass is a step forward.
Unknown

622

What is algebra, exactly? Is it those three-cornered things?   *J. M. Barrie (1860–1937)*

623

Computers are useless. They can only give you answers.
Pablo Picasso (1881–1973)

624

Peace, n. In international affairs, a period of cheating between two periods of fighting.
Ambrose Bierce (1842–1914?)

625

Let thy maid servant be faithful, strong, and homely.
Benjamin Franklin (1706–1790)

626

At twenty-six, Kate, though not promiscuous, had slept with most of the decent men in public life.
Renata Adler

627

The egg cream is psychologically the opposite of circumcision—it *pleasurably* reaffirms your Jewishness.

Mel Brooks

628

His absence is good company.   *Scottish saying*

629

The happiest liaisons are based on mutual misunderstanding. *La Rochefoucauld (1613–1680)*

630

So many beautiful women and so little time.
John Barrymore (1882–1942)

631

The art of *not* reading is extremely important. It consists in our not taking up whatever happens to occupy the larger public. *Arthur Schopenhauer (1788–1860)*

632

Nowadays the illiterates can read and write.
Alberto Moravia

633

A good man is always a beginner.
Martial (c. 40–c. 104)

634

I knew a very interesting Italian woman last winter, but now she's married.
Percy Bysshe Shelley (1792–1822)

635

How much money did you make last year? Mail it in.
*Simplified tax form
suggested by Stanton Delaplane*

636

Gray hair is God's graffiti. *Bill Cosby*

637

The gods too are fond of a joke.

Aristotle (*384–322* B.C.)

Sources, References, and Notes

Like other books of quotations, this one owes a heavy debt to anthologists who have gone before. The principal secondary sources I used in supplementing my own reading and eavesdropping are listed below and referred to in the citations by the letters assigned to them.

Readers who point out misquotations or supply missing sources will be thanked in future printings, if any. Favorite lines (nothing pompous, please) also will be gratefully received.

Collecting quotations is an insidious, even embarrassing habit, like ragpicking or hoarding rocks or trying on other people's laundry. I got into it originally while trying to break an addiction to candy. I kicked candy and now seem to be stuck with quotations, which are attacking my brain instead of my teeth. While I have no plans to compile a third sampler, I can't promise I won't, either.

A. H. L. Mencken, ed., *A New Dictionary of Quotations on Historical Principles* (New York: Alfred A. Knopf, 1952).
B. Jonathon Green, comp., *Morrow's International Dictionary of Contemporary Quotations* (New York: William Morrow and Company, 1982).
C. J. M. and M. J. Cohen, *The Penguin Dictionary of Modern Quotations*, 2nd ed. (Harmondsworth, England, and New York: Penguin Books, 1980).
D. John Gross, comp., *The Oxford Book of Aphorisms* (Oxford, England: Oxford University Press, 1983).
E. Gerald F. Lieberman, *3,500 Good Quotes for Speakers* (New York: Doubleday & Company, 1983).
F. Bob Chieger, *Was It Good for You, Too? Quotations on Love and Sex* (New York: Atheneum Publishers, 1983).
G. Jonathon Green, comp., *The Book of Political Quotes* (New York: McGraw-Hill Book Company, 1982).
H. Joe Franklin, *Joe Franklin's Encyclopedia of Comedians* (Secaucus, N.J.: Citadel Press, 1979).
I. Steve Allen, *More Funny People* (New York: Stein and Day, 1982).

Quotation
Number
2. As given in D.
3. *Notebooks,* 1912.
4. As given in C.
5. Quoted in the *New York Times Book Review,* October 30, 1983.
8. Linda Festa to RB.
9. As given in *Peter's Quotations* (New York: William Morrow and Company, 1977).
10. "The Tonight Show," September 31, 1982.
12. As given in D.
14. "The Tonight Show," August 11, 1982.
15. Thanks to Ms. Christopher B. Eubanks.
16. As given in E.
18. Thanks to Robert Machuta.
19. As given in F.
20. As given in D.
22. From *The Ladies Guide* (Battle Creek, Mich.: Modern Medicine Publishing Company, 1895). Dr. Kellogg helped invent cornflakes and peanut butter. In addition to denouncing masturbation, he believed that smoking caused cancer and that certain ailments could be cured by rolling a cannonball on the stomach.
23. As quoted by John Molloy in a San Francisco lecture in 1982.
24. A slightly different version is in E.
27. From the movie *Sleeper.*
28. As given in *Quotations for Writers and Speakers,* by A. Andrews.
29. As given in B.
32. Thanks to George Dushek.
35. As given in *Wilhelm Meisters Lehrjahre,* 1795.
37. As given in A.
38. Linda Festa to RB.
39. Quoted in the *San Francisco Chronicle,* August 14, 1982.
40. As given in Walter Wagner, *You Must Remember This.*
41. As given in F.
42. At Cobb's Pub, San Francisco, February 3, 1984.
43. During the San Francisco Standup Comedy Competition, 1983.
44. From the movie *Everything You Wanted to Know About Sex.*
45. As given in *The Sayings of Quentin Crisp.*
47. As given in B.
48. As given in Charlotte Chandler, *The Ultimate Seduction.*
49. As given in Joseph Weintraub, ed., *The Wit and Wisdom of Mae West.*
50. As given in E.
51, 52. As given in C.
57. Thanks to Arlene Heath.
59. As given in *Who Do You Think You Are?*
61. As given in *The Well-Tempered Sentence* (New York: Ticknor & Fields).
65. As given in H.
68. As given in F.
71. Don Rose is a San Francisco disk jockey.
72. Thanks to Arlene Heath.

73. Martin Cruz Smith to RB in jest.
76. As given in E.
78. As given in B.
79. Jim Samuels won the 1982 San Francisco Standup Comedy Competition.
80. *Newsweek*, 1980.
82. As given in B.
84. As given in *Comment*.
85. As given in F.
92. As quoted by Merla Zellerbach in the *San Francisco Chronicle*, December 21, 1982.
93. Thanks to Charles Deshong.
94. As given in *The Young Duke*, 1831.
96. Interview in the *Washington Post*, January 1983.
99, 100. As given in F.
101. From the movie *Manhattan*.
103. As given in *The Watched Pot*.
106. As given in *One Fat Englishman*.
107. As given in H.
109, 110. As given in A.
111. As given in Newbern and Rodebaugh, *Proverbs of the World*.
112. As given in *Vital Parts*. Thanks to Gerald Howard.
113, 114. As given in E.
115. As given in *The British Museum Is Falling Down*.
116. As given in *The Lonely Life*.
118. Robert Orben is a professional joke writer who publishes a newsletter called *Orben's Current Comedy* that is airmailed to subscribers. This is from the November 2, 1983, edition. The address is 700 Orange Street, Wilmington, Delaware 19801.
119. As given in E.
120. As given in *Last Words*, 1933.
123. As given in *The Measure of My Days*, 1972.
125. As given in *Newsweek*, 1978.
126. As given in B.
128. As given in Frank Muir, *The Frank Muir Book*.
129. As given in *The Old Woman*.
130. As recalled by Arlene Heath.
131. As given in *Time*, December 28, 1970.
133. As given in *Living It Up*.
134. From the movie *Annie Hall*.
135. As given in *Reginald in Russia*, 1910.
138. Thanks to Cyra McFadden.
139. Quoted by Georgia Hesse in the *San Francisco Chronicle*. Hesse added that Dom Pérignon was blind at the time.
144. As given in Herb Caen's *San Francisco Chronicle* column, November 24, 1983.
145. As given in B.
147, 148. As given in H.
149. As given in Gary Herman, comp., *The Book of Hollywood Quotes* (London: Omnibus Press, 1979). Thanks to Chris Arnold.

150. Quoted by Jimmy Breslin in his syndicated column, April 1983.
151. As given in B.
153. From *Rhinoceros*, Act II.
154. Bill Musselman is a basketball coach.
157. From the movie *Sleeper*.
160. As given in the *Observer*, April 19, 1957.
161. From *Death of a Salesman*.
162. From Larry Gelbart's introduction to I.
163. As given in *Funny, but Not Vulgar*, 1944.
164, 165. From Mordecai Richler's introduction to *The Best of Modern Humor* (New York: Alfred A. Knopf, 1983).
167. As given in Calvin Trillin's San Francisco lecture, January 18, 1984.
168. From a cable TV special called "Homage to Steve," 1984.
171. As given in *Sisterhood Is Powerful*.
174. As given in B.
175. As given in E.
176. As given in *Metropolitan Life*.
177. As given in E.
178. As given in *Kiss and Tell*.
179. As given in *Quote and Unquote*.
180. As given in B.
184. As given in *Esquire*, 1970.
184. See note 151.
189. See note 92.
190. As given in *The Saturday Evening Post*, 1952.
191. A slightly different version is given in F.
193. As given in *MS* (November 1983).
194. As given in the movie *The Culture of Narcissism* (1979).
195. As given in *I'm No Angel*.
196. From Gerald Nachman's column in the *San Francisco Chronicle*, August 1982.
197. As given in B.
201. As given in *The Big Book of Jewish Humor*.
202. From the Movie *My Favorite Year*.
203. As given by S. M. Ulam, *Adventures of a Mathematician* (New York: Charles Scribner's Sons, 1976).
207. As given in *The Conquest of Happiness*.
210. As given in B.
218. As given in *Jackie Mason's America* (Lyle Stuart, Inc., 1983).
219. As given in *The Painted Lady*.
220. Thanks to Linda Festa.
222. As given in *Careers for Women*.
227. See note 92.
232. Quoted by Herb Caen in the *San Francisco Chronicle*, May 17, 1983.
233. *New Yorker*, January 2, 1984.
234. As given in E.
236. As given in the *Village Voice*, April 1983.
238. As given in G.
240. As given in Joseph Heller, *Catch-22*.
242. As given in E.

243. As given in G.
244. From Will Rogers, *Autobiography*.
247. From *The Tonight Show*,
February 8, 1984.
248. At The Punch Line, San
Francisco, January
1984.
249. Herb Caen's column,
*San Francisco
Chronicle*, August 19,
1983.
251. From an article in *The
San Francisco Paper*,
February 1984.
252. As given in D.
253. As given in J. Green,
*The Book of Rock
Quotes*.
257. As given in A.
259. See note 218.
265. See note 218.
267. As given in *Orben's Current Comedy*, October
19, 1983.
268. See note 92.
272. Recalled by Calvin
Trillin.
274. Thanks to Arlene Heath.
275. As given in B.
276. As given in H.
278. As given in *The Daily
Herald*, October 5,
1962.
279. Quoted by Paul Burka in
Esquire (April 1983).
280. As given in Andy
Rooney, *And More by
Andy Rooney*.
281. See note 92.
283. *The Tonight Show*, September 26, 1983.
284. Gerald Nachman is a
columnist for the *San
Francisco Chronicle*.
285. As given in *The Hole*.
286. Quoted by Sir Laurence
Olivier on the BBC.

290. See note 92.
292, 293. See note 167.
294. As given in B.
296. As given in Herb Caen's
column, *San Francisco
Chronicle*, December 2,
1982.
297. As given in *The Letters
of Edna St. Vincent Mil-
lay*.
298. As given in *The Men's
Club*.
299. Quoted by Richard Con-
don in *Prizzi's Honor*.
303. Quoted by Paul Fussell
in *Class*.
304. See note 92.
305. As given in D.
306. As given in the
Observer, April 20,
1958.
307. As given in C.
310. As given in G.
311. *The Third Man* was written by Graham Greene.
313. From the TV show "Late
Night with David Letter-
man," January 6, 1984.
314. From his nightly com-
mentary on Channel 4
(NBC), San Francisco,
September 29, 1982.
315. From her San Francisco
lecture, November 4,
1983.
316. From "Late Night with
David Letterman," Feb-
ruary 9, 1984.
317. From a letter to Goodman Ace.
320. Will Durst won the 1983
San Francisco Standup
Comedy Competition.
322. See note 248.
324. "The Tonight Show,"
September 14, 1983.
327. As given in H.
328. As given in D.

333. As given in E.

337. As given in D.

342. Thanks to Tom Stewart.

349. As given in *The Critic as Artist*, 1891.

350. Written for a competition among the paper's sub-editors for "the world's most boring headline." Described by Claud Cockburn in his *Autobiography*.

351. Cecilia Bartholomew writes and teaches writing in the San Francisco area.

352. Quoted by George Will in his syndicated column, December 20, 1983.

353. In the *New York Times Book Review*, January 1, 1984.

355. As given in B.

360. As given in *The Nature and Aim of Fiction*. Thanks to Gerald Howard.

363. As given in the *New York Times Book Review*, June 6, 1982.

364. *Afterthoughts*, 1931.

365. As given in the *Observer*, October 14, 1951.

367. As given in the *Guardian*, March 21, 1973.

369. As given in F. Scott Fitzgerald, *The Last Tycoon*.

371. As given in the *Sunday Times* (London), October 16, 1977.

372. As given in *Time*, 1957.

373. Quoted by W. H. Auden in *A Certain World*.

378, 379, 380. See note 151.

381. As given in the *New York Times Book Review*, 1971.

382. As given in the *Observer*, October 8, 1961.

383. As given in H.

398. From the movie *All About Eve*, 1950.

400. As given in *San Francisco Chronicle*, December 21, 1982.

401. As given in *San Francisco Chronicle*, January 2, 1983.

402. Arthur Gingold wrote *Items from Our Catalog*.

403. Quoted by Gerald Nachman in the *San Francisco Chronicle*, September 22, 1983.

404. Quoted by Gerald Nachman in the *San Francisco Chronicle*, July 18, 1983.

405. Quoted by Gerald Nachman in the *San Francisco Chronicle*, December 21, 1983.

407. As given in the *New York Times Magazine*, January 9, 1966.

408. As given in B.

412. As given in E.

413. Martin Cruz Smith to RB.

415. As given in F.

416. As given in C.

419. Thanks to Maureen Connolly.

427. See note 79.

428. From a Hallmark card.

435. As given in *A Madman's Diary*.

436. Inge was dean of St. Paul's.

437. As given in *More in Anger*, 1958.

438. See note 79.
439. From the radio show *The Prairie Home Companion*, June 1983.
442. As given in *Cat Scan* (New York: Atheneum, 1983).
444. Thanks to Leslie Sheridan.
446. As given in *The Diary of Alice James*.
448. As given in I.
449. As given in E.
450. As given in *Jeeves and the Hard-boiled Egg*.
452. Quoted by Harry Zohn, *Karl Kraus*.
453. As given in the *Observer*, July 19, 1975.
455. "The Tonight Show," February 10, 1984.
456. As given in the *Atlantic Monthly*, 1981.
459. As given in A. Schlesinger, Jr., *A Thousand Days*.
460, 461. As given in G.
462. As given in H.
464. As given in B.
467. "The Tonight Show," November 17, 1982.
470. See note 315.
479. Thanks to Charles T. DeShong.
485. As given in *The Book of Laughter and Forgetting*.
487. Thanks to Dick Werthimer.
488. Thanks to Robert Machuta.
490. Thanks to Charles T. DeShong.
491. Darrin Weinberg to RB.
493. See note 248.
495. John Rostoni to Teressa Skelton to RB.
499. Often called Sturgeon's Law.
500. *Improvisation.*
503. As given in *The Naked Civil Servant*.
504. See note 61.
507. As given in D.
508. As given in *Psychology in the Wry*.
514. Don Quisenberry is a baseball pitcher.
517. Teressa Skelton to RB.
518. Thanks to Bob Hudson.
520. See note 92.
521. Quoted by Herb Caen in the *San Francisco Chronicle*, May 22, 1983.
523. As given in *Orben's Current Comedy*, September 21, 1983. See note 118.
525. As given in I.
526. As given in *My Saber Is Bent*, 1983. See note 118.
530. As given in *The Bald Twit Lion*.
532. As given in *Epistles*.
543. As given in *How to Become a Virgin*.
545. As given in *They and I*.
550. As given in *Present Laughter*, Act I.
552. As given in *Orben's Current Comedy*, November 17, 1983. See note 118.
556. As given in G.
557. See slightly different wording in D.
558. As given in C.
559. As given in I.
563. As given in the *Wall Street Journal*, 1975.
565. See note 151.
570. *Maxims*, 1665.
572. As given in George Robey, *Looking Back on Life*.

573. "The Tonight Show," September 14, 1983.
577. As given in *Unkempt Thoughts*.
581. As given in *Night Thought Book*, 1834.
586. Linda Festa to RB.
590. As given in *Ugly Trades*.
592. Jerry Bundsen is a former aide to Herb Caen, who quoted this line in his column in the *San Francisco Chronicle* in October 1983.
594. As given in H.
596. In the introduction to *Mother Night*.
597. As given in *Class*.
599. As given in I.
602. Quoted in the magazine *Friendly Exchange* (Winter 1982).
605. As given in *The Densa Quiz*.
606. As given in the *Observer*, 1974.
607. Thanks to Arlene Heath.
609. See note 151.
611. As given in *Social Studies*.

612, 613. As given in B.
615. Thanks to George Dushek.
618. As given in F.
622. As given in *Quality Street*, Act III.
623. As given in William Fifield, *In Search of Genius*.
624. As given in *The Devil's Dictionary*.
625. As given in *Poor Richard's Almanac*.
626. As given in *Speedboat*. Thanks to Gerald Howard.
629. Thanks to George Dushek.
631. As given in *On Reading and Books*, 1851.
634. As given in letter to T. J. Hogg, 1821.
635. As given in Stanton Delaplane's column in the *San Francisco Chronicle*, March 7, 1934.
636. "The Tonight Show," March 13, 1984.

Index of Authors

Abzug, Bella, 56
Adams, Joey, 180,
  594
Adler, Larry, 384
Adler, Renata, 626
Ajaye, Franklyn,
  248, 322, 493
Allen, Fred, 16,
  181, 411, 417,
  448, 559, 599
Allen, Woody, 25,
  27, 44, 53,
  101, 134, 157,
  158, 166, 331,
  568
Alzado, Lyle, 329,
  496
Amis, Kingsley,
  106, 358
Anderson, Sher-
  wood, 397
Aristotle, 637
Armour, Richard,
  169
Artaud, Antonin,
  362
Ashley, Elizabeth,
  39
Auden, W. H., 131
Awdrey, William
  Vere, 613
Bagehot, Walter,
  336
Baker, Russell, 19,
  288
Balzac, Honoré de,
  221
Bankhead, Tallu-
  lah, 506
Barrie, J. M., 622
Barrymore, John,
  630

Bartholomew,
  Cecilia, 351
Beach, Scott, 251
Beard, James, 282
Behan, Brendan,
  370
Belli, Melvin, 487
Benchley, Robert,
  262, 379, 429,
  431, 609
Benny, Jack, 261
Bergen, Edgar,
  211
Berger, Thomas,
  112
Bergman, Ingrid,
  542
Berle, Milton, 525
Bierce, Ambrose,
  345, 451, 624
Billings, Josh, 576
Bishop, Stephen,
  419
Bismarck, Otto
  von, 488
Blake, William,
  591
Blessington, Mar-
  guerite, 581
Blount, Roy G.,
  Jr., 295, 456,
  467
Bodenheim,
  Maxwell, 536
Boileau, Nicolas,
  257
Bok, Derek, 126
Boleyn, Anne, 155
Bombeck, Erma,
  444
Boosler, Elayne,
  54

Borge, Victor, 383
Bowman, Dr. Karl,
  32
Bradbury, Mal-
  colm, 59
Braver, Billy, 107
Brogan, Colm, 612
Brooks, Mel, 627
Brophy, Brigid,
  174
Brown, Larry, 42
Bruce, Lenny, 6,
  13, 201, 325
Bundsen, Jerry,
  592
Burns, George,
  133, 192, 565,
  585
Burns, Robert, 509
Burton, Richard,
  150
Butler, Samuel, 3,
  432
Butts, Anthony,
  389
Byrne, Robert,
  121, 198, 423,
  442, 516, 549,
  604
Caen, Herb, 318
Calhoun, Dr.
  George M., 21
Canrey, Jim, 602
Capone, Al, 479
Capote, Truman,
  26, 376
Carlin, George,
  518
Carlyle, Thomas,
  341
Carpenter, Don,
  410

Carson, Johnny,
14, 409, 440,
619
Cebrian, Katherine, 290
Chamfort, Sébastian, 473
Chandler, Raymond, 380
Charles V, 242
Chateaubriand,
588
Cher, 85
Chesterton, G. K.,
289, 348, 505
Child, Julia, 281
Churchill, Winston, 475
Ciardi, John, 560
Cicero, 394
Clark, Blake, 247
Clemenceau,
Georges, 238
Clerihew, Edmund,
571
Cockburn, Claud,
350
Cocteau, Jean, 528
Coleridge, Samuel
Taylor, 84
Commoner, Barry,
301, 554
Congreve, William,
143
Conrad, Joseph,
175
Conway, Tim, 99
Cooper, Tommy,
507
Corenk, Alan, 416
Corey, Irwin, 102,
569
Cosby, Bill, 636
Coward, Noel, 214,
550
Cozzens, James
Gould, 372
Crisp, Quentin,
45, 503, 543

Crosby, Norm, 486
cummings, e.e.,
231
Dane, Frank, 477
Dangerfield, Rodney, 105, 199
Darrow, Clarence,
114
Davis, Bette, 116
Davis, Evan, 43,
522
Day, Lillian, 178
De Gaulle,
Charles, 152
Delaplane, Stanton, 635
Depew, Chauncey,
263
De Vries, Peter, 93
Dewar, Thomas
Robert, 572
Diller, Phyllis,
501, 502, 618
Diogenes the
Cynic, 20
Diran, Richard,
521
Dirksen, Everett,
217
Disney, Walt, 40
Disraeli, Benjamin, 94
Donleavy, J. P.,
355
Douglas, Kirk, 183
Du Maurier,
Daphne, 357
Dumas, Alexandre,
the Younger,
538
Durst, Will, 320,
468
Edison, Thomas,
564
Edman, Irwin, 128
Eisenhower,
Dwight David,
458
Eliot, T. S., 374

Emerson, Ralph
Waldo, 254,
511
Ephron, Nora, 315,
470
Feiffer, Jules, 9,
375
Festa, Linda, 8,
38, 586
Fields, Totie, 276
Fields, W. C., 149,
182, 567
Firbank, Ronald,
307
Fitzgerald, F.
Scott, 144, 369
Flaubert, Gustave,
305, 547
Flynn, Errol, 228,
229
Forbes, Malcolm,
212
Forneret, Xavier,
557
Foxx, Redd, 268
Franklin, Benjamin, 625
Freud, Sigmund,
302
Frost, Robert, 406
Frumkes, Lewis
B., 117
Frye, David, 462
Fussell, Paul, 597
Gabor, Zsa Zsa, 80
Gandhi, Mahatma,
620
Garner, John
Nance, 472
Gelbart, Larry, 162
Gibbon, Edward,
359
Gilbert, W. S., 513
Gingold, Arthur,
402
Gobel, George,
147, 148
Godwin, Gail, 129

Goethe, Johann von, 35
Goldwater, Barry, 460
Goncourt, the Brothers, 337
Gonzo, Dr., 441
Goodman, Paul, 579
Gordon, Karen Elizabeth, 61, 504, 578
Grant, Cary, 96
Greene, Graham, 311
Gregory, Dick, 206
Grizzard, Lewis, 421, 424
Guedalla, Philip, 340
Guindon (cartoon), 361
Guitry, Sacha, 160
Gwenn, Edmond, 165
Hadas, Moses, 342
Halas, George, 494
Hampton, Christopher, 371
Hardy, Thomas, 37
Harper, Lucille S., 17
Harris, Phil, 146
Haskins, Ernest, 227
Heine, Heinrich, 391
Heller, Joseph, 240
Herbert, George, 109
Herford, Oliver, 338, 399
Hesse, Hermann, 328
Hildebrand, Joel, 616
Hirschfield, M., 33

Hoover, Herbert, 119
Hubbard, Kin, 385
Inge, W. R., 436
Ionesco, Eugène, 153, 500
Jagger, Mick, 253
James, Alice, 446
Jameson, Storm, 291
Jefferson, Thomas, 347
Jensen, John, 296
Jerome, Jerome K., 209, 545
Jerrold, Douglas, 590
Johnson, Lyndon, 243
Johnson, Samuel, 339, 425
Jones, Bobby, 492
Jones, Thomas, 563
Joseph, Michael, 366
Joyce, James, 23
Jung, C. G., 453
Kaufman, George S., 68
Keillor, Garrison, 439
Kellogg, Dr. J. H., 22
Kennedy, Florynce, 208
Kennedy, John F., 459
Kermit the Frog, 443
Kerr, Jean, 404
King, Alan, 74
King, Martin Luther, Jr., 204
Kissinger, Henry, 130, 480
Knebel, Fletcher, 266
Knight, Bobby, 352

Kovacs, Ernie, 417
Kraus, Karl, 334, 452
Kundera, Milan, 485
La Rochefoucauld, 570, 629
Landers, Ann, 415
Lardner, Ring, 346
Lasch, Christopher, 194
Lebowitz, Fran, 176, 611
Lem, Stanislaw, 577
Lennon, John, 582
Leonard, Jack E., 555
Lester, Jerry, 65
Letellier, Johnson, 601
Letterman, David, 316, 323, 330
Levant, Oscar, 333
Lewis, Joe E., 151
Lewis, Richard, 63, 313
Lichtenberg, Georg Christoph, 332, 583
Lincoln, Abraham, 519
Lodge, David, 115
Loelia, Duchess of Westminster, 197
Lowell, Robert, 498
Luther, Martin, 12
Mailer, Norman, 100
Mankiewicz, Joseph L, 398
Manners, Miss, 18
Mannes, Marya, 437
Mansfield, Jayne, 173
Manville, Tommy, 97

Marbury, Elisa-
beth, 222
Marcus Aurelius,
527
Marr, Bill, 10
Martial, 633
Martin, Judith, 18
Martin, Steve, 168
Marx, Chico, 51
Marx, Groucho,
179, 317
Marx, Karl, 24
Mason, Jackie, 91,
218, 259, 265
Maugham, W. Som-
erset, 365
McCabe, Charles,
87
McCarthy, Charlie,
211
McGuane, Tom, 41
McGuire, Al, 132
Mencken, H. L.,
30, 75, 76,
344, 386, 474,
534, 535
Michaels, Leonard,
298
Millay, Edna St.
Vincent, 297,
335
Miller, Arthur, 161
Milligan, Spike,
530
Mizner, Wilson,
575
Mondale, Walter,
469
Monroe, Marilyn,
286
Montand, Yves, 92
Moravia, Alberto,
632
Morgan, Robin,
171
Morley, Christo-
pher, 1
Morley, Robert,
210, 294, 306

Mostel, Zero, 272
Mull, Martin, 125
Munro, H. H., 77,
103, 135
Murphy, Maureen,
66
Musselman, Bill,
154
Nachman, Gerald,
196, 284
Napoleon, 7, 252
Nash, Ogden, 213
Nathan, George
Jean, 78
Nixon, Richard,
461
O'Connor, Flan-
nery, 360
Onassis, Aristotle,
225
Orben, Robert,
118, 267, 300,
523, 552
Orwell, George,
163, 515
Ovid, 541
Paar, Jack, 526
Paige, Satchel,
264, 553
Pante, Robert, 236
Pasternak, Joe,
378
Patton, George,
241
Pearl, Steven, 610
Perelman, S. J.,
28, 387
Pérignon, Dom,
139
Phelps, William
Lyon, 113
Picasso, Pablo,
623
Pierce, Charles, 58
Pliny the Younger,
532
Plummer, Christo-
pher, 191

Poore, Charles,
368
Presley, Elvis, 392
Price, Stephen,
605
Prynne, Hester, 57
Pryor, Richard, 89
Quisenberry, Don,
514
Radner, Gilda, 237
Rankin, Jeannette,
239
Rascoe, Judith,
353
Reagan, Ronald,
463
Reed, Jerry, 420
Reinhardt, Got-
tfried, 216
Renard, Jules, 356
Richler, Mordecai,
164
Rivers, Joan, 60,
64, 69, 86
Rogers, Will, 62,
184, 205, 244,
471, 481, 482,
537
Rooney, Andy, 280
Rose, Don, 71
Rostoni, John, 495
Rowland, Helen,
81, 82, 83, 172
Russell, Bertrand,
207
Ryan, Tom, 46
Sagan, Françoise,
219
Sahl, Mort, 403,
465
Saki, 77, 103, 132
Samuels, Jim, 79,
427, 438, 574
Santayana, George,
580
Sartre, Jean Paul,
529
Satie, Erik, 5
Schopenhauer,
Arthur, 631

Schulz, Charles, 377
Scott-Maxwell, Florida, 123
Secombe, Harry, 278
Sendak, Maurice, 224
Shakes, Ronnie, 455
Shannon, Wayne, 314
Shaw, George Bernard, 124, 142, 270, 393, 476, 562, 615
Sheehy, Gail, 275
Shelley, Percy Bysshe, 634
Shivers, Allan, 279
Shulman, Max, 587
Sibelius, Jean, 390
Sihanouk, Prince, 188
Simpson, N. F., 285
Sinatra, Frank, 186, 187
Skelton, Teressa, 517
Slezak, Walter, 405
Smith, Logan Persall, 120, 364
Smith, Martin Cruz, 73, 413
Spender, Stephen, 539
Stack, Peter, 400
Stack, Walt, 249
Stalin, Joseph, 310
Stark, John, 401
Stein, Gertrude, 223
Steinberg, David, 273

Steinem, Gloria, 98
Stengel, Casey, 490
Stevenson, Adlai, 556
Stoppard, Tom, 367
Stravinsky, Igor, 381, 382
Strindberg, August, 435
Sturgeon, Theodore, 499
Tacitus, 533
Thomas, Dylan, 145
Thomas, Marlo, 185, 193
Thoreau, Henry David, 235
Thurber, James, 29, 434
Tomlin, Lily, 215, 304, 327, 540
Toynbee, Arnold, 426
Trillin, Calvin, 167, 292, 293, 520
Truman, Harry S, 457, 484
Tuchman, Barbara, 464
Tucker, Sophie, 414
Twain, Mark, 137, 269, 309, 354, 510, 524
Tynan, Kenneth, 407
Valéry, Paul, 2, 31, 373
Van Buren, Abigail, 95, 200
Vidal, Gore, 122, 127, 466
Voltaire, 388, 430

Von Neumann, John, 203
Vonnegut, Kurt, Jr., 596
Ward, Artemus, 245
Warhol, Andy, 189
Warren, Earl, 489
Waugh, Evelyn, 497
Weber (cartoon), 233
Weinberg, Darrin, 491
Weinreich, Max, 608
Weissmuller, Johnny, 255
Wells, H. G., 159
West, Mae, 47, 48, 49, 50, 195
White, William Allen, 177
Whitehorn, Katharine, 606
Whitton, Charlotte, 170
Wilde, Oscar, 88, 234, 303, 349, 433, 561
Wilder, Billy, 308
Williamson, Nicol, 584
Winch, Marty, 508
Winchell, Walter, 408
Winters, Shelley, 190, 283
Wodehouse, P. G., 450
Wotton, Henry, 483
Wright, Steven, 324, 573
Yeats, William Butler, 140
York, Peter, 395
Ziggy (cartoon), 418

Index of Subjects and Key Words

Absence, 628
Accordion, 396
Acting, 399–402
Adultery, 57
Advertising, 515
Advice, 249–258
Agents, 412
Aïda, 307
Algebra, 622
Alimony, 97
Allah, 15
Ambassador, 483
America, 425–529,
    462
American Bar
    Association,
    487
Amiability, 94
Ancient times, 541
Animals, 382,
    430–443
Anorexia, 283
Apple, 57
Army, 246–247
Arrow, 551
Art, 560
Arthritis, 261
Authors, 351–380
Autobiography,
    340–341
Babies, 103–105
Bach, Johann
    Sebastian,
    383–384
Bachelors, 88
Bargains, 219
Baseball, 386, 490
Beauty, 519, 617,
    630
Bible, 553
Big cities, 315

Birch, 127
Bisexuality, 53
Blackmail, 612
Blacks, 493
Bondage, 60
Booing, 494
Books, 332–346,
    359, 376
Boredom, 102
Bowling, 125
Boy Scouts, 247
British, 159, 293,
    306
Brotherhood, 303
Bus, 197
California, 314
Calories, 282
Camel, 15
Canada, 312
Cannonball, 242
Captivity, 98
Car, 232
Car, parked, 42
Carnival, 557
Catholicism, 10
Catholics, 101
Cats, 439, 442
Celebrity, 183–193
Champagne, 139
Change, 299
Chastity, 67
Cheating, 91–92
Chicago, 147
Children,
    108–125, 382
Chile, 350
Chili, 278
Chinese food, 202
Christ, 9, 13
Christianity, 8
Christians, 599

Cincinnati, 287
Civilization, 244,
    620
Cleveland, 321
Closet, 546
Cocaine, 427
Coincidences, 505
Comedy, 165, 168
Comforting, 520
Communion, 10
Computers, 623
Consenting adults,
    127
Contraceptives, 52
Cookbooks, 280
Cooking, 275, 290,
    501
Cop, 42
Cork, 149
Corruption, 633
Country-western,
    192
Court, 486
Crap, 499
Creativity, 616
Crime, 221, 601
Critics, 371, 390,
    400–401, 407
Cuckoo clock, 311
Dahlias, 177
Dancing, 394, 527
Death, 152–159,
    295, 585, 590
Defeat, 154
Democracy,
    475–478
Depression, 564
Detroit, 321
Dialect, 608
Diet, 274,
    276–278, 280

Divorce, 96, 99, 100
Doberman pinschers, 248
Doctors, 444–456
Dogs, 431, 435, 600
Dreams, 507
Drinking, 136–151
Dutch elm disease, 418
Earthquake, 350
Eclipses, 595
Ecology, 554
Education, 126, 128, 132–135
Egg cream, 627
Egotism, 16–19, 333
Egypt, 307
Elbows, 73
Elections, 477
Emperor, 242
Enemies, 563, 591
Essayist, 368
Eve, 169
Exercise, 263
Existential, 324
Facts, 193
Failure, 196–199
Faith, 11
Fame, 185
Fanaticism, 580
Fashion, 234–237
Fast lane, 296
Fiction, 367
Fighting, 250
Fire, 71
Fire hydrants, 573
First aid, 450
Flattery, 526
Food, 269–295, 326
Fools, 257
Foreign food, 284
Forgiveness, 531, 591
France, 308–309

Friends, 70, 563, 587, 591
Frogs, 443
Fun, 214
Future, 514
Garbage, 362
George III, 571
God, 2–6, 59, 327, 575, 637
Golf, 492–493
Good examples, 524
Gorky Park (Smith), 413
Gourmet, 282, 287
Government, 473–474
Graffiti, 636
Granola, 319
Graveyards, 152
Gravity, 548
Gray hair, 636
Great men, 578–581
Great women, 582
Groping, 47
Groundhog Day, 440
Group sex, 59, 73
Guns, 380, 619
Hamlet (Shakespeare), 610
Happiness, 220, 542
Hatred, 533
Health, 259–268
Heart attack, 262
Hell, 406, 529
Hemingway, Ernest, 361
Hesitation, 50
Hick, 72
History, 131, 305, 314
Hollywood, 408–410
Honesty, 87, 205
Honor, 511

Hookers, 54
Horses, 436–437, 605
House, 545
Housecleaning, 501–503
Human beings, 302, 305
Humor, 160–168
Hunger, 20
Husband, 81, 86, 180
Ice, 151
Id, 454
Idiots, 547, 578, 582
Idling, 209
Ignorance, 126
Illegal aliens, 523
Illiteracy, 632
Imbeciles, 538
Immigration, 293, 526–527
Incest, 68
Income, 228, 231
Indians, 205, 523
Infidelity, 91
Insanity, 328, 330
Insult, 513
Intellectuals, 403
IQ, 117, 569
Irishman, 141
Israel, 248
Italy, 311
Jews, 200–202, 272, 599
Jobs, 208, 212
Jokes, 637
Jonah, 564
Joneses, 543
Journalism, 186–188, 347–350
Judges, 97
Jury duty, 486
Kansas, 314
Kansas City, 317
Kiss, 46, 51

Language, 608
Laps, 47
Last minute, 589
Late, 530
Laws, 488
Lawyers, 96, 456
Laziness, 249
Leftovers, 292
Lemmings, 558
Letting go, 253
Liaisons, 629
Library, 346
Lies, 512
Life, 297, 304,
    506, 523, 562
Lightning, 14
Literature, 115,
    361
Liver, 146
Living, 523
Livingstone, Dr.,
    607
Loneliness, 294
Los Angeles, 318,
    322
Losers, 299
Love, 28–40, 53,
    74, 595, 629
Lover, 58, 81
Luck, 528
Lying, 556
Macho, 66
Maids, 625
Manuscript,
    338–339
Map, 324
Marriage, 32, 74–
    102, 391, 634
Marseilles, 309
Marshmallow, 507
Mask, 557
Masochism, 61
Massenet, Jules,
    389
Masturbation,
    20–27
Matzo, 286

Melon patch, 256
Men and women,
    170–182
Mencken, H. L.,
    536
Metaphysics, 134
Mickey Mouse, 40
Mistakes, 506, 562
Mome raths, 584
Mondale, Walter,
    468
Money, 216–233,
    355, 635
Monogamy, 77
Morale, 598
Moralists, 138
Mothers, 123, 587
Murder, 508
Music, 381–396
Nachman's Rule,
    284
National debt, 119
New York, 201,
    316, 323
Newspapers, 337,
    347
Nice guys, 522
Nipple, 12
Nixon, Richard,
    459
Nouvelle cuisine,
    281
Novelists, 363
Novels, 343
Offenbach,
    Jacques, 383
Old age, 566, 584
Omniscience, 544
Opera, 386, 388
Oregon, 414
Organ, 27, 59
Overtures, 387
Oysters, 295
Parents, 114, 116
Parking, 574
Peace, 624
Peace of mind,
    583

Pedestals, 577
Pedestrians, 572
Penicillin, 65
Penis, 208
People, 305, 529
Permission, 531
Phone calls, 504,
    540
Pigeons, 101
Pimple, 36
Pizza, 58
Plagiarism, 375
Planning, 589
Plays, 367
Playwrights,
    397–398
Plotting, 379
Poetry, 373–374
Police dog, 434
Politicians, 480–
    484, 497, 626
Pollution, 552–554
Popularity, 532
Pork, 273
Postmen, 248
Prague, 485
Prayer, 327
Pregnant, 66
Presidents,
    457–472
Professions, 615
Promiscuity, 626
Psychiatrists, 363
Psychiatry, 454
Psychics, 600
Psychoanalysis,
    331, 452
Puke, 168
Rabbit, 66
Rat race, 215
Reading, 347, 568,
    631
Reagan, Ronald,
    465–467, 469
Real estate, 525,
    545
Reincarnation, 555

Relationship, 38
Relatives, 68, 533
Religion, 7
Retirement, 565
Rich, 219
Rock and roll, 395
Rock garden, 521
Rogues, 538
Rotarians, 535
Running, 264
San Francisco,
    318–320
Sandals, 256
Sanity, 329, 394,
    453
Santa Claus, 206
Sausages, 488
Schizophrenia,
    326, 327
Scientists, 497
Sculptor, 559
Seduction, 70
Sex, 44–45,
    59–60, 63–73,
    93, 95, 98,
    114, 157, 595,
    630
Sexism, 169, 170,
    470
Shakespeare,
    William, 610
Shopping, 220
Show business,
    397–414
Sin, 230
Sister, 576
Skeleton, 546
Small towns, 325
Smiling, 567, 614
Smoking, 266, 611
Snow White, 49
Solitude, 593–594,
    628
Song titles,
    419–424

Songs, 570
Soul, 134
Spaghetti, 294
Speed reading,
    568
Spelling, 602, 603
Spiritualism, 550
Spoons, 511
Sports, 489–495
Stars, 139
Statistics, 266
Steam engine, 613
Steinbeck, John,
    372
Stranger, 70
Strangers, 586
Stupidity, 273–332
Success, 194–199
Suffering, 202
Suicide, 509
Sunburn, 62
Superficiality, 189
Superiority, 588
Surgery, 451
Sweat, 71
Swine, 128
Switzerland, 311
Taxes, 635
Teaching, 129
Television,
    415–418
Texans, 313
Thanksgiving, 428
Theology, 1
Third World, 315
Thirst, 298
Thrift, 227
Toddling, 609
Togetherness, 617
Tourists, 306
Traffic signals,
    323
Tramp, 64
Transsexuals, 176

Trapeze, 72
Travel, 427
Truth, 354, 457,
    510, 512, 519
Tunnel, 300, 498
Turkey cocktail,
    144
Typing, 56
Typos, 602
Underwear, 178
Universe, 1
Universities, 360
University politics,
    130
Vagina, 208
Valentine, 191
Vanity, 364
Vice-presidents,
    470–472
Virginity, 90, 36
Voting, 478, 479
Wages, 230
Wallpaper, 561
War, 238–248,
    391, 624
Washington,
    George, 464
Waste, 67
Water, 137
Weather, 518
Wedding cake, 539
Weddings, 391
Weightlifters, 495
Wife, 79
Winning, 491
Winter, 516–517
Wit, 160
Women, 225
Women and men,
    170–182
Work, 207–215
Wrestling, 527
Writers, 351–380
Writing, 604–605

THE THIRD

—AND POSSIBLY THE BEST—

637

BEST THINGS

ANYBODY EVER SAID

For
Susan Richman
The best in the business

Contents

Introduction

PART ONE

Religion, Life Itself, Men and Women, Cats,
Clothes, Love, Sex, Marriage, Self-Abuse, Parents,
Kids, Work, Money, Crime, Old Age, Death,
and one thing and another

PART TWO

Cynicism, Happiness, Morality, Bores, Food,
Doctors, Parties, Alcohol, Music, Sports, Art,
Law, Travel, Airplanes, Science, War, Movies,
Politics, Presidents, Writers,
and various odds and ends

PART THREE

Miscellaneous

Sources, References, and Notes

Index of Authors

Index of Subjects and Key Words

Introduction

The first volume in this series appeared in 1982 and was called *The 637 Best Things Anybody Ever Said*. The title, I hoped, would provoke bookstore browsers into sampling the contents, after which they would be compelled to read a few lines to the cashier while fishing for their wallets. The number 637 was not entirely arbitrary—that's how many good quotes were left after I boiled down my own notebooks and gutted other people's collections. The book presented what I thought were the tastiest morsels from the world's wags and wits. Although I asked to hear from readers on the off chance that I might have missed something, I gave little thought to a sequel. A second serving, I felt sure, would be bland by comparison.

Well, a year later I was one red-faced compiler! I had continued compulsively jotting down good lines— once the eyes and ears are awakened to the possibilities they can't be put back to sleep—and readers were stuffing my mailbox with bon mots I had overlooked, some of them their own. Asking for contributions from readers, like the Treaty of Versailles following World War I, had turned out to be a tragic mistake that made a sequel inevitable.

The Other 637 Best Things Anybody Ever Said was published in 1984 and is one of the few sequels since the New Testament that is as good as the original, perhaps better in that it contains fewer of my own lines. It sold twice as many copies as the prequel, resulting in twice as many suggestions from readers and teaching me that the path to success in the literary world may lie in producing the same book over and over. I don't know about you, but when I hear or read a good line I can hardly wait to tell it to somebody else, so here I am again. I never would have believed four years ago that a third volume was possible or that I would be more or less forced by a sense of duty and money to compile it.

The number 637 has turned out to be more a measure of the narrowness of my original vision than an index of the world's wit and insight. Still, it is a pretty good number for a quote book designed to be read from cover to cover; bigger and the reader's eyes would begin to glaze, smaller and it would be hard to get published in hardcover.

It's amazing how much funny stuff there is. Funny people are everywhere, and not all of them belong to the army of some three thousand standup comedians now terrorizing America; some, in fact, have been dead for hundreds of years. Then there are the ordinary people who are funny only now and then, a point not interesting enough to pursue. In any event, a river of rich comedic milk is flowing across the land, and as fast as I skim off the cream more cream appears. That's fine for you, but I may be doomed to wade around forever in other people's pith. Not that it's such a bad life. I can go to a comedy club and deduct it as a business expense.

I considered calling this collection *The Third and Possibly the Last 637 Best Things Anybody Ever Said*, but I didn't want to have to eat those words as I have so many others. Like H. L. Mencken (1880–1956) before me, what I really want to do is write a book that weighs at least five pounds. I'll work on it between trips to the mailbox.

A few announcements. Dates are given only for people who strike me as being dead; others can fend for themselves. In Parts One and Two, quotes are grouped in rough, untitled categories. Use the indexes of subjects and authors if you want to locate a half-remembered quote. To facilitate reading in the normal front-to-back manner, categories generally follow one another in logical rather than alphabetical order . . . for example, Marriage follows Sex and Self-Abuse follows Marriage. In most books of this kind, Sex is followed by such unrelated topics as Shakespeare, Sickness, and Socialism, and there is no category for Self-Abuse at all. I'm uneasy about crediting lines to certain celebrities, for I sense the touch of the gag-writer's hidden hand. It would contribute to accuracy and completeness if those ghosts would step forward and identify themselves even if it costs them their jobs. Unless you are familiar with all three volumes, don't write to point out anything. Finally, some quotes are not numbered because they appeared earlier in the series ("Plato was a bore"), and quotes used more than once in the following pages are numbered on first appearance only ("Hemingway was a jerk").

Have fun—I did.

Robert Byrne

PART ONE

———⟨◆⟩———

Religion
Life Itself
Men and Women
Cats
Clothes
Love
Sex
Marriage
Self-Abuse
Parents
Kids
Work
Money
Crime
Old Age
Death
and one thing and another

1

The only thing that stops God from sending another flood is that the first one was useless.

Nicolas Chamfort (1741–1794)

2

The world is proof that God is a committee.

Bob Stokes

3

God is dead, but fifty thousand social workers have risen to take his place.

J. D. McCoughey

4

Which is it, is man one of God's blunders or is God one of man's?

Friedrich Nietzsche (1844–1900)

5

Nietzsche was stupid and abnormal.

Leo Tolstoy (1828–1910)

6

Millions long for immortality who don't know what to do on a rainy Sunday afternoon.

Susan Ertz

7

A pious man is one who would be an atheist if the king were.

Jean de La Bruyère (1645–1696)

8

I detest converts almost as much as I do missionaries.

H. L. Mencken (1880–1956)

9

Most of my friends are not Christians, but I have some who are Anglicans or Roman Catholics.

Dame Rose Macaulay (1881–1958)

1 0

Promise me that if you become a Christian you'll become a Presbyterian.

Lord Beaverbrook (1879–1964) to
Josef Stalin in 1941

1 1

The history of saints is mainly the history of insane people.

Benito Mussolini (1883–1945)

1 2

In Burbank there's a drive-in church called Jack-in-the-Pew. You shout your sins into the face of a plastic priest.

Johnny Carson

1 3

When I was a kid in the ghetto, a gang started going around harassing people, so some of the toughest kids formed a gang called The Sharks to stop them. The other gang was called The Jehovah's Witnesses.

Charles Kosar

1 4

Jesus was a Jew, yes, but only on his mother's side.

Archie Bunker

1 5

Unless you hate your father and mother and wife and brothers and sisters and, yes, even your own life, you can't be my disciple.

Jesus Christ (0?–32?), if St. Luke is to be believed. See Luke 14:26.

1 6

Jesus was a crackpot.

Bhagwan Shree Rajneesh

17

Let Bhagwans be Bhagwans.

*Headline considered by
the* Washington Post

18

Jesus died too soon. If he had lived to my age he would
have repudiated his doctrine.

Friedrich Nietzsche (1844–1900)

Nietzsche was stupid and abnormal.

Leo Tolstoy (1828–1910)

19

I'm not going to climb into the ring with Tolstoy.

Ernest Hemingway (1898–1961)

20

Hemingway was a jerk.

Harold Robbins

21

The purpose of life is a life of purpose.

Robert Byrne

2 2

I like life. It's something to do.

Ronnie Shakes

2 3

Life is divided into the horrible and the miserable.

Woody Allen

2 4

Life is just a bowl of pits.

Rodney Dangerfield

2 5

Life being what it is, one dreams of revenge.

Paul Gauguin (1848–1903)

2 6

If I had my life to live over, I'd live over a delicatessen.

Unknown

2 7
Man is more an ape than many of the apes.

Friedrich Nietzsche (1844–1900)

Nietzsche was stupid and abnormal.

Leo Tolstoy (1828–1910)

2 8
He who looketh upon a woman loseth a fender.

Sign in auto repair shop

2 9
Mahatma Gandhi was what wives wish their husbands
were: thin, tan, and moral.

Unknown

3 0
The only time a woman really succeeds in changing a
man is when he's a baby.

Natalie Wood (1938–1981)

31

I'm a disgrace to my sex. I should work in an Arabian palace as a eunuch.

Woody Allen

32

Girls are always running through my mind. They don't dare walk.

Andy Gibb

33

One good thing about being a man is that men don't have to talk to each other.

Peter Cocotas

34

Of all the wild beasts of land or sea, the wildest is woman.

Menander (342?–291? B.C.)

35

A woman is always buying something.

Ovid (43 B.C.–A.D. 18)

36

Nothing is more intolerable than a wealthy woman.

Juvenal (60?–140?)

37

A woman talks to one man, looks at a second, and thinks of a third.

Bhartrihari, ca. 625

38

Woman was God's second mistake.

Friedrich Nietzsche (1844–1900)

Nietzsche was stupid and abnormal.

Leo Tolstoy (1828–1910)

39

Women speak two languages, one of which is verbal.

Steve Rubenstein

40

Women who seek to be equal with men lack ambition.

Timothy Leary

41

Women are like elephants to me. I like to look at them but I wouldn't want to own one.

W. C. Fields (1880–1946)

4 2

Phyllis Schlafly speaks for all American women who oppose equal rights for themselves.

Andy Rooney

4 3

Housework can kill you if done right.

Erma Bombeck

4 4

What do women want? Shoes.

Mimi Pond

45

Shopping tip: You can get shoes for 85 cents at bowling alleys.

Al Clethen

46

Can you imagine a world without men? No crime and lots of happy fat women.

Sylvia (Nicole Hollander)

47

Veni, vidi, Visa. *(We came, we saw, we went shopping.)*

Jan Barrett

48

Any girl can be glamorous; all you have to do is stand still and look stupid.

Hedy Lamarr

49

If they could put one man on the moon, why can't they put them all?

Unknown

50

Good breeding consists of concealing how much we think of ourselves and how little we think of the other person.

Mark Twain (1835–1910)

51

Charm is a way of getting the answer yes without asking a clear question.

Albert Camus (1913–1960)

52

Good taste is the worst vice ever invented.

Dame Edith Sitwell (1887–1964)

53

We are all born charming, fresh, and spontaneous and must be civilized before we are fit to participate in society.

Miss Manners (Judith Martin)

54

Cats are smarter than dogs. You can't get eight cats to pull a sled through snow.

Jeff Valdez

55

Dogs come when they're called; cats take a message and get back to you.

Missy Dizick

56

If a cat spoke, it would say things like "Hey, I don't see the *problem* here."

Roy Blount, Jr.

57

A man who was loved by 300 women singled me out to live with him. Why? I was the only one without a cat.

Elayne Boosler

58

I take my pet lion to church every Sunday. He has to eat.

Marty Pollio

59

Cute rots the intellect.

Garfield (Jim Davis)

60

Distrust any enterprise that requires new clothes.
Henry David Thoreau (1817–1862)

61

Fashions are induced epidemics.
George Bernard Shaw (1856–1950)

62

You'd be surprised how much it costs to look this cheap.

Dolly Parton

63

There is a new awareness of style in the Soviet Union. The premier's wife recently appeared on the cover of *House and Tractor*.

Johnny Carson

64

I should warn you that underneath these clothes I'm wearing boxer shorts and I know how to use them.
Robert Orben

65

What you have when everyone wears the same play-clothes for all occasions, is addressed by nickname, expected to participate in Show and Tell, and bullied out of any desire for privacy, is not democracy; it is kindergarten.

Miss Manners (Judith Martin)

66

Being named as one of the world's best-dressed men doesn't necessarily mean that I am a bad person.

Anthony R. Cucci,
Mayor of Jersey City

6 7

In love there are two evils: war and peace.

Horace (65–8 B.C.*)*

6 8

Love is the crocodile on the river of desire.

Bhartrihari (ca. 625)

6 9

Love is what happens to men and women who don't know each other.

W. Somerset Maugham (1874–1965)

7 0

Love is blond.

Herbert Gold's mother

7 1

The trouble with loving is that pets don't last long enough and people last too long.

Unknown

7 2

A man always remembers his first love with special tenderness, but after that he begins to bunch them.

H. L. Mencken (1880–1956)

7 3

When you are in love with someone you want to be near him all the time, except when you are out buying things and charging them to him.

Miss Piggy, according to Henry Beard,
Miss Piggy's Guide to Life, *1981*

7 4

Better to have loved and lost a short person than never to have loved a tall.

David Chambless

7 5

One of the advantages of living alone is that you don't have to wake up in the arms of a loved one.

Marion Smith

7 6

Dear Sweetheart:
     Last night I thought of you.
     At least I think it was you.

Love letter by Snoopy (Charles Schulz)

7 7

In the race for love, I was scratched.

Joan Davis (1912–1961)

78

Outside every thin woman is a fat man trying to get in.

Katherine Whitehorn

79

Sex is natural, but not if it's done right.

Unknown

80

Sex is good, but not as good as fresh sweet corn.

Garrison Keillor

81

There is hardly anyone whose sexual life, if it were broadcast, would not fill the world at large with surprise and horror.

W. Somerset Maugham (1874–1965)

82

There is nothing a young man can get by wenching but duels, the clap, and bastards.

Kathleen Winsor

83

It is more fun contemplating somebody else's navel than your own.

Arthur Hoppe

84

Of all the sexual aberrations, perhaps the most peculiar is chastity.

Remy de Gourmont (1858–1915)

85

We may eventually come to realize that chastity is no more a virtue than malnutrition.

Alex Comfort

86

I used to be a virgin, but I gave it up because there was no money in it.

Marsha Warfield

87

A terrible thing happened again last night—nothing.

Phyllis Diller

88

Celibacy is not hereditary.

Guy Goden

89

Kissing is a means of getting two people so close together that they can't see anything wrong with each
other.

René Yasenek

9 0

Oh, what lies there are in kisses!

Heinrich Heine (1797–1856)

9 1

Whenever I'm caught between two evils, I take the one I've never tried.

Mae West (1892–1980)

9 2

It is better to copulate than never.

Robert Heinlein

9 3

Vasectomy means never having to say you're sorry.

Unknown

9 4

Last night I discovered a new form of oral contraceptive. I asked a girl to go to bed with me and she said no.

Woody Allen

9 5

I told my girl friend that unless she expressed her feelings and told me what she liked I wouldn't be able to please her, so she said, "Get off me."

Garry Shandling

96

She was so wild that when she made French toast she got her tongue caught in the toaster.

Rodney Dangerfield

97

I'm too shy to express my sexual needs except over the phone to people I don't know.

Garry Shandling

98

Sex Appeal—Give Generously

Bumper sticker

99

How did sex come to be thought of as dirty in the first place? God must have been a Republican.

Will Durst

100

Before we make love, my husband takes a pain killer.

Joan Rivers

101

My wife was in labor with our first child for thirty-two hours and I was faithful to her the whole time.

Jonathan Katz

102

My wife has cut our lovemaking down to once a month, but I know two guys she's cut out entirely.

Rodney Dangerfield

103

Chains required, whips optional.

California highway sign

104

The fantasy of every Australian man is to have two women—one cleaning and the other dusting.

Maureen Murphy

105

Ouch! You're on My Hair!

Sex manual title suggested by
Richard Lewis

106

The difference between pornography and erotica is lighting.

Gloria Leonard

107

If homosexuality were normal, God would have created Adam and Bruce.

Anita Bryant

108

Rub-a-dub-dub
Three men in a tub
And that's on a slow night.

Sign in a San Francisco bath house

109

Never play leapfrog with a unicorn.

Unknown

110

Get in good physical condition before submitting to bondage. You should be fit to be tied.

Robert Byrne

111

I caused my husband's heart attack. In the middle of lovemaking I took the paper bag off my head. He dropped the Polaroid and keeled over and so did the hooker. It would have taken me half an hour to untie myself and call the paramedics, but fortunately the Great Dane could dial.

Joan Rivers

112

A British mother's advice to her daughter on how to survive the wedding night: "Close your eyes and think of England."

Pierre Daninos

113

I have so little sex appeal that my gynecologist calls me "sir."

Joan Rivers

114

What men call gallantry and gods adultery
Is much more common where the climate's sultry.

Lord Byron (1788–1824)

115

Of all the tame beasts, I hate sluts.

John Ray (1627?–1705)

116

I'd like to have a girl, and I'm saving my money so I can get a good one.

Bob Nickman

117

A relationship is what happens between two people who are waiting for something better to come along.

Unknown

118

I have such poor vision I can date anybody.

Garry Shandling

119

It's relaxing to go out with my ex-wife because she already knows I'm an idiot.

Warren Thomas

120

I used to go out exclusively with actresses and other female impersonators.

Mort Sahl

121

The trouble with living in sin is the shortage of closet space.

Missy Dizick

122

The fickleness of the women I love is only equalled by the infernal constancy of the women who love me.

George Bernard Shaw (1856–1950)

123

Burt Reynolds once asked me out. I was in his room.

Phyllis Diller

124

He's the kind of man a woman would have to marry to get rid of.

Mae West (1892–1980)

125

Brains are an asset, if you hide them.

Mae West (1892–1980)

126

He promised me earrings, but he only pierced my ears.

Arabian saying

127

Marriage is a necessary evil.

Menander (342?–291? B.C.)

128

Marriage is the only war in which you sleep with the enemy.

Unknown

129

Nothing anybody tells you about marriage helps.

Max Siegel

130

There is so little difference between husbands you might as well keep the first.

Adela Rogers St. Johns

131

Marriage is really tough because you have to deal with feelings and lawyers.

Richard Pryor

132

Marriage could catch on again because living together is not quite living and not quite together. Premarital sex slowly evolves into premarital sox.

Gerald Nachman

133

Marriage is part of a sort of 50's revival package that's back in vogue along with neckties and naked ambition.

Calvin Trillin

134

I'll have to marry a virgin. I can't stand criticism.

From the movie Out of Africa, *1985*

135

If you are living with a man, you don't have to worry about whether you should sleep with him after dinner.

Stephanie Brush

136

I'd like to get married because I like the idea of a man being required by law to sleep with me every night.

Carrie Snow

137

Alimony is like buying oats for a dead horse.

Arthur Baer (1896–1975)

138

I hated my marriage, but I always had a great place to park.

Gerald Nachman

139

Where I come from, when a Catholic marries a Lutheran it is considered the first step on the road to Minneapolis.

Garrison Keillor

140

I was married by a judge. I should have asked for a jury.

George Burns

141

I wouldn't trust my husband with a young woman for five minutes, and he's been dead for 25 years.

Brendan Behan's mother

142

I want a girl just like the girl that married dear old Dad.

Lyrics by Oedipus Rex

143

Adultery is a meanness and a stealing, a taking away from someone what should be theirs, a great selfishness, and surrounded and guarded by lies lest it should be found out. And out of the meanness and selfishness and lying flow love and joy and peace beyond anything that can be imagined.

Dame Rose Macaulay (1881–1958)

144

I am a marvelous housekeeper. Every time I leave a man I keep his house.

Zsa Zsa Gabor

145

The happiest time in any man's life is just after the first divorce.

John Kenneth Galbraith

146

One reason people get divorced is that they run out of gift ideas.

Robert Byrne

147

I've married a few people I shouldn't have, but haven't we all?

Mamie Van Doren

148

What I like about masturbation is that you don't have to talk afterwards.

Milos Forman

149

If sex is so personal, why do we have to share it with someone?

Unknown

150

Enjoy yourself. If you can't enjoy yourself, enjoy somebody else.

Jack Schaefer

151

The only reason I feel guilty about masturbation is that I do it so badly.

David Steinberg

152

Philip Roth is a good writer, but I wouldn't want to shake hands with him.

Jacqueline Susann (1921–1974)
after reading Portnoy's Complaint

153

I can't believe I forgot to have children.

Unknown

154

If God wanted sex to be fun, He wouldn't have included children as punishment.

Ed Bluestone

155

I am determined my children shall be brought up in their father's religion, if they can find out what it is.

Charles Lamb (1775–1834)

156

I could now afford all the things I never had as a kid, if I didn't have kids.

Robert Orben

157

My mother had a great deal of trouble with me, but I think she enjoyed it.

Mark Twain (1835–1910)

158

I'll probably never have children because I don't believe in touching people for any reason.

Paula Poundstone

159

I take my children everywhere, but they always find their way back home.

Robert Orben

160

My parents put a live teddy bear in my crib.

Woody Allen

161

I phoned my dad to tell him I had stopped smoking. He called me a quitter.

Steven Pearl

162

Never lend your car to anyone to whom you have given birth.

Erma Bombeck

163

The best revenge is to live long enough to be a problem to your children.

Unknown

164

Children today are tyrants. They contradict their parents, gobble their food, and tyrannize their teachers.

Socrates (470–399 B.C.*)*

165

An ugly baby is a very nasty object, and the prettiest is frightful when undressed.

Queen Victoria (1819–1901)

166

What is more enchanting than the voices of young people when you can't hear what they say?

Logan Pearsall Smith (1865–1946)

167

At my lemonade stand I used to give the first glass away free and charge five dollars for the second glass. The refill contained the antidote.

Emo Philips

168

When you are eight years old, nothing is any of your business.

Lenny Bruce (1926–1955)

169

What is youth except a man or woman before it is fit to be seen?

Evelyn Waugh (1903–1966)

170

My eleven-year-old daughter mopes around the house all day waiting for her breasts to grow.

Bill Cosby

171

If you're not beguiling by age twelve, forget it.

Lucy (Charles Schulz)

172

I was so naive as a kid I used to sneak behind the barn and do nothing.

Johnny Carson

173

My schoolmates would make love to anything that moved, but I never saw any reason to limit myself.

Emo Philips

174

I almost got a girl pregnant in high school. It's costing me a fortune to keep the rabbit on a life-support system.

Will Shriner

175

The trouble with the 1980's as compared with the 1970's is that teenagers no longer rebel and leave home.

Marion Smith

176

Learning to dislike children at an early age saves a lot of expense and aggravation later in life.

Robert Byrne

177

Adolescence is the stage between infancy and adultery.

Unknown

178

I like work; it fascinates me. I can sit and look at it for hours.

Jerome K. Jerome (1859–1927)

179

Work is for cowards.

Pool hustler U. J. Puckett
in 1984 at age seventy-six

180

Always be smarter than the people who hire you.

Lena Horne

181

The trouble with unemployment is that the minute you wake up in the morning you're on the job.

Slappy White

182

The volume of paper expands to fill the available briefcases.

Jerry Brown

183

Any new venture goes through the following stages: enthusiasm, complication, disillusionment, search for the guilty, punishment of the innocent, and decoration of those who did nothing.

Unknown

184

When I realized that what I had turned out to be was a lousy, two-bit pool hustler and drunk, I wasn't depressed at all. I was glad to have a profession.

Danny McGoorty (1901–1970)

185

The reason American cities are prosperous is that there is no place to sit down.

Alfred J. Talley

186

Gardner's Law: Eighty-seven percent of all people in all professions are incompetent.

John Gardner

187

It is time I stepped aside for a less experienced and less able man.

Professor Scott Elledge
on his retirement from Cornell

188

The only way to succeed is to make people hate you.
Josef von Sternberg (1894–1969)

189

A man can't get rich if he takes proper care of his family.

Navajo saying

190

I believe that the power to make money is a gift from God.

John D. Rockefeller (1839–1937)

191

It is the wretchedness of being rich that you have to live with rich people.

Logan Pearsall Smith (1865–1946)

192

Never invest in anything that eats or needs repairing.

Billy Rose (1899–1966)

193

Every morning I get up and look through the Forbes list of the richest people in America. If I'm not there, I go to work.

Robert Orben

194

I enjoy being a highly overpaid actor.

Roger Moore

195

Buy old masters. They bring better prices than young mistresses.

Lord Beaverbrook (1879–1964)

196

The income tax has made liars out of more Americans than golf.

Will Rogers (1879–1935)

197

Why is there so much month left at the end of the money?

Unknown

198

Today you can go to a gas station and find the cash register open and the toilets locked. They must think toilet paper is worth more than money.

Joey Bishop

199

Enjoy money while you have it. Shrouds don't have pockets.

Virginia Esberg's grandmother

200

It is no disgrace to be poor, but it might as well be.

Jim Grue

201

So he's short . . . he can stand on his wallet.

Jewish mother

202

Business is a good game—lots of competition and a minimum of rules. You keep score with money.

Atari founder Nolan Bushnell

203

Economists are people who work with numbers but who don't have the personality to be accountants.

Unknown

204

An economist's guess is liable to be as good as anybody else's.

Will Rogers (1879–1935)

205

Mathematics has given economics rigor, but alas, also mortis.

Robert Heilbroner

206

Organized crime in America takes in over forty billion dollars a year and spends very little on office supplies.

Woody Allen

207

Getting caught is the mother of invention.

Robert Byrne

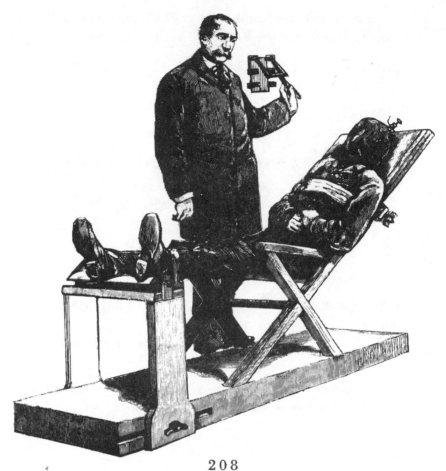

208

Capital punishment is either an affront to humanity or
a potential parking place.

Larry Brown

209

I believe that people would be alive today if there were
a death penalty.

Nancy Reagan

2 1 0

There is never enough time, unless you're serving it.

Malcolm Forbes

2 1 1

At age fifty, every man has the face he deserves.

George Orwell (1903–1950)

2 1 2

The secret of staying young is to live honestly, eat slowly, and lie about your age.

Lucille Ball

2 1 3

I am in the prime of senility.

Joel Chandler Harris (1848–1908)
at age fifty-eight

2 1 4

I am not young enough to know everything.

Oscar Wilde (1854–1900)

2 1 5

The closing years of life are like the end of a masquerade party, when the masks are dropped.

Arthur Schopenhauer (1788–1860)

216

Old age is not for sissies.

Variously ascribed

217

Old age is when the liver spots show through your gloves.

Phyllis Diller

218

Old age is like a plane flying through a storm. Once you are aboard there is nothing you can do.

Golda Meir (1898–1978)

219

When I was young there was no respect for the young, and now that I am old there is no respect for the old. I missed out coming and going.

J. B. Priestley (1894–1984)

220

Middle age begins with the first mortgage and ends when you drop dead.

Herb Caen

221

You know you're old when you notice how young the derelicts are getting.

Jeanne Phillips

222

My grandfather used to make home movies and edit out the joy.

Richard Lewis

223

I smoke cigars because at my age if I don't have something to hang onto I might fall down.

George Burns

224

The hardest years in life are those between ten and seventy.

Helen Hayes at age eighty-three

225

After age seventy it's patch, patch, patch.

Jimmy Stewart

226

You have to be an antique to appreciate them.

Fay Madigan Lange

227

Death is just a distant rumor to the young.

Andy Rooney

228

They say such nice things about people at their funerals that it makes me sad to realize that I'm going to miss mine by just a few days.

Garrison Keillor

229

Big deal! I'm used to dust.

Gravestone epitaph requested
by Erma Bombeck

230

There is no reason for me to die. I already died in Altoona.

George Burns

231

I know a man who gave up smoking, drinking, sex, and rich food. He was healthy right up to the time he killed himself.

Johnny Carson

232

The only thing wrong with immortality is that it tends to go on forever.

Herb Caen

233

There will be sex after death; we just won't be able to feel it.

Lily Tomlin

234

Dying ought to be done in black and white. It is simply not a colorful activity.

Russell Baker

235

What Einstein was to physics, what Babe Ruth was to home runs, what Emily Post was to table manners . . . that's what Edward G. Robinson was to dying like a dirty rat.

Russell Baker

PART TWO

Cynicism
Happiness
Morality
Bores
Food
Doctors
Parties
Alcohol
Music
Sports
Art
Law
Travel
Airplanes
Science
War
Movies
Politics
Presidents
Writers
and various odds and ends

236

Idealism is what precedes experience; cynicism is what follows.

David T. Wolf

237

The cynics are right nine times out of ten.

H. L. Mencken (1880–1956)

238

No matter how cynical you get, it is impossible to keep up.

Lily Tomlin

239

When there are two conflicting versions of a story, the wise course is to believe the one in which people appear at their worst.

H. Allen Smith (1906–1976)

240

Half the people in America are faking it.

Robert Mitchum

241

Ignorance is the mother of admiration.

George Chapman (1599?–1634)

242

I was going to buy a copy of *The Power of Positive Thinking*, and then I thought: What the hell good would that do?

Ronnie Shakes

243

Nothing matters very much, and few things matter all.

Arthur Balfour (1848–1930)

244

Doing a thing well is often a waste of time.

Robert Byrne

245

Happiness is a Chinese meal; sorrow is a nourishment forever.

Carolyn Kizer

246

There is no happiness; there are only moments of happiness.

Spanish proverb

247

I am a kind of paranoiac in reverse. I suspect people of plotting to make me happy.

J. D. Salinger

248

Happiness is having a large, loving, caring, close-knit family in another city.

George Burns

249

O Lord, help me to be pure, but not yet.

St. Augustine (354–430)

250

An evil mind is a constant solace.

Unknown

251

A thing worth having is a thing worth cheating for.

W. C. Fields (1880–1946)

252

He without benefit of scruples
His fun and money soon quadruples.

Ogden Nash (1902–1971)

2 5 3

Living with a conscience is like driving a car with the brakes on.

Budd Schulberg

2 5 4

In order to preserve your self-respect, it is sometimes necessary to lie and cheat.

Robert Byrne

2 5 5

It has been my experience that folks who have no vices have very few virtues.

Abraham Lincoln (1809–1865)

2 5 6

The price of purity is purists.

Calvin Trillin

2 5 7

A bore is someone who, when you ask him how he is, tells you.

Variously ascribed

258

Some people stay longer in an hour than others do in a month.

William Dean Howells (1837–1920)

259

There are very few people who don't become more interesting when they stop talking.

Mary Lowry

260

The opposite of talking isn't listening. The opposite of talking is waiting.

Fran Lebowitz

261

When the Emperor Constantine turned Christian, he banned the eating of sausage, which of course immediately created a whole army of sausage bootleggers and may explain why Al Capone always looked like a sausage.

Donald E. Westlake

262

A louse in the cabbage is better than no meat at all.

Pennsylvania Dutch proverb

263

The food in Yugoslavia is fine if you like pork tartare.

Ed Begley, Jr.

264

Eating an artichoke is like getting to know someone really well.

Willi Hastings

265

I will not eat oysters. I want my food dead—not sick, not wounded—dead.

Woody Allen

266

Only Irish coffee provides in a single glass all four essential food groups: alcohol, caffeine, sugar, and fat.

Alex Levine

267

Cogito ergo dim sum. (*Therefore I think these are pork buns.*)

Robert Byrne

268

Anybody who doesn't think that the best hamburger place in the world is in his home town is a sissy.

Calvin Trillin

269

You can find your way across the country using burger joints the way a navigator uses stars.

Charles Kuralt

270

Part of the secret of success in life is to eat what you like and let the food fight it out inside.

Mark Twain (1835–1910)

271

We didn't starve, but we didn't eat chicken unless we were sick, or the chicken was.

Bernard Malamud (1914–1986)

272

In Mexico we have a word for sushi: bait.

José Simon

273

Everything you see I owe to spaghetti.

Sophia Loren

274

Blow in its ear.

*Johnny Carson on the best
way to thaw a frozen turkey*

2 7 5

If you want to look young and thin, hang around old fat people.

Jim Eason

2 7 6

The cherry tomato is a marvelous invention, producing as it does a satisfactorily explosive squish when bitten.

Miss Manners (Judith Martin)

2 7 7

I prefer Hostess fruit pies to pop-up toaster tarts because they don't require so much cooking.

Carrie Snow

2 7 8

You are where you eat.

Unknown

2 7 9

No diet will remove all the fat from your body because the brain is entirely fat. Without a brain you might look good, but all you could do is run for public office.

Covert Bailey

2 8 0

I can get along with anybody . . . provided they're fat.

Susan Richman

281

Anybody who believes that the way to a man's heart is through his stomach flunked geography.

Robert Byrne

282

The waist is a terrible thing to mind.

Ziggy (Tom Wilson)

283

I have learned to spell hors d'oeuvres,
Which grates on many people's nerves.

Unknown

284

The trouble with eating Italian food is that five or six days later you're hungry again.

George Miller

285

There is no love sincerer than the love of food.

George Bernard Shaw (1856–1950)

286

Statistics show that of those who contract the habit of eating, very few survive.

Wallace Irwin (1875–1959)

287

Marriage is not merely sharing the fettucini, but sharing the burden of finding the fettucini restaurant in the first place.

Calvin Trillin

288

My wife and I tried to breakfast together, but we had to stop or our marriage would have been wrecked.

Winston Churchill (1874–1965)

289

My doctor gave me two weeks to live. I hope they're in August.

Ronnie Shakes

290

The trouble with heart disease is that the first symptom is often hard to deal with: sudden death.

Michael Phelps, M.D.

291

One of my problems is that I internalize everything. I can't express anger; I grow a tumor instead.

Woody Allen

292

A male gynecologist is like an auto mechanic who has never owned a car.

Carrie Snow

293

After a year in therapy, my psychiatrist said to me, "Maybe life isn't for everyone."

Larry Brown

294

Half of analysis is anal.

Marty Indik

295

Why should I tolerate a perfect stranger at the bedside of my mind?

Vladimir Nabokov (1899–1977)
on psychoanalysis

296

People who say you're just as old as you feel are all wrong, fortunately.

Russell Baker

297

To reduce stress, avoid excitement. Spend more time with your spouse.

Robert Orben

298

Nancy Reagan has agreed to be the first artificial heart donor.

Andrea C. Michaels

299

Be true to your teeth or your teeth will be false to you.

Dental proverb

300

You're ugly. Not only that, you need a root canal.

James J. Garrett, D.D.S.

301

Attention to health is life's greatest hindrance.

Plato (427?–347 B.C.*)*

Plato was a bore.

Friedrich Nietzsche (1844–1900)

Nietzsche was stupid and abnormal.

Leo Tolstoy (1828–1910)

302

Never give a party if you will be the most interesting person there.

Mickey Friedman

303

Support wildlife. Throw a party.

Unknown

304

Cockroaches and socialites are the only things that can stay up all night and eat anything.

Herb Caen

305

Never mistake endurance for hospitality.

Unknown

3 0 6

Nothing spoils a good party like a genius.

Elsa Maxwell (1883–1963)

3 0 7

For a single woman, preparing for company means wiping the lipstick off the milk carton.

Elayne Boosler

3 0 8

In America, you can always find a party. In Russia, the party always finds you.

Yakov Smirnoff

309

The best thing about a cocktail party is being asked to it.

Gerald Nachman

310

There is nothing for a case of nerves like a case of beer.

Joan Goldstein

311

Reminds me of my safari in Africa. Somebody forgot the corkscrew and for several days we had to live on nothing but food and water.

W. C. Fields (1880–1946)

312
Sometimes too much to drink is barely enough.
Mark Twain (1835–1910)

313
Like a camel, I can go without a drink for seven days
—and have on several horrible occasions.

Herb Caen

314

My grandmother is over eighty and still doesn't need glasses. Drinks right out of the bottle.

Henny Youngman

315

There is no law against composing music when one has no ideas whatsoever. The music of Wagner, therefore, is perfectly legal.

The National, *Paris, 1850*

316

The prelude to *Tristan and Isolde* sounded as if a bomb had fallen into a large music factory and had thrown all the notes into confusion.

The Tribune, *Berlin, 1871*

317

The prelude to *Tristan and Isolde* reminds me of the Italian painting of the martyr whose intestines are slowly being unwound from his body on a reel.

Eduard Hanslick (1825–1904), 1868

318

Wagner drives the nail into your head with swinging hammer blows.

P. A. Fiorentino (1806–1864), Paris, 1867

9W.

Answer to the question: Do you spell your
name with a V, Mr. Vagner?

Steve Allen

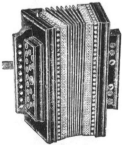

3 2 0

A gentleman is a man who can play the accordion but
doesn't.

Unknown

3 2 1

There are some experiences in life which should not be demanded twice from any man, and one of them is listening to the Brahms Requiem.

George Bernard Shaw (1856–1950)

3 2 2

Classical music is music written by famous dead foreigners.

Arlene Heath

3 2 3

The main thing the public demands of a composer is that he be dead.

Arthur Honegger (1892–1955)

3 2 4

Do it big or stay in bed.

Opera producer Larry Kelly

325

Assassins!

Arturo Toscanini (1867–1957)
to his orchestra

326

I only know two pieces—one is *Clair de Lune* and the
other one isn't.

Victor Borge

327

Elvis Presley had nothing to do with excellence, just myth.

Marlon Brando

328

Anybody who has listened to certain kinds of music, or read certain kinds of poetry, or heard certain kinds of performances on the concertina, will admit that even suicide has its brighter aspects.

Stephen Leacock (1869–1944)

3 2 9

MTV is the lava lamp of the 1980's.

Doug Ferrari

3 3 0

When I was young we didn't have MTV; we had to take drugs and go to concerts.

Steven Pearl

3 3 1

Music is essentially useless, as life is.

George Santayana (1863–1952)

3 3 2

Show me a good loser and I'll show you a loser.

Unknown

3 3 3

Show me a good loser and I'll show you an idiot.

Leo Durocher

3 3 4

Try to hate your opponent. Even if you are playing your grandmother, try to beat her fifty to nothing. If she already has three, try to beat her fifty to three.

Danny McGoorty (1901–1969),
billiard player

335

I probably couldn't play for me. I wouldn't like my attitude.

John Thompson, Georgetown basketball coach

336

A team should be an extension of the coach's personality. My teams were arrogant and obnoxious.

Al McGuire, former basketball coach

337

My toughest fight was with my first wife.

Muhammad Ali

338

Hurting people is my business.

Sugar Ray Robinson

339

Football players, like prostitutes, are in the business of ruining their bodies for the pleasure of strangers.

Merle Kessler

340

I'm no different from anybody else with two arms, two legs, and forty-two-hundred hits.

Pete Rose

341

Any pitcher who throws at a batter and deliberately
tries to hit him is a communist.

Alvin Dark, former baseball coach

342

The highlight of my baseball career came in Philadelphia's Connie Mack Stadium when I saw a fan fall out of the upper deck. When he got up and walked away the crowd booed.

Bob Uecker

343

One night we play like King Kong, the next night like Fay Wray.

*Terry Kennedy, catcher for the
San Diego Padres*

344

If I ever needed a brain transplant, I'd choose a sportswriter because I'd want a brain that had never been used.

Norm Van Brocklin (1926–1983)

345

Stuffed deer heads on walls are bad enough, but it's worse when they are wearing dark glasses and have streamers and ornaments in their antlers because then you know they were enjoying themselves at a party when they were shot.

Ellen DeGeneris

346

Golf is a game with the soul of a 1956 Rotarian.

Bill Mandel

347

Golf is the most fun you can have without taking your clothes off.

Chi Chi Rodríguez

348

If Borg's parents hadn't liked the name, he might never have been Bjorn.

Marty Indik

349

The Rose Bowl is the only bowl I've ever seen that I didn't have to clean.

Erma Bombeck

350

How could I lose to such an idiot?

A shout from chess grandmaster
Aaron Nimzovich (1886–1935)

351

I hate all sports as rabidly as a person who likes sports
hates common sense.

H. L. Mencken (1880–1956)

352

Running is an unnatural act, except from enemies and
to the bathroom.

Unknown

353

I believe that professional wrestling is clean and everything else in the world is fixed.

Frank Deford

3 5 4

Art, like morality, consists of drawing the line somewhere.

G. K. Chesterton (1874–1936)

3 5 5

These is not art to me, all these squares and things.
Real art has, you know, like a madonna in it.

*Unknown (from the guest book at
an exhibition of modern art)*

3 5 6

I'm glad the old masters are all dead, and I only wish
they had died sooner.

Mark Twain (1835–1910)

3 5 7

Give me a museum and I'll fill it.

Pablo Picasso (1881–1973)

3 5 8

Agree, for the law is costly.

William Camden (1551–1623)

359

It is better to be a mouse in a cat's mouth than a man in a lawyer's hands.

Spanish proverb

360

Two farmers each claimed to own a certain cow. While one pulled on its head and the other pulled on its tail, the cow was milked by a lawyer.

Jewish parable

361

Whatever their other contributions to our society, lawyers could be an important source of protein.

Guindon cartoon caption

362

Law school is the opposite of sex. Even when it's good it's lousy.

Unknown

363

How to win a case in court: If the law is on your side, pound on the law; if the facts are on your side, pound on the facts; if neither is on your side, pound on the table.

Unknown

364

Injustice is relatively easy to bear; what stings is justice.

H. L. Mencken (1880–1956)

365

Nobody wants justice.

Alan Dershowitz

366

I'm not an ambulance chaser. I'm usually there before the ambulance.

Melvin Belli

367

I never travel without my diary. One should always have something sensational to read.

Oscar Wilde (1854–1900)

368

The Irish are a fair people—they never speak well of one another.

Samuel Johnson (1709–1784)

369

There are still parts of Wales where the only concession to gaiety is a striped shroud.

Gwyn Thomas

370

I don't have any idea what I'm doing here. I didn't even know Alaska Airlines had a flight to Leningrad.

Bob and Ray

371

In Italy a woman can have a face like a train wreck if she's blonde.

Unknown

372

If you are going to America, bring food.

Fran Lebowitz

373

California is a great place to live if you're an orange.

Fred Allen (1894–1956)

374

In California you lose a point off your IQ every year.

Truman Capote (1924–1984)

375

Nothing is wrong with Southern California that a rise in the ocean level wouldn't cure.

Ross MacDonald (1915–1983)

376

There are two million interesting people in New York and only seventy-eight in Los Angeles.

Neil Simon

377

It is true that I was born in Iowa, but I can't speak for my twin sister.

Abigail Van Buren (Dear Abby)

378

Parts of Texas look like Kansas with a goiter.

Unknown

379

I have just returned from Boston. It is the only thing to do if you find yourself there.

Fred Allen (1894–1956)

380

Thanks to the Interstate Highway System, it is now possible to travel from coast to coast without seeing anything.

Charles Kuralt

381

One of the first things schoolchildren in Texas learn is how to compose a simple declarative sentence without the word *shit* in it.

Unknown

382

The town was so dull that when the tide went out it refused to come back.

Fred Allen (1894–1956)

383

If you don't miss a few planes during the year you are spending too much time at airports.

Paul C. Martin

384

It is now possible for a flight attendant to get a pilot pregnant.

Richard J. Ferris, president, United Airlines

385

The odds against there being a bomb on a plane are a million to one, and against two bombs a million times a million to one. Next time you fly, cut the odds and take a bomb.

Benny Hill

386

If God had intended us to fly he would never have given us railways.

Michael Flanders

387

There are two kinds of air travel in the United States, first class and third world.

Bobby Slayton

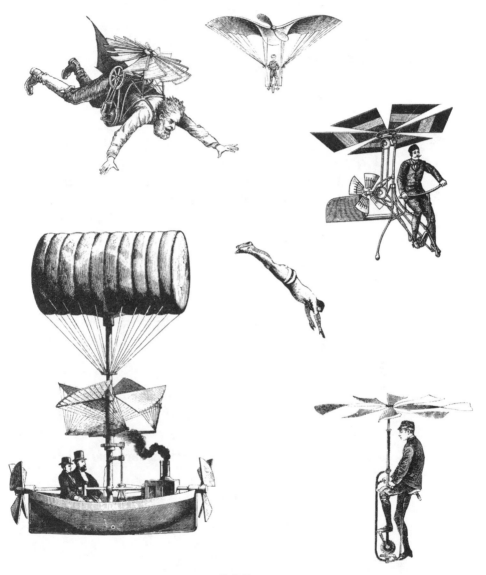

388

Thank God men cannot as yet fly and lay waste the sky
as well as the earth!

Henry David Thoreau (1817–1862)

389

Art is I; science is we.

Claude Bernard (1813–1878)

390

Life is extinct on other planets because their scientists were more advanced than ours.

Unknown

391

A stitch in time would have confused Einstein.

Unknown

392

Great moments in science: Einstein discovers that time is actually money.

Gary Larson cartoon caption

393

Technological progress is like an axe in the hands of a pathological criminal.

Albert Einstein (1879–1955)

394

Technology is a way of organizing the universe so that man doesn't have to experience it.

Max Frisch

395

Horsepower was a wonderful thing when only horses had it.

Unknown

396

Men have become the tools of their tools.

Henry David Thoreau (1817–1862)

397

The computer is down. I hope it's something serious.

Stanton Delaplane

398

Rivers in the United States are so polluted that acid rain makes them cleaner.

Andrew Malcolm

399

A two-pound turkey and a fifty-pound cranberry— that's Thanksgiving dinner at Three-Mile Island.

Johnny Carson

400

The scientific theory I like best is that the rings of Saturn are composed entirely of lost airline luggage.

Mark Russell

401

Energy experts have announced the development of a new fuel made from human brain tissue. It's called assohol.

George Carlin

402

What a beautiful fix we are in now; peace has been declared.

Napoleon Bonaparte (1769–1821)
after the Treaty of Amiens, 1802

403

I thoroughly disapprove of duels. If a man should challenge me, I would take him kindly and forgivingly by the hand and lead him to a quiet place and kill him.

Mark Twain (1835–1910)

404

There is nothing more exhilarating than to be shot at without result.

Winston Churchill (1874–1965)

405

Nobody ever forgets where he buried the hatchet.

Kin Hubbard (1868–1930)

406

Will the last person out of the tunnel turn out the light?

Graffito in Saigon, 1973

407

We are what we are.

Motto of Lake Wobegone,
according to Garrison Keillor

408

You gotta live somewhere.

Motto for Cleveland
suggested by Jimmy Brogan

409

It's a living.

Motto for the U.S. Army
suggested by Mort Sahl

410

What died?

Motto for New Jersey
suggested by Steven Pearl

411

What the hell are you looking at?

License plate slogan for New York
suggested by Steven Pearl

412

Eat cheese or die.

Motto for Wisconsin
suggested by Joel McNally

413

Not you.

Bumper sticker in the state where the
license plate slogan is You've Got a
Friend in Pennsylvania

414

You appeal to a small, select group of confused people.
Message in fortune cookie

415

Ignore previous cookie.

Message in fortune cookie

416

You make God sick.

Message in fortune cookie
received by Rick Reynolds

417

There is nothing wrong with Hollywood that six first-class funerals wouldn't solve.

Unknown

418

The length of a film should be directly related to the endurance of the human bladder.

Alfred Hitchcock (1899–1980)

419

A team effort is a lot of people doing what I say.

Michael Winner, British film director

420

You just gotta save Christianity, Richard! You gotta!

*Loretta Young to Richard the Lionhearted
in the movie* The Crusades, *1935*

421

Yer beautiful in yer wrath! I shall keep you, and in responding to my passions, yer hatred will kindle into love.

*John Wayne as Genghis Khan to Susan
Hayward in the movie* The Conqueror, *1956*

422

I've met a lot of hard-boiled eggs in my time, but you—
you're twenty minutes!

From the movie Ace in the Hole, *1951*

423

When Elizabeth Taylor meets a man she takes him and
squeezes the life out of him and then throws away the
pulp.

Eddie Fisher's mother

424

Elsa Lanchester looks as though butter wouldn't melt
in her mouth, or anywhere else.

Maureen O'Hara

425

They used to photograph Shirley Temple through
gauze. They should photograph me through linoleum.

Tallulah Bankhead (1903–1968)

426

Clark Gable's ears make him look like a taxicab with
the doors open.

Howard Hughes (1905–1976)

427

I saw the sequel to the movie *Clones*, and you know
what? It was the same movie!

Jim Samuels

428

If you get to be a really big headliner, you have to be prepared for people throwing bottles at you in the night.

Mick Jagger

429

You have to have a talent for having talent.

Ruth Gordon (1897–1985)

430

Now that I'm over sixty I'm veering toward respectability.

Shelley Winters

431

A starlet is any woman under thirty not actively employed in a brothel.

Unknown

432

The human race is faced with a cruel choice: work or daytime television.

Unknown

433

Television is democracy at its ugliest.
Paddy Chayevsky (1923–1982)

434

Television enables you to be entertained in your home by people you wouldn't have in your home.
David Frost

435

Imitation is the sincerest form of television.
Fred Allen (1894–1956)

436

Never miss a chance to have sex or appear on television.
Gore Vidal

437

The cable TV sex channels don't expand our horizons, don't make us better people, and don't come in clearly enough.
Bill Maher

438

Babies on television never spit up on the Ultrasuede.
Erma Bombeck

439

Men and nations behave wisely once they have exhausted all the other alternatives.

Abba Eban

440

What luck for rulers that men do not think.

Adolf Hitler (1889–1945)

441

Every government is run by liars and nothing they say should be believed.

I. F. Stone

442

It is dangerous to be right when the government is wrong.

Voltaire (1694–1778)

443

Patriotism is the veneration of real estate above principles.

George Jean Nathan (1882–1958)

444

Patriotism is a pernicious, psychopathic form of idiocy.

George Bernard Shaw (1856–1950)

445

There is but one way for a newspaperman to look at a politician and that is down.

Frank H. Simonds (1878–1936)

446

Don't burn the flag; wash it.

Norman Thomas (1884–1968)

447

The reason there are so few female politicians is that it is too much trouble to put makeup on two faces.

Maureen Murphy

448

Democracy is being allowed to vote for the candidate you dislike least.

Robert Byrne

449

Diplomacy is the art of saying "Nice doggie" until you can find a rock.

Will Rogers (1879–1935)

450

An honest politician is one who when he is bought will stay bought.

Simon Cameron (1799–1889)

451

A communist is a person who publicly airs his dirty Lenin.

Jack Pomeroy

452

A conservative is a man who wants the rules changed so that no one can make a pile the way he did.

Gregory Nunn

453

Liberals feel unworthy of their possessions. Conservatives feel they deserve everything they've stolen.

Mort Sahl

454

A conservative doesn't want anything to happen for the first time; a liberal feels it should happen, but not now.

Mort Sahl

455

Conservatives are satisfied with present evils; liberals want to replace them with new ones.

Unknown

456

They dug up an ancient Chinese emperor a while back who was encased in jade. I prefer gold.

Ed Koch, mayor of New York City

457

Too bad the only people who know how to run the country are busy driving cabs and cutting hair.

George Burns

458

Those who are too smart to engage in politics are punished by being governed by those who are dumber.

Plato (427?–347 B.C.)

Plato was a bore.

Friedrich Nietzsche (1844–1900)

Nietzsche was stupid and abnormal.

Leo Tolstoy (1828–1910)

459

If the Republicans will stop telling lies about the Democrats, we will stop telling the truth about them.

Adlai Stevenson (1900–1965)

460

In America, anyone can become president. That's one of the risks you take.

Adlai Stevenson (1900–1965)

461

Calvin Coolidge didn't say much, and when he did he didn't say much.

Will Rogers (1879–1935)

462

I think the American public wants a solemn ass as president. And I think I'll go along with them.

Calvin Coolidge (1872–1933)

463

He's alive but unconscious, just like Gerald Ford.

From the movie Airplane, *1980*

464

Your public servants serve you right.

Adlai Stevenson (1900–1965)

465

It's the responsibility of the media to look at the president with a microscope, but they go too far when they use a proctoscope.

Richard M. Nixon

466

When we got into office, the thing that surprised me the most was that things were as bad as we'd been saying they were.

John F. Kennedy (1917–1963)

467

It's our fault. We should have given him better parts.

Jack Warner on hearing that Ronald Reagan had been elected governor of California

468

I have left orders to be awakened at any time in case of national emergency, even if I'm in a cabinet meeting.

Joke by Ronald Reagan, current president of the United States

469

Ronald Reagan is the first president to be accompanied by a Silly Statement Repair Team.

Mark Russell

470

I'm glad Reagan is president. Of course, I'm a professional comedian.

Will Durst

471

Reagan is proof that there is life after death.

Mort Sahl

472

There is no distinctly American criminal class—except Congress.

Mark Twain (1835–1910)

473

They should stop calling Reagan and Gorbachev the two most powerful men in the world. Between the two of them they couldn't bench press a hundred pounds.

Al Ordover

474

Gary Hart is just Jerry Brown without the fruit flies.

Robert Strauss

475

Author's Prayer:
        Our Father, which art in heaven,
        And has also written a book . . .

Unknown

476

The only reason for being a professional writer is that you can't help it.

Leo Rosten

477

In Hollywood, writers are considered only the first drafts of human beings.

Frank Deford

478

What an author likes to write most is his signature on the back of a check.

Brendan Francis

479

Very few things happen at the right time and the rest do not happen at all. The conscientious historian will correct these defects.

Herodotus (484–425 B.C.)

480

History will be kind to me for I intend to write it.

Winston Churchill (1874–1965)

481

It is a mean thief or a successful author that plunders the dead.

Austin O'Malley (1858–1932)

482

The best part of the fiction in many novels is the notice that the characters are purely imaginary.

Franklin P. Adams (1881–1960)

483

A detective digs around in the garbage of people's lives. A novelist invents people and then digs around in their garbage.

Joe Gores

484

Fiction is obliged to stick to possibilities. Truth isn't.

Mark Twain (1835–1910)

485

Truth is shorter than fiction.

Irving Cohen

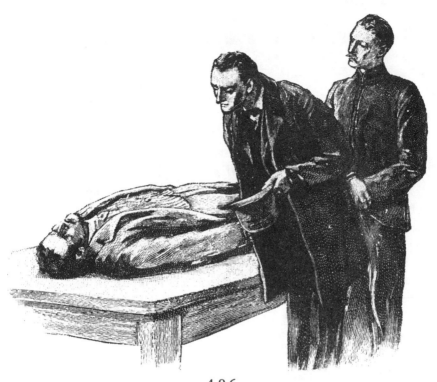

486

The only good author is a dead author.

Book editor Patrick O'Connor

487

In six pages I can't even say "hello."

James Michener

488

Copy from one, it's plagiarism; copy from two, it's research.

Wilson Mizner (1876–1933)

489

Originality is the art of concealing your sources.

Unknown

490

There are three rules for writing a novel. Unfortunately, no one knows what they are.

W. Somerset Maugham (1874–1965)

491

Get your facts first, then you can distort them as you please.

Mark Twain (1835–1910)

492

Why don't you write books people can read?

Nora Joyce to her husband, James (1882–1941)

493

A Treasury of Filthy Religious Art Masterpieces.

Book once proposed to Simon & Schuster

494

Changing literary agents is like changing deck chairs on the *Titanic*.

Unknown

495

You can always tell book people. They are well dressed and their hair is really clean.

Overheard by Constance Casey
at a booksellers' convention

496

Teaching has ruined more American novelists than drink.

Gore Vidal

497

I felt like poisoning a monk.

Umberto Eco
on why he wrote the novel
The Name of the Rose

498

With the single exception of Homer, there is no eminent writer, not even Sir Walter Scott, whom I despise so entirely as I despise Shakespeare.

George Bernard Shaw (1856–1950)

499

I feel very old sometimes . . . I carry on and would not like to die before having emptied a few more buckets of shit on the heads of my fellow men.

Gustave Flaubert (1821–1880)

To read your own poetry in public is a kind of mental incest.

Brendan Behan's father

501

Nobody ever committed suicide while reading a good book, but many have while trying to write one.

Robert Byrne

502

All newspaper editorial writers ever do is come down from the hills after the battle is over and shoot the wounded.

Unknown

503

The difference between literature and journalism is that journalism is unreadable and literature is not read.

Oscar Wilde (1854–1900)

504

Advertisements contain the only truths to be relied on in a newspaper.

Thomas Jefferson (1743–1826)

505

Never argue with people who buy ink by the gallon.

Tommy Lasorda

506

Some editors are failed writers, but so are most writers.

T. S. Eliot (1888–1965)

507

Every great man has his disciples, and it is always Judas who writes the biography.

Oscar Wilde (1854–1900)

508

Biography lends to death a new terror.

Oscar Wilde (1854–1900)

509

Autobiography is now as common as adultery and hardly less reprehensible.

Lord Altrincham

510

Autobiography is the last refuse of scoundrels.

Henry Gray

511

It's not a bad idea to get in the habit of writing down one's thoughts. It saves one having to bother anyone else with them.

Isabel Colegate

512

Book reviewers are little old ladies of both sexes.

John O'Hara (1905–1970)

5 1 3

Any reviewer who expresses rage and loathing for a novel is preposterous. He or she is like a person who has put on full armor and attacked a hot fudge sundae.

Kurt Vonnegut

5 1 4

People who like this sort of thing will find this the sort of thing they like.

Book review by Abraham Lincoln (1809–1865)

5 1 5

A bad review is like baking a cake with all the best ingredients and having someone sit on it.

Danielle Steel

5 1 6

Criticism is prejudice made plausible.

H. L. Mencken (1880–1956)

5 1 7

Praise and criticism are both frauds.

Unknown

5 1 8

I am sitting in the smallest room in the house. I have your review in front of me. Soon it will be behind me.

Max Reger (1873–1916)

519

Quotations are a columnist's bullpen. Stealing someone else's words frequently spares the embarrassment
of eating your own.

Peter Anderson

520

It is better to be quotable than to be honest.

Tom Stoppard

521

This isn't much of a quote book if I'm in it.

Richard Dowd,
quoted here for the first time anywhere

PART THREE

Miscellaneous

5 2 2

There will be a rain dance Friday night, weather permitting.

George Carlin

5 2 3

Gifts are like hooks.

Martial (40?–102?)

5 2 4

Every time a friend succeeds, I die a little.

Gore Vidal

5 2 5

The goal of all inanimate objects is to resist man and ultimately defeat him.

Russell Baker

5 2 6

Cleaning anything involves making something else dirty, but anything can get dirty without something else getting clean.

Lawrence J. Peter

527

You know it's not a good wax museum when there are wicks coming out of people's heads.

Rick Reynolds

528

Everything changes but the avant garde.

Paul Valéry (1871–1945)

529

If you can't laugh at yourself, make fun of other people.

Bobby Slayton

530

The world is divided into two classes—invalids and nurses.

James McNeill Whistler (1834–1903)

531

Never mistake motion for action.

Ernest Hemingway (1889–1961)

Hemingway was a jerk.

Harold Robbins

532

I wish everybody would go back into the closet.

Josefa Heifetz

533

Some luck lies in not getting what you thought you wanted but getting what you have, which once you have got it you may be smart enough to see is what you would have wanted had you known.

Garrison Keillor

534

All God's children are not beautiful. Most of God's children are, in fact, barely presentable.

Fran Lebowitz

535

Providence protects children and idiots. I know because I have tested it.

Mark Twain (1835–1910)

536

The easiest kind of relationship for me is with ten thousand people. The hardest is with one.

Joan Baez

537

Five Kids Who Make Your Kids Look Sick

Magazine article suggested by Garrison Keillor

538

I'll not listen to reason. Reason always means what someone else has to say.

Elizabeth Cleghorn Gaskell (1810–1865)

539

Suggested magazines:

Crotch: The International Sex Weekly

Thomas Berger

Cocker Spaniel Annual Manual

Luther Vrettos

Gimme! The Magazine of Money

Robert Byrne

The Shining (Formerly Bald World)

Robert Byrne

Beautiful Spot: A Magazine of Parking

Calvin Trillin

Poor Housekeeping (ten times the circulation of Good Housekeeping)

Robert Byrne

540

Nothing is impossible for the man who doesn't have to do it himself.

A. H. Weiler

541

A censor is a man who knows more than he thinks you ought to.

Granville Hicks (1901–1982)

542

A committee is a cul-de-sac down which ideas are lured and then quietly strangled.

Sir Barnett Cocks (ca. 1907)

543

As scarce as truth is, the supply has always been in excess of the demand.

Josh Billings (1818–1885)

544

I never forget a face, but in your case I'll be glad to make an exception.

Groucho Marx (1895–1977)

545

I can mend the break of day, heal a broken heart, and provide temporary relief to nymphomaniacs.

Larry Lee

546

Hell is paved with Good Samaritans.

William M. Holden

547

Enough.

Definition of "Once."

Ambrose Bierce (1842–1914?)

548

Anybody who thinks of going to bed before 12 o'clock is a scoundrel.

Samuel Johnson (1709–1784)

549

A fanatic is a man who does what he thinks the Lord would do if He knew the facts of the case.

Finley Peter Dunne (1867–1936)

550

All movements go too far.

Bertrand Russell (1872–1970)

551

Never engage in a battle of wits with an unarmed person.

Unknown

552

Flies spread disease—keep yours zipped.

Unknown

553

Ya gotta do what ya gotta do.

Sylvester Stallone in the movie Rocky IV, *1985*

554

There is one thing to be said for country clubs; they drain off a lot of people you wouldn't want to associate with anyway.

Joseph Prescott

555

I do not want people to be agreeable, as it saves me the trouble of liking them.

Jane Austen (1775–1817)

556

A friend in need is a friend to dodge.

Unknown

557

Analyzing humor is like dissecting a frog. Few people are interested and the frog dies of it.

E. B. White (1899–1985)

558

A lot of people like snow. I find it to be an unnecessary freezing of water.

Carl Reiner

559

I've only met four perfect people in my life and I didn't like any of them.

Unknown

5 6 0

I dote on his very absence.
William Shakespeare (1564–1616)

Shakespeare is crude, immoral, vulgar, and senseless.
Leo Tolstoy (1828–1910)

5 6 1

Often it does seem a pity that Noah and his party did not miss the boat.
Mark Twain (1835–1910)

5 6 2

You can't depend on your eyes when your imagination is out of focus.
Mark Twain (1835–1910)

5 6 3

Only dead fish swim with the stream.
Unknown

5 6 4

I wish people wouldn't say, "Excuse me," when I *want* them to step on my feet.
Karen Elizabeth Gordon

5 6 5

Either I've been missing something or nothing has been going on.
Karen Elizabeth Gordon

5 6 6

There are 350 varieties of shark, not counting loan and pool.

L. M. Boyd

5 6 7

When in doubt, duck.

Malcolm Forbes

5 6 8

American college students are like American colleges —each has half-dulled faculties.

James Thurber (1894–1961)

5 6 9

It took me twenty years of studied self-restraint, aided by the natural decay of my faculties, to make myself dull enough to be accepted as a serious person by the British public.

George Bernard Shaw (1856–1950)

5 7 0

The longer I live the more I see that I am never wrong about anything, and that all the pains I have so humbly taken to verify my notions have only wasted my time.

George Bernard Shaw (1856–1950)

5 7 1

I don't care what you ♥.

Bumper sticker

5 7 2

I ♠ my pets.

Bumper sticker

5 7 3

Love your enemies in case your friends turn out to be a bunch of bastards.

R. A. Dickson

5 7 4

One should forgive one's enemies, but not before they are hanged.

Heinrich Heine (1797–1856)

5 7 5

Experience teaches you to recognize a mistake when you've made it again.

Unknown

5 7 6

Good judgment comes from experience, and experience comes from bad judgment.

Barry LePatner

5 7 7

The trouble with using experience as a guide is that the final exam often comes first and then the lesson.

Unknown

It's not what we don't know that hurts, it's what we know that ain't so.

Will Rogers (1879–1935)

The world is a madhouse, so it's only right that it is patrolled by armed idiots.

Brendan Behan

580

Consistency requires you to be as ignorant today as you were a year ago.

Bernard Berenson (1865–1959)

581

Correct me if I'm wrong, but hasn't the fine line between sanity and madness gotten finer?

George Price

582

The reason lightning doesn't strike twice in the same place is that the same place isn't there the second time.

Willie Tyler

583

The nail that sticks up gets hammered down.

Japanese proverb

584

You can lead a horse to water, but you can't make him float.

Unknown

585

If you want a place in the sun, prepare to put up with a few blisters.

Abigail Van Buren

586

I don't know, I've never been kippled.

> Answer to the question: Do you like Kipling?
> *Unknown*

587

Ford used to have a better idea; now they don't have a clue.

> *Steve Kravitz*

588

I can't believe that out of 100,000 sperm, you were the quickest.

> *Steven Pearl*

589

Honesty is the best image.

> *Ziggy (Tom Wilson)*

590

Silence is argument carried on by other means.

> *Ernesto "Che" Guevara (1928–1967)*

591

Soderquist's Paradox:

> There are more horse's asses than horses.
> *From* 1,001 Logical Laws,
> *compiled by John Peers*

592

Do Not Disturb signs should be written in the language of the hotel maids.

Tim Bedore

593

What ought to be done to the man who invented the celebrating of anniversaries? Mere killing would be too light.

Mark Twain (1835–1910)

594

Status quo. Latin for the mess we're in.

Jeve Moorman

595

Never put off until tomorrow what you can do the day after tomorrow.

Mark Twain (1835–1910)

596

Nobody can make you feel inferior without your consent.

Eleanor Roosevelt (1884–1962)

597

An intellectual is a person whose mind watches itself.

Albert Camus (1913–1960)

598

The average person thinks he isn't.

Father Larry Lorenzoni

599

Sleep is an eight-hour peep show of infantile erotica.

J. G. Ballard

600

No man can think clearly when his fists are clenched.

George Jean Nathan (1882–1958)

601

Propaganda is the art of persuading others of what you don't believe yourself.

Abba Eban

602

Never believe anything until it has been officially denied.

Claud Cockburn (1904–1981)

603

There are only two ways of telling the complete truth—anonymously and posthumously.

Thomas Sowell

604

There is only one thing about which I am certain, and that is that there is very little about which one can be certain.

W. Somerset Maugham (1874–1965)

605

Before they made S. J. Perelman they broke the mold.

Unknown

606

Here's to our wives and sweethearts—may they never meet.

John Bunny (1866–1939)

607

Man Robs, Then Kills Himself.

Headline in Vancouver Province, *June 21, 1978*

608

Don't jump on a man unless he's down.

Finley Peter Dunne (1867–1936)

609

Just because your voice reaches halfway around the world doesn't mean you are wiser than when it reached only to the end of the bar.

Edward R. Murrow (1908–1965)

6 1 0

Glory is fleeting, but obscurity is forever.

Napoleon Bonaparte (1769–1821)

6 1 1

It is fun being in the same decade with you.

Franklin Delano Roosevelt (1882–1945)
in a letter to Churchill, 1942

6 1 2

Although prepared for martyrdom, I preferred that it be postponed.

Winston Churchill (1874–1965)

6 1 3

The higher a monkey climbs, the more you see of its behind.

General Joseph "Vinegar Bend" Stilwell (1883–1946)

6 1 4

Marie Osmond makes Mother Teresa look like a slut.

Joan Rivers

6 1 5

What a strange illusion it is to suppose that beauty is goodness.

Leo Tolstoy (1828–1910)

I'm not going to climb into the ring with Tolstoy.

Ernest Hemingway (1889–1961)

Hemingway was a jerk.

Harold Robbins

6 1 6

As Miss America, my goal is to bring peace to the entire world and then to get my own apartment.

Jay Leno

6 1 7

I hate the outdoors. To me the outdoors is where the car is.

Will Durst

6 1 8

The other day a dog peed on me. A bad sign.

H. L. Mencken (1880–1956)

619

He grounds the warship he walks on.
John Bracken on Captain Barney Kelly,
who ran the USS Enterprise *into the mud of*
San Francisco Bay in May of 1983

620

These are the souls that time men's tries.
Sports Illustrated *on*
official timers at track meets

621

Astrology is Taurus.

F. W. Dedering

622

Nobody outside of a baby carriage or a judge's chamber believes in an unprejudiced point of view.

Lillian Hellman (1907–1984)

623

If I don't get a part for my artificial heart
I'm gonna stop caring for you.

Lyrics by Bernie Sheehan

624

I Can't Give You Anything But Love and a Baby

Song title by Willie Tyler

625

If the Phone Doesn't Ring, It's Me

Song title by Jimmy Buffet

626

It isn't that gentlemen really prefer blondes, it's just that we look dumber.

Anita Loos (1893–1981)

627

She was what we used to call a suicide blonde—dyed by her own hand.

Saul Bellow

628

For people who like peace and quiet: a phoneless cord.

Unknown

629

The best audience is intelligent, well-educated, and a little drunk.

Alben W. Barkley (1877–1956)

630

What is this, an audience or an oil painting?

Milton Berle

631

Civilization exists by geological consent, subject to change without notice.

Will Durant (1885–1981)

632

In Biblical times, a man could have as many wives as he could afford. Just like today.

Abigail Van Buren

633

The first human being who hurled an insult instead of a stone was the founder of civilization.

Attributed to Sigmund Freud (1856–1939)

634

The only paradise is paradise lost.

Marcel Proust (1871–1922)

635

Historical reminder: always put Horace before Descartes.

Donald O. Rickter

636

Most of our future lies ahead.

Denny Crum, Louisville basketball coach

637

If there is another way to skin a cat, I don't want to know about it.

Steve Kravitz

Sources, References, and Notes

Quotations are indexed here only when I have something useful to add. Readers with corrections or who can supply missing information are urged to write to me in care of Scribner, 1230 Avenue of the Americas, New York, New York 10020.

Quotation
Number

2. BS in a letter to RB.
3. JDM in the *Bulletin*, 1974
5. LT in *What Is Religion?*, 1902.
8. HLM in an Associated Press interview, 1941.
9. RM in *The Towers of Trebizond*, 1956.
10. Quoted by G. M. Thomson in *Vote of Censure*, 1968.
11. BM in a speech in Lausanne, 1904.
13. CK is a standup comedian.
14. From the television series "All in the Family." Thanks to George Aronek.
16. Quoted in the *San Francisco Chronicle*, December 17, 1985.
17. According to William Safire in his syndicated column, December 8, 1985.
18. FN in *Thus Spake Zarathustra*.
19. EH in a letter.
20. HR as quoted in Leslie Halliwell's *The Filmgoer's Companion*, 1984.
22. RS is a standup comedian.
25. From *The Cynic's Lexicon*, compiled by Jonathon Green, 1982.
26. Thanks to David Huard.
27. FN in *Thus Spake Zarathustra*, 1891.
28. Quoted in *3500 Good Quotes for Speakers*, compiled by Gerald F. Lieberman, 1983.
30. NW quoted in *Was It Good for You, Too?* compiled by Bob Chieger, 1983.
31. WA in *Play It Again, Sam*, 1969.
33. Quoted in the *San Francisco Sunday Chronicle-Examiner*, September 1, 1985.
35. O in *Ars Amatoria*.
36. J in *Satires*, A. D. 110.
37. From *A New Dictionary of Quotations on Historical Principles*, compiled by H. L. Mencken, 1952.
39. SR in the *San Francisco Chronicle*, August 2, 1985.
44. Taken from the jacket of MP's 1985 book *Shoes Never Lie*.
45. AC is a standup comedian.

47. Quoted in the comedy trade paper *Just for Laughs*, August 1985.
51. Quoted in *Forbes*, September 16, 1985.
53. JM in *Miss Manners' Guide to Excruciatingly Correct Behavior*, 1985.
54. JV is a standup comedian.
55. MD in *Dogs Are Better Than Cats*, 1985.
56. RB in the *Atlantic Monthly*, February 1985.
57. EB is a standup comedian.
58. MP is a standup comedian.
62. Quoted in the *San Francisco Chronicle*, December 31, 1984.
63. "The Tonight Show," January 10, 1985.
64. RO in *Orben's Current Comedy*, a weekly newsletter of topical gags, November 6, 1985.
65. JM in *Common Courtesy*, 1985.
66. ARC was interviewed by the *New York Times* in December 1985. He was quoted further as saying that he didn't rule out the possibility that the honor bestowed on him was political smear.
68. See note 37.
70. Quoted by HG in his autobiographical novel *Family*.
72. Thanks to H. Peter Metzger.
73. From *Miss Piggy's Guide to Life*, 1981, as told to HB.
74. From *Quote*, November 1, 1985.
75. MS to RB.
76. From the Peanuts comic strip, April 1984.
78. KW is a popular columnist in Great Britain.
80. GK on his radio show "A Prairie Home Companion," July 21, 1985.
83. AH in the *San Francisco Chronicle*, November 25, 1985.
84. Quoted in *The Cynic's Lexicon*, compiled by Jonathon Green, 1982.
85. AC in the *New York Times*, February 18, 1968.
86. MW at the San Francisco Standup Comedy Competition, 1979.
88. GG in a letter to the *Journal of Irreproducible Results*.
89. RY in *Family Weekly*, 1977.
92. Thanks to Marty Indik.
95. GS is a standup comedian.
97. GS on "The Tonight Show," August 17, 1985.
98. Seen in London by Herb Caen.
99. WD won the 1983 San Francisco Standup Comedy Competition.
100. Given in *Was It Good for You, Too?* compiled by Bob Chieger, 1983.
101. JK is a standup comedian.
104. MM is a standup comedian.
105. Quoted by Peter Stack in the *San Francisco Chronicle*, October 4, 1985. RL is a standup comedian.

106. GL is publisher of *High Society*.

107. AB in *Rolling Stone*, July 14, 1977.

112. PD in his 1955 novel *Major Thompson Lives in France and Discovers the French*.

114. LB in *Don Juan*, 1819.

116. BN is a standup comedian. Thanks to Pete Harley.

117. Thanks to Lee Simon.

118. GS is a standup comedian.

119. WT is a standup comedian.

121. MD to RB.

124. From the movie *She Done Him Wrong* (1933), screenplay by MW.

129. MS in the *New York Times Book Review*, November 6, 1985.

132. GN is a columnist and critic for the *San Francisco Chronicle*.

134. *Out of Africa*, screenplay by Kurt Luedtke based on books by and about Isak Dinesen.

135. SB in *Men: An Owner's Manual*, 1984.

136. CS is a standup comedian.

138. GN in the *San Francisco Chronicle*, February 26, 1985.

139. GK in his San Francisco lecture, December 13, 1984.

141. Thanks to Susan Richman.

142. Thanks to Arlene Heath.

143. RM in *The Towers of Trebizond*, 1956.

145. Quoted in *Was It Good for You, Too?* compiled by Bob Chieger, 1983.

147. Thanks to Merla Zellerbach.

149. Thanks to Susan Richman.

150. Quoted by Herb Caen in the *San Francisco Chronicle*, December 23, 1983.

151. DS on "The Tonight Show," 1972.

156. See note 65.

158. PP is a standup comedian.

159. See note 65.

161. SP is a standup comedian.

165. In *Letter and Journals* (New York: Viking, 1985).

166. LPS in *Afterthoughts*, 1934.

167. EP is a standup comedian.

174. WS is a standup comedian.

175. MS to RB.

180. LH on "Freeman Reports," November 30, 1985.

181. Thanks to Joe Gores.

184. In RB's biography *McGoorty*, 1972, and 1984.

186. JG in *Esquire*, April 1983.

187. Thanks to Knox Burger.

191. LPS in *All Trivia*, 1949.

193. See note 65.

194. RM at a San Francisco press conference, May 21, 1985.

199. Quoted by Merla Zellerbach in the *San Francisco Chronicle*, March 7, 1984.

200. Quoted in the *Little Dublin News*, March 1985, published in Dubuque, Iowa.

208. LB in the *San Francisco Examiner*, July 15, 1984.
220. HC in the *San Francisco Chronicle*, April 28, 1985.
226. FML to RB.
228. GK in his San Francisco lecture, December 13, 1984.
231. JC on "The Tonight Show," November 20, 1984.
232. HC in the *San Francisco Chronicle*, December 11, 1985.
234–235. RB in his syndicated *New York Times* column, September 22, 1985.
236. OTW to RB.
238. LT in her one-woman Broadway show, 1985.
239. HAS in *Let the Crabgrass Grow*, 1960.
241. GC in *The Widow's Tears*, 1612.
242. RS is a standup comedian.
245. CK won the Pulitzer Prize for poetry in 1985.
246. Quoted in *Hot News*, published periodically by Lyle Stuart.
251. Thanks to David Huard.
252. Thanks to Marty Indik.
253. BS in *What Makes Sammy Run?* 1941.
256. CT in *American Fried*, 1979.
259. ML in the *Pacific Sun*, November 15, 1985.
260. FL in *Social Studies*, 1981.
261. DL in *A Likely Story*, 1984.
262. EB on "The Tonight Show," September 25, 1985.
264. Quoted by Herb Caen in the *San Francisco Chronicle*, May 6, 1985.
265. WA in *Please Don't Drink the Water*, 1967.
266. Quoted by Herb Caen in the *San Francisco Chronicle*, December 13, 1984.
268. CT in *American Fried*, 1979.
271. BM in *Idiots First*, 1963.
272. JS is a standup comedian.
275. JE is a San Francisco radio talk-show host.
277. CS is a standup comedian.
279. CB in his San Rafael, California, lecture, February 1985.
282. GM is a standup comedian.
283. Thanks to H. Peter Metzger.
289. RS is a standup comedian.
290. MP on the BBC World Service.
292–293. Delivered on Comedy Celebration Day, July 20, 1985, when sixty standup comedians performed for a total of seven hours in San Francisco's Golden Gate Park.
296. RB in his syndicated *New York Times* column, August 27, 1985.
297. See note 64.
298. Quoted by Herb Caen in the *San Francisco Chronicle*, March 7, 1985.
299. Thanks to Dr. Stephen F. Goodman.
300. JJG to RB in jest; RB didn't need a root canal.

302. Thanks to Collin Wilcox.

305. Thanks to Audrey Stanley, KARN, Little Rock.

307. EB is a standup comedian.

308. YS is a Soviet comedian who emigrated to the United States in 1981. He also said that in the United States you watch television, but in Russia television watches you.

309. GN in the *San Francisco Chronicle*, August 27, 1985.

314. HC in the *San Francisco Chronicle*, December 29, 1985. The quote is out of context, for it appeared in a column in which HC argued that drunk jokes aren't really funny and vowed to use fewer of them in his widely read column.

315–318. Many quotes of this sort can be found in *The Lexicon of Musical Invective*, compiled by Nicolas Slonimsky, 1969.

319. From the Question Man segment of the old "Steve Allen Show."

320. Thanks to Kitty Sprague.

322. AH to RB.

327. MB in *Playboy*, 1979.

328. SL in *The Mariposa Bank Mystery*, 1912.

330. SP is a standup comedian.

331. GS in *The Life of Reason*, 1954.

332. Thanks to Leonard Tong.

333. As quoted by RB in *McGoorty*, 1972 and 1984.

337. Quoted by Bob Greene in *Cheeseburgers*. Thanks to Tom Winston.

338. RR to the New York State Boxing Commission, May 23, 1962.

339. Quoted by Patricia Holt in the *San Francisco Chronicle*, November 13, 1985.

341. Thanks to Marty Indik.

342. BU on "Larry King Live," September 17, 1985.

345. EG is a standup comedian.

346. BD in the *San Francisco Examiner*, February 10, 1985.

349. EB was the grand marshal of the 1986 Rose Bowl Parade.

353. FD on Cable News Network, November 4, 1985.

357. Quoted by Barnaby Conrad III in the *San Francisco Chronicle*, November 24, 1985.

362–363. Thanks to Arlene Heath.

366. Quoted in the *San Francisco Chronicle*, August 10, 1985.

369. GT in *Punch*, June 18, 1958.

370. From a sketch titled *Fern Ock Veek, Sickly Whale Oil Processor*, reprinted in *The New! Improved! Bob and Ray Book*, 1985.

371. Quoted by Stephanie von Buchau in the *Pacific Sun*, February 8, 1985.

372. FL in *Social Studies*, 1981.

373. From *Conversations with Capote*, by Lawrence Grobel.

375. RM in *The Drowning Pool*, 1951.

376. NS in *Playboy*, February 1979.

377. Letter to RB.

379. Letter to Groucho Marx, June 12, 1953.

383. Thanks to Susan Richman.

386. MF in the *New York Times*, April 16, 1975.

387. BS is a standup comedian.

388. HDT in *Journal,* January 3, 1861.

391. From *The Journal of Irreproducible Results*. Thanks to D. O. Rickter.

397. SD in the *San Francisco Chronicle*, July 11, 1984.

398. AM is the author of *The Canadians*, 1985.

399. JC on "The Tonight Show," November 20, 1984.

404. Thanks to Gary Muldoon.

406. Thanks to Harry Roach.

410. SP is a standup comedian.

412. Quoted by Leah Garchik in the *San Francisco Chronicle*, December 6, 1985.

420–421. Quoted in *The Hollywood Hall of Shame* by Harry and Michael Medved, 1984.

422. Screenplay by Billy Wilder, Lesser Samuels, and Walter Newman.

423. Quoted in *The Jewish Mother's Hall of Fame*, by Fred Bernstein, 1986.

428. Thanks to Mary Indik.

430. SW on "The Tonight Show," February 28, 1985.

437. BM is a standup comedian.

442. Wording by RB.

451. JP in a letter to RB.

456. EK at the opening of an exhibition of jade in January 1985.

462. CC to Ethel Barrymore, according to *Time*, March 6, 1955.

463. Screenplay by Jim Abrahams and Jim and Jerry Zucker.

464. Thanks to Tom Stewart.

465. RN during an interview on CBS in 1984.

470. See note 99.

473. Al Ordover is a close personal friend of Knox Burger.

474. RS is former chairman of the Democratic party.

477. FD in *Sports Illustrated*, July 9, 1984.

478. From *The Cynic's Lexicon*, compiled by Jonathon Green, 1982.

480. Quoted by Richard Nixon to Barbara Walters, May 8, 1985.

487. JM in the introduction to Hemingway's *The Most Dangerous Summer*, 1985.

495. CC is book editor of the *San Jose Mercury-News*.

496. GV in *Oui*, April 1975.

499. GF in a letter to Ivan Turgenev, November 8, 1879.

500. Quoted by Shay Duffrin in his one-man show *Confessions of an Irish Rebel*, 1984.

504. TJ in a letter, 1819.

505. TL is the coach of the Los Angeles Dodgers.

507. OW in *The Critic as Artist*, 1890.

509. LA in the *Sunday Times*, London, February 28, 1962.

511. IC in her 1981 novel *The Shooting Party*.

513. Quoted by Thomas Fleming in the *New York Times Book Review*, January 6, 1985.

514. Thanks to Hugh Parker.

515. Quoted by Merla Zellerbach in the *San Francisco Chronicle*, December 21, 1982.

518. Quoted in *New York* magazine, July 8, 1974.

519. PA reviewing *The Other 637 Best Things Anybody Ever Said* in the *San Rafael Independent Journal*, March 21, 1985.

521. RD is chiefly known as the former roommate of Marty Indik, who himself is not particularly well known.

524. GV in the *New York Times*, February 4, 1973.

525. RB in the *New York Times*, June 18, 1968.

527. RR in the *San Francisco Examiner*, July 1, 1984.

531. Thanks to Harry Roach.

532. JH as quoted in the *Pacific Sun*, November 28, 1985.

533. GK in *Lake Wobegone Days*, 1985.

534. FL in *Metropolitan Life*, 1978.

540. AHW in the *New York Times*, 1968.

542. From *The Cynic's Lexicon*, compiled by Jonathon Green, 1982.

543. JB in *Affurisms*, 1869.

545. Thanks to Lee Simon.

546. WMH in a letter to RB.

552. Quoted by Rob Morse in the *San Francisco Examiner*, January 5, 1986.

554. JP in *Aphorisms*, privately printed in 1985.

556. Thanks to Arlene Heath.

558. Thanks to Marty Indik.

560. WS in *The Merchant of Venice*.

565. KEG in *The Well-Tempered Sentence*, 1984.

566. LMB in his syndicated column, May 5, 1985.

568. Thanks to David L. Huard.

569. GBS as quoted by Ulick O'Connor in *All the Olympians*, 1984.

570. GBS in a letter to H. G. Wells.

573. Quoted by Herb Caen in the *San Francisco Chronicle*, November 17, 1985.

577. Thanks to Robert Gordon.

579. BB as quoted by Shay Duffrin in his one-man show *Confessions of an Irish Rebel*.

581. Cartoon caption in the *New Yorker*, January 6, 1986.

582. WT is a professional ventriloquist.

584. Thanks to Jim Eason.

586. Steve Allen remembers this line from the 1930s. Letter to RB.

587. SK is a standup comedian.
588. SP is a standup comedian.
590. Thanks to Marty Indik.
594. As given in *The Dictionary of Humorous Economics*.
597. AC in *Notebooks*, 1965.
598. Quoted by Herb Caen in the *San Francisco Chronicle*, February 2, 1985.
601. AE as quoted in *The Book of Political Quotes*, compiled by Jonathon Green, 1982.
606. JB as quoted by Joe Franklin in his *Encyclopedia of Comedy*, 1979.
609. ERM as quoted by Harry Reasoner.

613. JS as quoted in *The Book of Political Quotes*, compiled by Jonathon Green, 1982.
616. JL is a standup comedian.
617. See note 99.
618. HLM in a letter. Thanks to Mary Indik.
619. Quoted by Herb Caen in the *San Francisco Chronicle*, May 19, 1983.
621. Thanks to Bob Engan.
624. WT is a ventriloquist.
626. From the movie *Gentlemen Prefer Blondes*, 1953.
627. SB in a lecture in San Francisco, November 1984.
634. Thanks to Oakley Hall.
637. SK is a standup comedian.

Index of Authors

Adams, Franklin P., 482
Ali, Muhammad, 337
Allen, Fred, 373, 381, 382, 435
Allen, Steve, 319
Allen, Woody, 23, 31, 94, 160, 206, 265, 291
Altrincham, Lord, 509
Anderson, Peter, 519
Augustine, St., 249
Austen, Jane, 555
Baer, Arthur, 137

Baez, Joan, 536
Bailey, Covert, 279
Baker, Russell, 234, 235, 296, 525
Balfour, Arthur, 243
Ball, Lucille, 212
Ballard, J. G., 599
Bankhead, Tallulah, 425
Barkley, Alben W., 629
Barrett, Jan, 47
Beard, Henry, 73
Beaverbrook, Lord, 10, 195
Bedore, Tim, 592

Begley, Ed, Jr., 263
Behan, Brendan, (mother) 141, (father) 500, 579
Belli, Melvin, 366
Bellow, Saul, 627
Berenson, Bernard, 580
Berger, Thomas, 539
Berle, Milton, 630
Bernard, Claude, 389
Bhartrihari, 37, 68
Bierce, Ambrose, 547

Billings, Josh, 543
Bishop, Joey, 198
Blount, Roy, Jr.,
    56
Bluestone, Ed, 154
Bob and Ray
    (Elliot and
    Goulding), 370
Bombeck, Erma,
    43, 162, 229,
    349, 438
Bonaparte,
    Napoleon, 402,
    610
Boosler, Elayne,
    57, 307
Borge, Victor, 326
Boyd, L. M., 566
Bracken, John,
    619
Brando, Marlon,
    327
Brogan, Jimmy,
    408
Brown, Jerry, 182
Brown, Larry, 208,
    293
Bruce, Lenny, 168
Brush, Stephanie,
    135
Bryant, Anita, 107
Buffet, Jimmy, 625
Bunker, Archie, 14
Bunny, John, 606
Burns, George,
    140, 223, 230,
    248, 457
Bushnell, Nolan,
    202
Byrne, Robert, 21,
    110, 146, 176,
    207, 244, 254,
    267, 281, 448,
    501, 539
Byron, Lord, 114
Caen, Herb, 220,
    232, 305, 313
Camden, William,
    358

Cameron, Simon,
    450
Camus, Albert, 51,
    597
Capote, Truman,
    374
Carlin, George,
    401, 522
Carson, Johnny,
    12, 63, 172,
    231, 274, 399
Casey, Constance,
    495
Chambless, David,
    74
Chamfort, Nicolas,
    1
Chapman, George,
    241
Chayevsky, Paddy,
    433
Chesterton, G. K.,
    354
Christ, Jesus, 15
Churchill, Win-
    ston, 288, 404,
    480, 612
Clethen, Al, 45
Cockburn, Claud,
    602
Cocks, Sir Barnett,
    542
Cocotas, Peter, 33
Cohen, Irving, 486
Colegate, Isabel,
    511
Comfort, Alex, 85
Coolidge, Calvin,
    462
Cosby, Bill, 170
Crum, Denny, 636
Cucci, Anthony R.,
    66
Dangerfield, Rod-
    ney, 24, 96,
    102
Daninos, Pierre,
    112

Dark, Alvin, 341
Davis, Jim, 59
Davis, Joan, 77
Dedering, F. W.,
    621
Deford, Frank,
    353, 477
DeGeneris, Ellen,
    345
Delaplane, Stan-
    ton, 397
Dershowitz, Alan,
    365
Dickson, R. A.,
    573
Diller, Phyllis, 87,
    123, 217
Dizick, Missy, 55,
    121
Dowd, Richard,
    521
Dunne, Finley
    Peter, 549, 608
Durant, Will, 631
Durocher, Leo,
    333
Durst, Will, 99,
    470, 617
Eason, Jim, 275
Eban, Abba, 439,
    601
Eco, Umberto, 497
Einstein, Albert,
    393
Eliot, T. S., 506
Elledge, Scott, 187
Ertz, Susan, 6
Esberg, Virginia,
    (grandmother)
    199
Ferrari, Doug, 329
Ferris, Richard J.,
    384
Fields, W. C., 41,
    251, 311
Fiorentino, P. A.,
    318
Fisher, Eddie,
    (mother) 423

Flanders, Michael, 386

Flaubert, Gustave, 499

Forbes, Malcolm, 210, 567

Forman, Milos, 148

Francis, Brendan, 478

Freud, Sigmund, 633

Friedman, Mickey, 302

Frisch, Max, 394

Frost, David, 434

Gabor, Zsa Zsa, 144

Galbraith, John Kenneth, 145

Gardner, John, 186

Garfield (Jim Davis), 59

Garrett, James J., 300

Gaskell, Elizabeth Cleghorn, 538

Gauguin, Paul, 25

Gibb, Andy, 32

Goden, Guy, 88

Gold, Herbert, (mother) 70

Goldstein, Joan, 310

Gordon, Karen Elizabeth, 564, 565

Gordon, Ruth, 429

Gores, Joe, 483

Gourmont, Remy de, 84

Gray, Henry, 510

Grue, Jim, 200

Guevara, "Che," 590

Guindon (cartoon), 361

Hanslick, Eduard, 317

Harris, Joel Chandler, 213

Hastings, Willi, 264

Hayes, Helen, 224

Heath, Arlene, 322

Heifetz, Josefa, 532

Heilbroner, Robert, 205

Heine, Heinrich, 90, 574

Heinlein, Robert, 92

Hellman, Lillian, 622

Hemingway, Ernest, 19, 531

Herodotus, 479

Hicks, Granville, 541

Hill, Benny, 385

Hitchcock, Alfred, 418

Hitler, Adolf, 440

Holden, William M., 546

Hollander, Nicole, 46

Honegger, Arthur, 323

Hoppe, Arthur, 83

Horace, 67

Horne, Lena, 180

Howells, William Dean, 258

Hubbard, Kin, 405

Hughes, Howard, 426

Indik, Marty, 294, 348

Irwin, Wallace, 286

Jagger, Mick, 428

Jefferson, Thomas, 504

Jerome, Jerome K., 178

Johnson, Samuel, 368, 548

Joyce, Nora, 492

Juvenal, 36

Katz, Jonathan, 101

Keillor, Garrison, 80, 139, 228, 407, 533, 537

Kelly, Larry, 324

Kennedy, John F., 466

Kennedy, Terry, 343

Kessler, Merle, 339

Kizer, Carolyn, 245

Koch, Ed, 456

Kosar, Charles, 13

Kravitz, Steve, 587, 637

Kuralt, Charles, 269, 380

La Bruyère, Jean de, 7

Lamarr, Hedy, 48

Lamb, Charles, 155

Lange, Fay Madigan, 226

Larson, Gary, 392

Lasorda, Tommy, 505

Leacock, Stephen, 328

Leary, Timothy, 40

Lebowitz, Fran, 260, 372, 534

Lee, Larry, 545

Leno, Jay, 616

Leonard, Gloria, 106

LePatner, Barry, 576

Levine, Alex, 266

Lewis, Richard, 105, 222

Lincoln, Abraham, 255, 514
Loos, Anita, 626
Loren, Sophia, 273
Lorenzoni, Father Larry, 598
Lowry, Mary, 259
Lucy (Charles Schulz), 171
Macaulay, Dame Rose, 9, 143
MacDonald, Ross, 375
Maher, Bill, 437
Malamud, Bernard, 271
Malcolm, Andrew, 398
Mandel, Bill, 346
Manners, Miss (Judith Martin), 53, 65, 276
Martial, 523
Martin, Judith, 53, 65, 276
Martin, Paul C., 383
Marx, Groucho, 544
Maugham, W. Somerset, 69, 81, 490, 604
Maxwell, Elsa, 306
McCoughey, J. D., 3
McGoorty, Danny, 184, 334
McGuire, Al, 336
McNally, Joel, 412
Meir, Golda, 218
Menander, 34, 127
Mencken, H. L., 8, 72, 237, 351, 364, 516, 618
Michaels, Andrea C., 298
Michener, James, 487
Miller, George, 284

Mitchum, Robert, 240
Mizner, Wilson, 488
Moore, Roger, 194
Mooreman, Jeve, 594
Murphy, Maureen, 104, 447
Murrow, Edward R., 609
Mussolini, Benito, 11
Nabokov, Vladimir, 295
Nachman, Gerald, 132, 138, 309
Nash, Ogden, 252
Nathan, George Jean, 443, 600
Nickman, Bob, 116
Nietzsche, Friedrich, 4, 18, 27, 38
Nimzovich, Aaron, 350
Nixon, Richard M., 465
Nunn, Gregory, 452
O'Connor, Patrick, 486
O'Hara, John, 512
O'Hara, Maureen, 424
O'Malley, Austin, 481
Orben, Robert, 64, 156, 159, 193, 297
Ordover, Al, 473
Orwell, George, 211
Ovid, 35
Parton, Dolly, 62
Pearl, Steven, 161, 330, 410, 411, 588

Peter, Laurence J., 526
Phelps, Michael, 290
Philips, Emo, 167, 173
Phillips, Jeanne, 221
Picasso, Pablo, 357
Piggy, Miss (Henry Beard), 73
Plato, 301, 458
Pollio, Marty, 58
Pomeroy, Jack, 451
Pond, Mimi, 44
Poundstone, Paula, 158
Prescott, Joseph, 554
Price, George, 581
Priestley, J. B., 219
Proust, Marcel, 634
Pryor, Richard, 131
Puckett, U. J., 179
Rajneesh, Bhagwan Shree, 16
Ray, John, 115
Reagan, Nancy, 209
Reagan, Ronald, 468
Reger, Max, 518
Reiner, Carl, 558
Reynolds, Rick, 416, 527
Richman, Susan, 280
Rickter, Donald O., 635
Rivers, Joan, 100, 111, 113, 614
Robbins, Harold, 20
Robinson, Sugar Ray, 338

Rockefeller, John
D., 190
Rodríguez, Chi
Chi, 347
Rogers, Will, 196,
204, 449, 461,
578
Rooney, Andy, 42,
227
Roosevelt,
Eleanor, 596
Roosevelt,
Franklin
Delano, 611
Rose, Billy, 192
Rose, Pete, 340
Rosten, Leo, 476
Rubenstein, Steve,
39
Russell, Bertrand,
550
Russell, Mark,
400, 469
Sahl, Mort, 120,
409, 453, 454,
471
Salinger, J. D., 247
Samuels, Jim, 427
Santayana, George,
331
Schaefer, Jack,
150
Schopenhauer,
Arthur, 215
Schulberg, Budd,
253
Schulz, Charles,
76, 171
Shakes, Ronnie,
22, 242, 289
Shakespeare,
William, 560
Shandling, Garry,
95, 97, 118
Shaw, George
Bernard, 61,
122, 285, 321,
444, 498, 569,
570

Sheehan, Bernie,
623
Shriner, Will, 174
Siegel, Max, 129
Simon, José, 272
Simon, Neil, 376
Simond, Frank H.,
445
Sitwell, Dame
Edith, 52
Slayton, Bobby,
387, 529
Smirnoff, Yakov,
308
Smith, H. Allen,
239
Smith, Logan
Pearsall, 166,
191
Smith, Marion, 75,
175
Snoopy (Charles
Schulz), 76
Snow, Carrie, 136,
277, 292
Socrates, 164
Sowell, Thomas,
603
Stallone, Sylvester,
553
Steel, Danielle,
515
Steinberg, David,
151
Steinberg, Josef
von, 188
Stevenson, Adlai,
459, 460, 464
Stewart, Jimmy,
225
Stilwell, Joseph,
613
St. Johns, Adela
Rogers, 130
Stokes, Bob, 2
Stone, I. F., 441
Stoppard, Tom,
520

Strauss, Robert,
474
Susann, Jacque-
line, 152
Sylvia (Nicole Hol-
lander), 46
Talley, Alfred J.,
185
Thomas, Gwyn,
369
Thomas, Norman,
446
Thomas, Warren,
119
Thompson, John,
335
Thoreau, Henry
David, 60, 388,
396
Thurber, James,
568
Tolstoy, Leo, 5,
615
Tomlin, Lily, 233,
238
Toscanini, Arturo,
325
Trillin, Calvin,
133, 256, 268,
287, 539
Twain, Mark, 50,
157, 270, 312,
356, 403, 472,
484, 491, 535,
561, 562, 593,
595
Tyler, Willie, 582,
624
Uecker, Bob, 342
Valdez, Jeff, 54
Valéry, Paul, 528
Van Brocklin,
Norm, 344
Van Buren, Abi-
gail, 377, 585,
632
Van Doren, Mamie,
147
Victoria, Queen,
165

Vidal, Gore, 436,
496, 524
Voltaire, 442
Vonnegut, Kurt,
513
Vrettos, Luther,
539
Warfield, Marsha,
86
Warner, Jack, 467
Waugh, Evelyn,
169
Wayne, John, 421
Weiler, A. H., 540
West, Mae, 91,
124, 125

Westlake, Donald
E., 261
Whistler, James
McNeill, 530
White, E. B., 557
White, Slappy, 181
Whitehorn,
Katherine, 78
Wilde, Oscar, 214,
367, 503, 507,
508
Wilson, Tom
(Ziggy), 282,
589
Winner, Michael,
419

Winsor, Kathleen,
82
Winters, Shelley,
430
Wolf, David T.,
236
Wood, Natalie, 30
Yasenek, René, 89
Young, Loretta,
420
Youngman, Henny,
314
Ziggy (Tom Wil-
son), 282, 589

Index of Subjects and Key Words

Absence, 560
Accordion, 320
Accountant, 203
Acid rain, 398
Action, 531
Actor, 194, 467
Actress, 120
Admiration, 241
Adolescence, 177
Adultery, 114,
143, 177, 509
Advertising, 504
Africa, 311
Agents, 494
Aging, 211–226,
296, 499, 570
Airports, 383
Alaska Airlines,
370
Alcohol, 266,
310–314
Alimony, 137
Altoona, 230
Ambulance chaser,
366
America, 460
Amiability, 555

Analysis, 294–295
Anglican, 9
Anniversaries, 593
Antidote, 167
Antique, 226
Apartment, 616
Ape, 27
Apologies, 564
Argument, 590
Art, 354–357, 389,
493
Artichoke, 264
Ass, 591, 613
Ass, solemn, 462
Assassins, 325
Asset, 125
Assohol, 401
Astrology, 621
Atheist, 7
Audience,
629–630
Australian, 104
Autobiography,
509–510
Avant garde, 528
Average person,
598

Babe Ruth, 235
Babies, 438
Baby, 165
Baby carriage, 622
Bait, 272
Baldness, 539
Barbers, 457
Baseball, 340–343
Bastard, 82, 573
Bathroom, 352
Battle of wits, 551
Beauty, 615
Beer, 310
Bench press, 473
Bhagwan, 17
Biography, 507,
508
Birth, 101
Black and white,
234
Bladder, 418
Blisters, 585
Blonde, 70, 371,
626
Blunders, 4
Bomb, 386
Bondage, 110–111

Book people, 495
Book reviews, 512,
514–518
Bootlegger, 261
Bore, 257–260
Borg, Bjorn, 348
Boston, 381
Bottles, 428
Boxer shorts, 65
Boxing, 337–338
Brahms, 321
Brains, 125, 279,
401
Brain transplant,
344
Brakes, 253
Breakfast, 288
Breasts, 170
Breeding, 50
Briefcases, 182
British public, 569
Brown, Jerry, 474
Burbank, 12
Business, 202
Butter, 424
Cabbage, 262
Cabinet meeting,
468
Cabs, 457
Caffeine, 266
California, 12,
373–375
Camel, 313
Capital punish-
ment, 208–209
Capone, Al, 261
Car, 162
Cash register, 198
Catholic, 139
Cats, 54–59, 359,
637
Celibacy, 88
Censor, 541
Certainty, 604
Chains, 105
Change, 528
Charm, 51
Chastity, 84–85

Cheating, 251, 254
Cheese, 412
Cherry tomato, 276
Chess, 350
Chicken, 271
Children,
153–177,
534–535, 537
Chinese emperor,
456
Chinese food, 245
Christian, 9, 10,
261
Christianity, 420
Churchill, 611
Cigars, 223
Cities, 185
Civilization, 631
Clair de Lune, 326
Clap, 82
Classical music,
322
Cleaning, 526
Clones, 427
Closet, 532
Closet space, 121
Clothes, 60–66
Coach, 335–336
Cocker spaniel,
539
Cockroaches, 304
Cocktail party, 309
Comedian, 470
Committee, 2, 542
Common sense,
351
Communist, 341,
451
Complaining, 632
Composer, 323
Compulsion, 553
Computer, 397
Concertina, 328
Congress, 472
Connie Mack Sta-
dium, 342
Conscience, 253
Conservatives,
452–455

Consistency, 580
Constantine, 261
Contraceptive, 94
Converts, 8
Coolidge, Calvin,
461
Copulate, 92
Corkscrew, 311
Corn, 80
Country clubs, 554
Court, 363
Cow, 360
Cranberry, 399
Crime, 46,
206–210
Criminal, 393
Criminal class,
472
Criticism, 134,
516–517
Crocodile, 68
Cul-de-sac, 542
Cuteness, 59
Cynicism,
236–239
Dating, 118–120
Death, 227–235,
290
Death penalty,
208–209
Deer heads, 345
Defloration, 112
Delicatessen, 26
Democracy, 433,
448
Democrats, 459
Derelicts, 221
Descartes, 635
Diary, 367, 511
Diet, 279
Digestion, 270
Dim sum, 267
Diplomacy, 449
Dirty, 526
Disciple, 15, 507
Disturb, 592
Divorce, 130,
144–147

Doctor, 289
Dogs, 54–55, 618
Doubt, 567
Drink, 496
Drunk, 184, 629
Duels, 82, 403
Dullness, 382, 569
Dust, 229
Duty, 553
Earrings, 126
Economist,
    203–205
Editors, 506
Eggs, 422
Einstein, 235, 391
Elephant, 41
Endurance, 306
Enemies, 352,
    573–574
Energy, 401
England, 112
Enough (See
    "Once")
Envy, 524
Epidemic, 61
Equality, 40, 42
Erotica, 106, 599
Eunuch, 31
Evil, 67, 91, 127,
    250
Excellence, 327
Experience, 236,
    575–577
Ex-wife, 119
Eyes, 562
Face, 544
Faculties, 568
Faking, 240
False teeth, 299
Family, 189, 248
Fanatic, 549
Farmers, 360
Fashion, 61
Fat, 46, 266, 275,
    279
Fat man, 78
Father, 142, 161
Feelings, 95, 131

Feet, 564
Female imperson-
    ators, 120
Fettucini, 287
Fickleness, 122
Fiction, 482, 484
Fifty, 211
Film, 418
Fish, 563
Fists, 600
Flag, 446
Flies, 552
Flight attendant,
    384
Flood, 1
Flying, 386
Food, 261–288,
    311
Football, 339
Ford, 587
Ford, Gerald, 463
Foreigners, 322
Forgetfulness, 153,
    544
Fortune cookies,
    414–416
Freezing, 558
French toast, 96
Friend, 556
Frog, 557
Fun, 154, 252
Funeral, 228, 417
Future, 636
Gable, Clark, 426
Gandhi, Mahatma,
    29
Gas station, 198
Gauze, 425
Genius, 306
Gentleman, 320
Geography, 281
Geology, 631
Ghetto, 13
Gifts, 146, 190,
    523
Girls, 32, 116
Glamour, 48
Glory, 610

God, 1–4, 190,
    386
Goiter, 378
Gold, 456
Golf, 196,
    346–347
Good Samaritans,
    546
Goodness, 615
Gorbachev, 473
Government,
    439–474
Grandfather, 222
Grandmother, 314
Guess, 204
Guilt, 151
Gynecologist, 113,
    292
Hair, 105
Hamburger, 268,
    269
Happiness, 145,
    245–248
Hard-boiled eggs,
    422
Hart, Gary, 474
Hatchet, 405
Hate, 15, 188
Headliner, 428
Health, 289–301
Heart, 281
Heart, artificial,
    298, 623
Heart attack, 111
Heart disease, 290
Hell, 546
Hemingway, 20
History, 477,
    479–480,
Home movies, 222
Homer, 498
Homosexuality,
    107
Honesty, 520, 589
Hooker, 111
Hooks, 523
Horace, 635
Hors d'oeuvres,
    283

Horse, 395, 584
Horsepower, 395
Hospitality, 305
Hostess fruit pies, 277
Hot fudge sundae, 513
Housekeeper, 144
Housekeeping, 539
Housework, 43
Humor, 557
Hunger, 284
Husband, 20, 130, 141
Idealism, 236
Idiocy, 444
Idiot, 119, 350, 535, 579
Ignorance, 241, 580
Illusion, 615
Imagination, 562
Imitation, 435
Immortality, 6, 232
Inanimate objects, 525
Incest, 142, 500
Incompetence, 151
Infancy, 177
Inferiority, 596
Infidelity, 37
Injustice, 364
Ink, 505
Insanity, 11
Insult, 633
Intellect, 59
Intellectual, 597
Interstate Highways, 380
Invalids, 530
Invention, 207
Iowa, 377
IQ, 374
Irish, 368
Irish coffee, 266
Italian food, 284
Italy, 371
Jack-in-the-Pew, 12

Jade, 456
Jehovah's Witnesses, 13
Jesus, 14, 16, 18
Jew, 14
Journalism, 503
Judas, 507
Judge, 140, 622
Judgment, 576
Jury, 140
Justice, 364–365
Kansas, 378
Kill, 403
Kindergarten, 65
King Kong, 343
Kipling, 586
Kissing, 89–90
Knowledge, 578
Lanchester, Elsa, 424
Language, 39
Latin, 594
Lava lamp, 328
Law, 358–366
Law school, 362
Lawyer, 131, 360–361
Leapfrog, 109
Lemonade, 167
Lenin, 451
Leningrad, 370
Lesson, 577
Liars, 196, 441
Liberals, 453–455
Lies, 459
Life, 21–26, 331, 390
Life-support system, 174
Lightning, 582
Linoleum, 425
Lion, 58
Lipstick, 307
Listening, 260
Literature, 503
Liver spots, 217
Living, 409
Living together, 121, 132, 135
Loan, 566

Lord, 249, 549
Los Angeles, 376
Loser, 332–333
Louse, 262
Love, 67–66, 285, 421, 571, 573
Luck, 533
Luggage, 400
Lutheran, 139
Lying, 212, 254
Madhouse, 579
Madness, 581
Madonna, 355
Magazine titles, 537, 539
Maids, 592
Makeup, 447
Man, 27, 30, 33
Manners, 53
Marriage, 124, 127–147, 287
Martyr, 317
Martyrdom, 612
Masquerade party, 215
Masturbation, 148–152
Mathematics, 205
Meat, 262
Media, 465
Mexico, 272
Microscope, 465
Middle age, 220
Milk carton, 307
Mind, 597
Minneapolis, 139
Miss America, 616
Missionaries, 8
Mistake, 575
Mistresses, 195
Money, 190–202, 252, 392, 539
Monk, 497
Monkey, 613
Month, 197
Moon, 49
Morality, 354
Mortgage, 220
Motion, 531
Mottos, 407–412

Mouse, 359
Movements, 550
MTV, 329–330
Museum, 357
Music, 315–331
Myth, 327
Nail, 583
Naiveté, 172
Nations, 439
Navel, 83
Neckties, 133
Needs, 97
Nerves, 310
Newspapermen,
    445
New York, 377
Nietzsche, 5
Noah, 561
Novels, 482, 483,
    490, 513
Nurses, 530
Nymphomaniacs,
    545
Obscurity, 610
Office supplies,
    206
Old age, 215–226
Old masters, 195,
    356
Omens, 618
Once, 547
Opera, 324
Opponent, 334
Orange, 373
Originality, 489
Osmond, Marie,
    614
Outdoors, 617
Oysters, 265
Pain killer, 100
Painting, 630
Paperwork, 182
Paradise, 634
Paradox, 591
Paramedic, 110
Paranoia, 247
Parking, 138, 208,
    537
Party, 302–308,
    345

Passions, 421
Patriotism,
    443–444
Peace, 67, 402,
    616
Perelman, S. J.,
    605
Perfection, 559,
    570
Pets, 572
Phone, 97, 625
Phoneless cord,
    628
Piety, 7
Pilot, 384
Pitching, 341
Plagiarism, 481,
    488
Planes, 383–388,
    400
Planets, 390
Pockets, 199
Poetry, 328, 500
Poisoning, 497
Polaroid, 111
Politician, 445,
    447, 450
Politics, 439–474
Pool hustler, 184
Pool shark, 566
Poor, 200
Pop-up toaster
    tarts, 277
Pork buns, 267
Pork tartare, 263
Pornography, 106
Prayer, 475
Pregnant, 174
Presbyterian, 10
Presidents,
    460–473
Presley, Elvis, 326
Principles, 443
Prison, 210
Procrastination,
    595
Proctoscope, 465
Profession,
    185–186
Progress, 393

Propaganda,
    601–602
Protein, 361
Providence, 535
Psychiatrist,
    293–295
Public, 462
Public office, 279
Public servants,
    464
Pulp, 423
Puns, 619–620
Purity, 249, 256
Purpose, 21
Quitter, 161
Quotations,
    519–521
Railways, 386
Rain dance, 522
Rat, dirty, 235
Reading, 501
Reagan, Nancy,
    298
Reagan, Ronald,
    467, 473
Real estate, 443
Reason, 538
Rebel, 175
Relationships,
    117, 536
Republicans, 459
Requiem, 321
Respect, 219
Respectability,
    430
Restaurant, 278
Retirement, 187
Revenge, 25, 163
Reynolds, Burt,
    123
Rich, 189, 191,
    193
Richard the Lion-
    hearted, 420
Ridicule, 529
Rigor mortis, 205
Rivers, 398
Robbery, 607
Robinson, Edward
    G., 235

Roman Catholic, 9
Root canal, 300
Rose Bowl, 349
Rotarian, 346
Roth, Philip, 152
Rulers, 440
Rumor, 227
Running, 352
Russia, 308
Ruth, Babe, 235
Safari, 311
Saints, 11, 559
Sanity, 581
Saturn, 400
Sausage, 261
Schoolchildren,
    381
Science, 289–401
Scott, Sir Walter,
    498
Scoundrel, 548
Scruples, 252
Self-abuse,
    148–152
Self-respect, 254
Senility, 213
Seventy, 225
Sex, 78–115, 154,
    173, 233, 362,
    436, 539
Sex appeal, 98,
    113
Shakespeare, 498
Shark, 566
Shit, 381, 499
Shoes, 44–45
Shopping, 35, 47,
    73
Short person, 74,
    201
Shot, 404
Show business
    417–438
Shrouds, 199, 369
Silence, 590
Silly statement,
    469
Sins, 12, 121

Sissies, 216, 268
Sister, 377
Sixty, 430
Sky, 388
Sleep, 599
Sluts, 115, 614
Smoking, 231
Snow, 558
Socialites, 304
Social workers, 3
Songs, 623–625
Sorrow, 245
Souls, 620
Southern Califor-
    nia, 375
Soviet Union, 63
Spaghetti, 273
Spayed, 572
Sperm, 588
Sports, 332–353
Sports Illustrated,
    620
Sportswriter, 344
Spouse, 297
Stalin, 10
Starlet, 431
Starvation, 271
Statistics, 286
Status quo, 594
Stitch, 391
Stomach, 281
Stress, 297
Students, 568
Stupidity, 48
Style, 63
Success, 188, 524
Sugar, 266
Suicide, 231, 328,
    501, 607
Suicide blonde,
    627
Sun, 585
Sushi, 272
Sweethearts, 606
Talent, 429
Taste, 52
Taxes, 196
Taxicab, 426

Taylor, Elizabeth,
    423
Teaching, 496
Team, 419, 336
Technology,
    393–401
Teddy bear, 160
Teeth, 299–300
Television,
    432–438
Temple, Shirley,
    425
Teresa, Mother,
    614
Texas, 378, 381
Thanksgiving, 399
Thaw, 274
Therapy, 293
Thief, 481
Thin, 275
Thin woman, 78
Thinking, 600
Three-Mile Island,
    399
Tide, 382
Time, 392
Timers, 620
Titanic, 494
Toaster, 96
Toilets, 198
Tolstoy, 19
Tomato, 276
Tomorrow, 595
Tools, 396
Touching, 158
Train wreck, 371
Tranquillity, 628
Travel, 367–382
Tristan and Isolde,
    316–317
Trust, 141
Truth, 543, 603
Tub, 108
Tumor, 291
Tunnel, 406
Turkey, 274, 399
Twin sister, 377
Tyrants, 164

Ugly, 300
Ultrasuede, 438
Unconscious, 463
Unemployment, 181
Unicorn, 109
Universe, 394
Vasectomy, 93
Vice, 52, 255
Violence, 553
Virgin, 86, 134
Virtue, 255
Vision, 118
Voice, 609
Wagner, 315–319
Waist, 282

Wales, 369
Wallet, 201
War, 67, 128
Warship, 619
Waste of time, 244
Water, 584
Wax museum, 527
Wealth, 36, 189
Weather, 522
Wedding night, 112
Whips, 105
Wicks, 527
Wife, 337
Wildlife, 303
Wits, 551

Wives, 606, 632
Woman, 34–48, 122
Work, 178–185, 432
World, 579
Wounded, 502
Wray, Fay, 343
Wrestling, 353
Writers, 152, 475–511
Youth, 169–177, 214
Yugoslavia, 263

THE FOURTH
– AND BY FAR THE MOST RECENT –
637
BEST THINGS
ANYBODY EVER SAID

*Dedicated with love
to anybody who has ever
invited me to dinner*

Contents

Introduction

PART ONE

God and the Universe, Life Itself,
Men and Women, Hair,
Love and Courtship, Blondes, Sex, Marriage,
Offspring, Christmas, Work, Success,
and that's just for starters

PART TWO

Lawyers and Money, Food and Drink,
Health, Politics, Celebrities and Boredom,
Sports, Books and Authors, Places,
Art and Music, War, Aging, Death,
just to mention a few things

PART THREE

One thing and another

Sources, References, and Notes

Index of Authors

Index of Subjects and Key Words

Introduction

What? Another collection of the 637 best things anybody ever said? Surely this time the bottom of the barrel has been reached. Not so! Quality is still above the bung, and much of it is in the cream zone. I think this new assortment is as good as any of the previous three. Readers who don't agree are invited to go back to whatever slime pit they came from.

Just kidding! I love my readers. Without them I wouldn't be able to do what I do, the legitimacy of which is borderline, in the opinion of my relatives. Hearing from readers keeps me going—that and the money, which has grown over the years to nearly a trickle. From an R. G. Fisher in New Orleans: "Everyone knows that life is not worth living, as Camus pointed out, so why not waste it compiling meaningless quote books?" I don't know. An attorney in Bucharest, Romania (the farthest-flung fan to date), who has an indecipherable signature, pointed out that "In every language there are only 637 best things anybody ever said. The 638th is always the start of another series of 637."

Another reader, on noting that I quote myself, suggested that "Robert Byrne should be gagged." Although gagging wouldn't stop me from typing, the remark does have merit and is therefore included in the pages that follow.

Which is not to say readers are never a problem. Take the case of the man who calls himself, for some reason, Strange de Jim. He has contributed many splendid lines to Herb Caen's column in *The San Francisco Chronicle*, only two of which I repeat here. The problem comes with the Index of Authors. Is Strange his first or his last name? You'll find him alphabetized as Jim, Strange de.

Or take Hal Lee Luyah, who mailed me dozens of well-crafted zingers, five of which are included among the 637 presented here. Is Hal Lee Luyah a pseudonym or did his parents really call him that in order to have something to shout on Easter Sunday? He won't tell.

The reasons quality has held up are severalfold. One is that twice as much time—four years—was invested in compiling this sequel as in either of the previous two. Another is that the audience for them has grown, and a larger audience means more contributions. There are people who have sent me hundreds of their favorite lines. Such generosity is stunning. Beyond crediting and thanking contributors who have been especially helpful, I should send them some sort of prize or gift. Well, maybe not.

Third, comedy and comedians are growing in number and are churning out a river of material. Odds are that if you knock a random person down, it will be a standup comedian . . . or somebody who thinks he is. The country is awash in one-liners. Part of what I do is sit on the shore and take potluck from the flotsam.

A final factor is that I'm much older than I was when the series began and better able to pick quotes and drawings. There is more bile and acid in my blood. Socially and mentally, I'm much more twisted than before, doctors agree, and therefore in closer harmony with the rest of you.

A word about the antique line cuts, since nobody asked. They are taken from several dozen collections, most of them put out by Dover Publications, which contain between 15,000 and 20,000 drawings. It's not easy finding a good match between a quote and a drawing, and I think I deserve more credit than I've been getting. When I do find a match, I'm happy for up to a minute at a time, and my craggy face is wreathed in smiles. It's then that you should ask for favors.

A few announcements for readers unfamiliar with the earlier volumes: In Part One and Part Two, the quotes are loosely grouped according to subjects, which tend to follow one another according to the rules of life rather than the alphabet. For example, Hair follows Women, Loneliness follows Truth, and Boredom follows Celebrities. The result is a book best read from front to back, though browsing is permitted. Indexes are provided for those who want a quote on a particular subject or who are trying to locate a quote half-remembered.

Birth and death dates are given only for dead people. Quotes aren't numbered if they appeared in the earlier volumes or if they don't deserve a number. I don't know why certain topics are so much better represented than others, and I don't care. It's just the way it turned out.

I'm sorry about the number of quotes ascribed to Unknown. I relied more this time on contributions from readers, many of whom don't swing on scholarly apparatus. If you can supply a missing ascription, or correct a wrong one, or have a good line I missed, speak up. If you do send me something I can use in a future tome, you'll be mentioned somewhere in the text, a practice called *quid pro quote.*

For help in tracking down missing ascriptions, I wish

to thank Steve Allen, Stanley Ralph Ross, and Harry Crane. Thanks also to Abby Adams, compiler of the newly published *An Uncommon Scold*, who let me rummage through her manuscript in search of quotes by women.

Robert Byrne

PART ONE

God and the Universe
Life Itself
Men and Women
Hair
Love and Courtship
Blondes
Sex
Marriage
Offspring
Christmas
Work
Success
and that's just for starters

1

God created man, but I could do better.

Erma Bombeck

2

If there is a supreme being, he's crazy.

Marlene Dietrich

3

Only two things are infinite, the universe and human stupidity, and I'm not sure about the former.

Albert Einstein (1879–1955)

4

We are here on earth to do good to others. What the others are here for, I don't know.

W. H. Auden (1907–1973)

5

I don't know, I don't care, and it doesn't make any difference.

Jack Kerouac (1922–1969)

6

There ain't no answer. There ain't going to be any answer. There never has been an answer. That's the answer.

Gertrude Stein (1874–1946)

7

The meek shall inherit the earth . . . if you don't mind.

Graffito

8

If you don't count some of Jehovah's injunctions, there is no humor in the Bible.

Mordecai Richler

9

Woe unto you who laugh now, for you shall mourn and weep.

Jesus Christ, according to Luke 6:25

10

I sometimes worry that God has Alzheimer's and has forgotten us.

Lily Tomlin and Jane Wagner

11

God seems to have left the receiver off the hook.

Arthur Koestler

12

If God listened to every shepherd's curse, our sheep would all be dead.

Russian proverb

13

What can you say about a society that says that God is dead and Elvis is alive?

Irv Kupcinet

14

To Jesus Christ! A splendid chap!
Toast by Sir Ralph Richardson (1902–1983)

15

If Jesus was Jewish, how come he has a Mexican name?

Unknown

16

Churches welcome all denominations, but most prefer fives and tens.

Unknown

17

The Vatican is against surrogate mothers. Good thing they didn't have that rule when Jesus was born.

Elayne Boosler

18

A difference of opinion is what makes horse racing and missionaries.

Will Rogers (1879–1935)

19

Do television evangelists do more than lay people?

Stanley Ralph Ross

20

Sin is geographical.

Bertrand Russell (1872–1970)

21

Even when I'm sick and depressed, I love life.

Artur Rubenstein (1887–1982)

22

Life! Can't live with it, can't live without it.

Cynthia Nelms

23

Life is something that happens when you can't get to sleep.

Fran Lebowitz

24

There is no cure for birth or death except to try to enjoy the interval.

George Santayana (1863–1952)

25

Why torture yourself when life will do it for you?

Laura Walker

26

It may be that we have all lived before and died, and this is hell.

A. L. Prusick

27

Life's a bitch, and then you meet one.

Unknown

28

Always look out for Number One and be careful not to step in Number Two.

Rodney Dangerfield

29

It's not what you are, it's what you don't become that hurts.

Oscar Levant (1906–1972)

30

The ethical argument regarding abortion hinges on the question of exactly when life begins. Some believe that life begins at forty.

Kevin Nealon

31

It is said that life begins when the fetus can exist apart from its mother. By this definition, many people in Hollywood are legally dead.

Jay Leno

32

Some mornings it just doesn't seem worth it to gnaw through the leather straps.

Emo Philips

33

Everything I did in my life that was worthwhile I caught hell for.

Earl Warren (1891–1974)

34

It's a dog-eat-dog world, and I'm wearing Milk Bone shorts.

Kelly Allen

35

You have to live life to love life, and you have to love life to live life. It's a vicious circle.

Unknown

36

In a fight between you and the world, bet on the world.

Franz Kafka (1883–1924)

37

Man was predestined to have free will.

Hal Lee Luyah

38

Swallow a toad in the morning if you want to encounter nothing more disgusting the rest of the day.

Nicolas Chamfort (1741–1794)

39

If you want a place in the sun, you must leave the shade of the family tree.

Osage saying

40

In spite of the cost of living, it's still popular.

Kathleen Norris (1880–1966)

41

If you're already in a hole, it's no use to continue digging.

Roy W. Walters

42

The longer you stay in one place, the greater your chances of disillusionment.

Art Spander

43

The optimist proclaims that we live in the best of all possible worlds, and the pessimist fears this is true.

James Branch Cabell (1879–1958)

44

An optimist is someone who thinks the future is uncertain.

Unknown

45

I always wanted to be somebody, but I should have been more specific.

Lily Tomlin and Jane Wagner

46

Dawn! A brand new day! This could be the start of something average.

Ziggy (Tom Wilson)

47

"That would be nice."

Charlie Brown on hearing that in life you win some and lose some.

Charles Schulz

48

The second half of the 20th Century is a complete flop.

Isaac Bashevis Singer

49

The more unpredictable the world becomes, the more we rely on predictions.

Steve Rivkin

50

There are few problems in life that wouldn't be eased by the proper application of high explosives.

Unknown

51

Reality is a collective hunch.

Lily Tomlin and Jane Wagner

5 2

Humankind cannot bear very much reality.

T. S. Eliot (1888–1965)

5 3

You've got to take the bitter with the sour.

Samuel Goldwyn (1882–1974)

5 4

Strife is better than loneliness.

Irish saying

55

Truth is more of a stranger than fiction.

Mark Twain (1835–1910)

56

It is annoying to be honest to no purpose.

Ovid (43 B.C.–A.D. 18)

57

Truth is the safest lie.

Unknown

58

I have seen the truth, and it doesn't make sense.

Unknown

59

Never let a computer know you're in a hurry.

Unknown

60

My theory of evolution is that Darwin was adopted.

Steven Wright

61

Never try to walk across a river just because it has an average depth of four feet.

Martin Friedman

62

Physics lesson: When a body is submerged in water, the phone rings.

Unknown

63

I like trees because they seem more resigned to the way they have to live than other things do.

Willa Cather (1873–1947)

64

I am at two with nature.

Woody Allen

65

Men are nicotine-soaked, beer-besmirched, whiskey-greased, red-eyed devils.

Carry Nation (1846–1911)

66

Many men die at twenty-five and aren't buried until they are seventy-five.

Benjamin Franklin (1706–1790)

67

Men are superior to women. For one thing, they can urinate from a speeding car.

Will Durst

68

Men are irrelevant.

Fay Weldon

69

I require three things in a man. He must be handsome, ruthless, and stupid.

Dorothy Parker (1893–1967)

70

His mother should have thrown him away and kept the stork.

Mae West (1892–1980)

71

I have yet to hear a man ask for advice on how to combine marriage and a career.

Gloria Steinem

72

When a man brings his wife flowers for no reason— there's a reason.

Molly McGee

73

Men! You can't live with them and you can't
1. Dip them in batter for tempura,
2. Use them for collateral on a loan,
3. Put in new batteries.

"Sylvia" (Nicole Hollander)

74

The main difference between men and women is that
men are lunatics and women are idiots.

Rebecca West (1892–1983)

75

Any young man who is unmarried at the age of twenty-
one is a menace to the community.

Brigham Young (1801–1877)

76

Talking with a man is like trying to saddle a cow. You
work like hell, but what's the point?

Gladys Upham

77

Men read maps better than women because only men can understand the concept of an inch equaling a hundred miles.

Roseanne Barr

78

A dork is a dork is a dork.

Judy Markey

79

I have known more men destroyed by the desire to have wife and child and to keep them in comfort than I have seen destroyed by drink and harlots.

William Butler Yeats (1865–1939)

80

I grew up to have my father's looks, my father's speech patterns, my father's posture, my father's opinions, and my mother's contempt for my father.

Jules Feiffer

81

A woman who takes things from a man is called a girlfriend. A man who takes things from a woman is called a gigolo.

Ruthie Stein

82

The main result of feminism has been the Dutch Treat.

Nora Ephron

83

Men should think twice before making widowhood wo-men's only path to power.

Gloria Steinem

84

You make the beds, you do the dishes, and six months later you have to start all over again.

Joan Rivers

85

Women have the feeling that since they didn't make the rules, the rules have nothing to do with them.

Diane Johnson

86

Women are cursed, and men are the proof.

Roseanne Barr

87

When a woman behaves like a man, why doesn't she behave like a nice man?

Edith Evans (1888–1976)

88

If a woman has to choose between catching a fly ball and saving an infant's life, she will choose to save the infant's life without even considering if there are men on base.

Dave Barry

89

Woman in Hurricane Has Same Baby Three Times
Tabloid headline suggested by Tracey Ullman

90

Women can do any job men can and give birth while doing it.

Allan Heavey

91

Women complain about premenstrual syndrome, but I think of it as the only time of the month I can be myself.

Roseanne Barr

92

My plastic surgeon told me my face looked like a bouquet of elbows.

Phyllis Diller

93

She was so ugly she could make a mule back away from an oat bin.

Will Rogers (1879–1935)

94

I don't consider myself bald. I'm simply taller than my hair.

Tom Sharp

95

You're only as good as your last haircut.

Susan Lee

96

I am my hair.

Woman overheard by Roy Blount, Jr.

97

Every time I look at you I get a fierce desire to be lonesome.

Oscar Levant (1906–1972)

98

I hate people. People make me pro-nuclear.

Margaret Smith

99

Love is an exploding cigar we willingly smoke.

Lynda Barry

100

You need someone to love while you're looking for someone to love.

Shelagh Delaney

101

God is love, but get it in writing.

Gypsy Rose Lee (1914–1970)

1 0 2

Abstinence makes the heart grow fonder.

Knox Burger

1 0 3

It is better to have flunked your Wasserman than never to have loved at all.

Jim Stark

1 0 4

Boy meets girl. So what?

Bertolt Brecht (1898–1956)

1 0 5

Men and women, women and men. It will never work.

Erica Jong

1 0 6

If you want to catch a trout, don't fish in a herring barrel.

Ann Landers on singles bars

107

The animals most often encountered in the singles jungle are pigs, dogs, wolves, skunks, slugs, and snakes. The fox is imaginary.

Robert Byrne

Robert Byrne should be gagged.

Tracy Chreene

108

I go from stool to stool in singles bars hoping to get lucky, but there's never any gum under any of them.

Emo Philips

109

A "Bay Area Bisexual" told me I didn't quite coincide with either of her desires.

Woody Allen

110

PERSONALS:
Famous Writer needs woman to organize his life and spend his money. Loves to turn off Sunday football and go to the Botanical Gardens with that special someone. Will obtain plastic surgery if necessary.

Sure-fire singles ad by Joe Bob Briggs

111

When I meet a man I ask myself, "Is this the man I want my children to spend their weekends with?"

Rita Rudner

112

Oh God, in the name of Thine only beloved Son, Jesus Christ, Our Lord, let him phone me now.

Dorothy Parker (1893–1967)

113

I enjoy dating married men because they don't want anything kinky, like breakfast.

Joni Rodgers

114

Women with pasts interest men because they hope history will repeat itself.

Mae West (1892–1980)

115

I turned down a date once because I was looking for someone a little closer to the top of the food chain.

Judy Tenuta

116

Have you ever dated someone because you were too lazy to commit suicide?

Judy Tenuta

117

Never date a woman you can hear ticking.

Mark Patinkin

118

There is one thing I would break up over, and that is if she caught me with another woman. I won't stand for that.

Steve Martin

119

My boyfriend and I broke up. He wanted to get married and I didn't want him to.

Rita Rudner

120

I'm dating a woman now who, evidently, is unaware of it.

Garry Shandling

121

Necessity is the mother of attraction.

Luke McKissack

122

When confronted with two evils, a man will always choose the prettier.

Unknown

123

Blondes have more fun because they're easier to find in the dark.

Unknown

124

When I was giving birth, the nurse asked, "Still think blondes have more fun?"

Joan Rivers

125

It is possible that blondes also prefer gentlemen.

Mamie Van Doren

126

Gentlemen prefer bonds.

Andrew Mellon (1855–1937)

127

Is sex better than drugs? That depends on the pusher.

Unknown

128

For birth control I rely on my personality.

Milt Abel

129

Condoms aren't completely safe. A friend of mine was wearing one and got hit by a bus.

Bob Rubin

130

When the clerk tried to sell me condoms that were made of sheep intestines because they have a more natural feel, I said, "Not for northern women."

Elayne Boosler

131

Some condoms are made of sheep intestines, but I was so scared the first time I wore the whole sheep.

Danny Williams

132

Some condom packages are stamped "Reservoir." You mean those things can generate hydroelectric power?

Elayne Boosler

133

National Condom Week is coming soon. Hey, there's a parade you won't want to miss.

Jay Leno

134

This gum tastes funny.

Sign on condom machine

135

"I don't know, I never looked."
Answer to the question: "Do you smoke after sex?"

Unknown

136

I don't even masturbate anymore, I'm so afraid I'll give myself something. I just want to be friends with myself.

Richard Lewis

137

The advantage of masturbation over intercourse is that it's less competitive.

Robert Byrne

138

Before sleeping together today, people should boil themselves.

Richard Lewis

139

Mr. Right is now a guy who hasn't been laid in fifteen years.

Elayne Boosler

140

I finally had an orgasm, and my doctor told me it was the wrong kind.

Woody Allen

141

My wife and I don't have mutual orgasms. We have State Farm.

Milton Berle

142

Erogenous zones are either everywhere or nowhere.

Joseph Heller

143

During sex I fantasize that I'm someone else.

Richard Lewis

144

I don't mind sleeping on an empty stomach provided it isn't my own.

Philip J. Simborg

145

"I don't know, what's the record?"
Answer to the question: "How horny can you get?"

Neil Simon

146

The difference between sex and love is that sex relieves tension and love causes it.

Woody Allen

147

I always thought of you as, at best, asexual, but maybe I was being kind.

From the television show "Slap Maxwell"

148

The late porn star Johnny Wadd claimed to have been laid 14,000 times. He died of friction.

Larry Brown

149

I'm not kinky, but occasionally I like to put on a robe and stand in front of a tennis ball machine.

Garry Shandling

150

Kinky sex involves the use of duck feathers. Perverted sex involves the whole duck.

Lewis Grizzard

151

One figure can sometimes add up to a lot.

Mae West (1892–1980)

152

I wouldn't let him touch me with a ten-foot pole.

Mae West (1892–1980)

153

Mae West had a voice like a vibrating bed.

John Kobal

154

It's okay to laugh in the bedroom so long as you don't point.

Will Durst

1 5 5

Sex is a powerful aphrodisiac.

Keith Waterhouse

1 5 6

What do I know about sex? I'm a married man.

Tom Clancy

1 5 7

Some are born to greatness, some achieve greatness, and some have greatness thrust within them.

Hal Lee Luyah

1 5 8

Warning signs that your lover is bored:
1. Passionless kisses
2. Frequent sighing
3. Moved, left no forwarding address.

Matt Groening

1 5 9

I once made love for an hour and fifteen minutes, but it was the night the clocks are set ahead.

Garry Shandling

160

In the old days, women wore so many girdles, corsets, pantaloons, bloomers, stockings, garters, step-ins and God knows what all that you had to practically be a *prospector* to get to first base . . . to even *find* first base.

Danny McGoorty (1903–1970)

161

Ooooh. Ahhhh. Get out.

Andrew Dice Clay's impression of a one-night stand.

162

It is a gentleman's first duty to remember in the morning who it was he took to bed with him.

Dorothy Sayers (1893–1957)

163

I would never go to bed with a man who had so little regard for my husband.

From a novel by Dan Greenburg

164

Oysters are supposed to enhance your sexual performance, but they don't work for me. Maybe I put them on
too soon.

Garry Shandling

165

My wife gives good headache.

Rodney Dangerfield

166

Oral sex is like being attacked by a giant snail.

Germaine Greer

167

Once while we were making love, a curious optical illusion occurred, and it almost looked as though she were moving.

Woody Allen

168

He gave her a look you could have poured on a waffle.

Ring Lardner (1885–1933)

169

In breeding cattle you need one bull for every twenty-five cows, unless the cows are known sluts.

Johnny Carson

170

After making love I said to my girl, "Was it good for you, too?" And she said, "I don't think this was good for anybody."

Garry Shandling

171

In sex as in banking there is a penalty for early withdrawal.

Cynthia Nelms

172

The mirror over my bed reads: Objects appear larger than they are.

Garry Shandling

173

I was a virgin till I was twenty, then again till I was twenty-three.

Carrie Snow

174

Losing my virginity was a career move.

Madonna

175

Sex after ninety is like trying to shoot pool with a rope. Even putting my cigar in its holder is a thrill.

George Burns

176

Sometimes a cigar is just a cigar.

Sigmund Freud (1856–1939)

177

This is my last year to fool around. Then I'm going to settle down and marry a rock star.

From the 1986 movie Modern Girls

178

Dating means doing a lot of fun things you will never do again if you get married. The fun stops with marriage because you're trying to save money for when you split up your property.

Dave Barry

179

There's nothing like a Catholic wedding to make you wish that life had a fast forward button.

Dan Chopin

180

I married the first man I ever kissed. When I tell my children that, they just about throw up.

Barbara Bush

181

Until I got married, I was my own worst enemy.

Unknown

182

The poor wish to be rich, the rich wish to be happy, the single wish to be married, and the married wish to be dead.

Ann Landers

183

Marriage is like paying an endless visit in your worst clothes.

J. B. Priestley (1894–1984)

184

Marriage is like a besieged fortress. Everyone outside wants to get in, and everyone inside wants to get out.

Quitard

185

The chains of marriage are so heavy it takes two to carry them, and sometimes three.

Alexandre Dumas (1802–1870)

186

Marriage is ridiculous.

Goldie Hawn

187

Instead of getting married again, I'm going to find a woman I don't like and give her a house.

Lewis Grizzard

188

Love is blind, and marriage is a real eye-opener.

Unknown

189

My divorce came as a complete surprise to me. That will happen when you haven't been home in eighteen years.

Lee Trevino

190

The secret of a happy marriage is to tell your spouse everything but the essentials.

Cynthia Nelms

191

All men make mistakes, but married men find out about them sooner.

Red Skelton

192

In marriage a man becomes slack and selfish and undergoes a fatty degeneration of the spirit.

Robert Louis Stevenson (1850–1894)

193

Conrad Hilton was very generous to me in the divorce settlement. He gave me 5,000 Gideon Bibles.

Zsa Zsa Gabor

194

The only thing that holds a marriage together is the husband being big enough to step back and see where the wife is wrong.

Archie Bunker

195

I've been married so long I'm on my third bottle of Tabasco sauce.

Susan Vass

196

There is nothing like living together for blinding people to each other.

Ivy Compton Burnett (1884–1969)

197

Always get married early in the morning. That way, if it doesn't work out, you haven't wasted a whole day.

Mickey Rooney

198

There are pigtails on the pillow in the morning that weren't there before.

Martin Luther (1483–1546) on marriage

199

I'm going to marry a Jewish woman because I like the idea of getting up on Sunday morning and going to the deli.

Michael J. Fox

200

That married couples can live together day after day is a miracle the Vatican has overlooked.

Bill Cosby

201

My wife and I were happy for twenty years. Then we met.

Rodney Dangerfield

202

My husband said he needed more space, so I locked him outside.

Roseanne Barr

203

You may marry the man of your dreams, but fifteen years later you're married to a reclining chair that burps.

Roseanne Barr

204

I grew up in a very large family in a very small house.
I never slept alone until after I was married.

Lewis Grizzard

205

My parents stayed together for forty years, but that was
out of spite.

Woody Allen

206

If it weren't for marriage, men and women would have
to fight with total strangers.

Unknown

207

Monogamous is what one partner in every relationship
wants to be.

Strange de Jim

208

Monogamous and monotonous are synonymous.

Thaddeus Golas

209

Monogamy leaves a lot to be desired.

Unknown

210

If you want monogamy, marry a swan.

From the movie Heartburn, *1987*

211

When Sears comes out with a riding vacuum cleaner, then I'll clean the house.

Roseanne Barr

212

My mom was fair. You never knew whether she was going to swing with her right or her left.

Herb Caen

213

As a housewife, I feel that if the kids are still alive when my husband gets home from work, then hey, I've done my job.

Roseanne Barr

214

My mother always phones me and asks, "Is everything all wrong?"

Richard Lewis

2 1 5

I'd get pregnant if I could be assured I'd have puppies.

Cynthia Nelms

2 1 6

Giving birth is like trying to push a piano through a transom.

Alice Roosevelt Longworth (1884–1980)

2 1 7

When I was born I was so surprised I didn't talk for a year and a half.

Gracie Allen (1906–1964)

2 1 8

I have never understood the fear of some parents about babies getting mixed up in the hospital. What difference does it make as long as you get a good one?

Heywood Broun (1888–1939)

2 1 9

A soiled baby with a neglected nose cannot be conscientiously regarded as a thing of beauty.

Mark Twain (1835–1910)

2 2 0

Babies don't need vacations, but I still see them at the beach.

Steven Wright

221

When childhood dies, its corpses are called adults.

Brian Aldiss

222

Adults are obsolete children.

Dr. Seuss

223

It's a dull child that knows less than its father.

Unknown

224

Before I was married I had three theories about raising children. Now I have three children and no theories.

John Wilmot, Earl of Rochester (1647–1680)

225

When my kids become wild and unruly, I use a nice, safe playpen. When they're finished, I climb out.

Erma Bombeck

226

My children love me. I'm like the mother they never had.

Roseanne Barr

227

The highlight of my childhood was making my brother laugh so hard that food came out of his nose.

Garrison Keillor

228

We had a quicksand box in our back yard. I was an only child, eventually.

Steven Wright

229

I was the kid next door's imaginary friend.

Emo Philips

230

As parents, my wife and I have one thing in common. We're both afraid of children.

Bill Cosby

231

My father was frightened of his father, I was frightened of my father, and I am damned well going to see to it that my children are frightened of me.

King George V (1865–1936)

232

If a child shows himself to be incorrigible, he should be decently and quietly beheaded at the age of twelve lest he grow to maturity, marry, and perpetuate his kind.

Don Marquis (1878–1937)

233

I reached puberty at age thirty. At age twelve I looked like a fetus.

Dave Barry

234

My niece was in *The Glass Menagerie* at school. They used Tupperware.

Cathy Ladman

235

Reasoning with a child is fine if you can reach the child's reason without destroying your own.

John Mason Brown (1900–1969)

236

There is nothing wrong with teenagers that reasoning with them won't aggravate.

Unknown

237

If Abraham's son had been a teenager, it wouldn't have been a sacrifice.

Scott Spendlove

238

If you want to recapture your youth, cut off his allowance.

Al Bernstein

239

Anybody who has survived his childhood has enough information about life to last him the rest of his days.

Flannery O'Connor (1925–1964)

240

Ask your child what he wants for dinner only if he's buying.

Fran Lebowitz

241

If you must hold yourself up to your children, hold yourself up as an object lesson and not as an example.

George Bernard Shaw (1856–1950)

242

My parents were too poor to have children, so the neighbors had me.

Buddy Hackett

243

Have children while your parents are still young enough to take care of them.

Rita Rudner

244

Children despise their parents until the age of forty, when they suddenly become just like them, thus preserving the system.

Quentin Crewe

2 4 5
Roses are reddish
Violets are bluish
If it weren't for Christmas
We'd all be Jewish.

Benny Hill

2 4 6
I stopped believing in Santa Claus when my mother took
me to see him in a department store, and he asked for
my autograph.

Shirley Temple

2 4 7
The three stages of a man's life:
1. He believes in Santa Claus;
2. He doesn't believe in Santa Claus;
3. He is Santa Claus.

Unknown

2 4 8
You can't beat the gentiles in December. We were stupid to make Hanukkah then.

Ralph Schoenstein's grandfather

2 4 9
Santa Claus has the right idea: Visit people once a year.

Victor Borge

250

Thanksgiving comes *after* Christmas for people over thirty.

Peter Kreeft

251

Christmas is Christ's revenge for the crucifixion.

Unknown

252

Setting a good example for children takes all the fun out of middle age.

William Feather

253

There is no such thing as fun for the whole family.

Jerry Seinfeld

254

In order to influence a child, one must be careful not to be that child's parent or grandparent.

Don Marquis (1878–1937)

255

The time not to become a father is eighteen years before a war.

E. B. White (1899–1985)

256

A married man with a family will do anything for money.
Charles Maurice de Talleyrand-Perigord
(1754–1838)

257

To be a successful father, there's one absolute rule:
When you have a kid, don't look at it for the first two
years.
Ernest Hemingway (1899–1961)

Hemingway was a jerk.
Harold Robbins

Harold Robbins doesn't sound like an author, he sounds
like a company brochure.
The New Yorker

258

You should have seen what a fine-looking man he was
before he had all those children.
Arapesh tribesman

259

Parenthood remains the greatest single preserve of the
amateur.
Alvin Toffler

260

I have over 42,000 children, and not one comes to visit.
Mel Brooks as The 2000-Year-Old Man

261

It behooves a father to be blameless if he expects his son to be.

Homer (circa 1000 B.C.)

262

Any father whose son raises his hand against him is guilty of having produced a son who raised his hand against him.

Charles Péguy (1873–1914)

263

Parents are not interested in justice, they are interested in quiet.

Bill Cosby

264

My parents only had one argument in forty-five years. It lasted forty-three years.

Cathy Ladman

265

My parents have been visiting me for a few days. I just dropped them off at the airport. They leave tomorrow.

Margaret Smith

266

I've been promoted to middle management. I never
thought I'd sink so low.

Tim Gould

267

Do it my way or watch your butt.

Management philosophy from the movie
Raising Arizona, *1987*

268

No man ever listened himself out of a job.

Calvin Coolidge (1872–1933)

269

Canadians shouldn't come down to Southern California
and take jobs away from our Mexicans.

Stanley Ralph Ross

270

There ain't no rules around here! We're trying to accomplish something!

Thomas Edison (1847–1931)

271

A career is a job that has gone on too long.

Cartoon caption by Jeff MacNelly

272

I used to work at The International House of Pancakes. It was a dream, and I made it happen.

Paula Poundstone

273

Tell your boss what you think of him, and the truth shall set you free.

Unknown

2 7 4

A holding company is a thing where you hand an accomplice the goods while the policeman searches you.

Will Rogers (1879–1935)

2 7 5

A criminal is a person with predatory instincts without
sufficient capital to form a corporation.

Howard Scott

2 7 6

The economy of Houston is so bad right now that two
prostitutes the police arrested turned out to be virgins.

Bill Abeel

2 7 7

Success isn't permanent, and failure isn't fatal.

Mike Ditka

2 7 8

Success has many fathers, failure is a mother.

Jeanne Phillips

279
The worst part of success is trying to find someone who is happy for you.

Bette Midler

280
Success is women you don't even know walking around your house.

From "Saturday Night Live"

281
If at first you don't succeed, find out if the loser gets anything.

Bill Lyon

282
Success in life means not becoming like your parents.

Louise Bowie

283
To make a small fortune, invest a large fortune.

Bruce Cohn

284
Formula for success: Rise early, work hard, strike oil.

J. Paul Getty, allegedly

285

The penalty of success is to be bored by the people who used to snub you.

Nancy, Lady Astor (1879–1964)

PART TWO

Lawyers and Money
Food and Drink
Health
Politics
Celebrities and Boredom
Sports
Books and Authors
Places
Art and Music
War
Aging
Death
just to mention a few things

286

Talk is cheap until you hire a lawyer.

Unknown

287

I've never been in love. I've always been a lawyer.

Unknown

288

There are three reasons why lawyers are replacing rats as laboratory research animals. One is that they're plentiful, another is that lab assistants don't get attached to them, and the third is that there are some things rats just won't do.

Unknown

289

A tragedy is a busload of lawyers going over a cliff with an empty seat.

Unknown

290

Lawyer Drowning in Bay Rescued

Headline nominated by George de Shazer as the saddest of the year

291

Lawsuit, n. A machine you go into as a pig and come out of as a sausage.

Ambrose Bierce (1842–1914)

292

Is it a bigger crime to rob a bank or to open one?

Ted Allan

293

Two can live as cheaply as one. Take the bird and the horse, for example.

Unknown

294

I don't like money, but it quiets my nerves.

Joe Louis (1914–1981)

295

I wish Karl would accumulate some capital instead of just writing about it.

Karl Marx's mother, allegedly

296

Money can't buy friends, but it can get you a better class of enemy.

Spike Milligan

297

Money won is twice as sweet as money earned.

From the movie The Color of Money, *1986*

298

Alimony is always having to say you're sorry.

Philip J. Simborg

299

Never get deeply in debt to someone who cried at the end of *Scarface*.

Robert S. Wieder

300

The rule is not to talk about money with people who have much more or much less than you.

Katherine Whitehorn

301

The way to make money is to buy when blood is running in the streets.

John D. Rockefeller (1839–1937)

302

I don't know much about being a millionaire, but I'll bet I'd be darling at it.

Dorothy Parker (1893–1967)

303

I don't have a bank account, because I don't know my mother's maiden name.

Paula Poundstone

304

I had plastic surgery last week. I cut up my credit cards.

Henny Youngman

305
Consequences, shmonsequences, as long as I'm rich.
Daffy Duck

306

A foundation is a large body of money surrounded by people who want some.

Dwight Macdonald (1906–1983)

307

The upper crust is a bunch of crumbs held together by dough.

Joseph A. Thomas (1906–1977)

308

I no longer prepare food or drink with more than one ingredient.

Cyra McFadden

309

Eternity is two people and a roast turkey.

James Dent

310

Do you hunt your own truffles or do you hire a pig?

Conversational icebreaker suggested by Jean McClatchy

3 1 1

I refuse to spend my life worrying about what I eat. There is no pleasure worth forgoing just for an extra three years in the geriatric ward.

John Mortimer

3 1 2

I asked the clothing store clerk if she had anything to make me look thinner, and she said, "How about a week in Bangladesh?"

Roseanne Barr

3 1 3

Diets are mainly food for thought.

N. Wylie Jones

3 1 4

Avoid fruits and nuts. You are what you eat.

Garfield (Jim Davis)

3 1 5

I'm on a grapefruit diet. I eat everything but grapefruit.

Chi Chi Rodriguez

3 1 6

In two decades I've lost a total of 789 pounds. I should be hanging from a charm bracelet.

Erma Bombeck

317

The toughest part of being on a diet is shutting up about it.

Gerald Nachman

318

My idea of heaven is a great big baked potato and someone to share it with.

Oprah Winfrey

319

If it tastes good, it's trying to kill you.

Roy Qualley

320

Everything I want is either illegal, immoral, or fattening.

Alexander Woollcott (1887–1943)

3 2 1

Eating an anchovy is like eating an eyebrow.

Unknown

3 2 2

A favorite dish in Kansas is creamed corn on a stick.

Jeff Harms

3 2 3

Meat is murder, but fish is justifiable homicide.

Jeremy Hardy

3 2 4

I smell a rat. Did you bake it or fry it?

Bill Hoest

325

Why should we take up farming when there are so many mongongo nuts in the world?

African Bushman quoted by Jared Diamond

326

You'll be hungry again in an hour.

Fortune cookie opened by Ziggy (Tom Wilson)

327

Your request for no MSG was ignored.

Fortune cookie opened by Merla Zellerbach

328

A vegetarian is a person who won't eat meat unless someone else pays for it.

Al Clethan

329

Cannibals aren't vegetarians, they're humanitarians.

Unknown

330

I'm not a vegetarian because I love animals; I'm a vegetarian because I hate plants.

A. Whitney Brown

331

Never order anything in a vegetarian restaurant that ordinarily would have meat in it.

Tom Parker

332

Where there's smoke, there's toast.

Unknown

333

Never eat anything whose listed ingredients cover more than one-third of the package.

Joseph Leonard

334

I don't eat snails. I prefer fast food.

Strange de Jim

335

It's okay to be fat. So you're fat. Just be fat and shut up about it.

Roseanne Barr

336

Come in, or we'll both starve

Sign in restaurant window

337

I hate to eat and eat and eat and run.

Neila Ross

338

Some people like to eat octopus. Liberals, mostly.

Russell Baker

3 3 9

Do not make a stingy sandwich
Pile the cold-cuts high
Customers should see salami
Coming through the rye.

Allan Sherman (1924–1973)

3 4 0

Plant carrots in January, and you'll never have to eat carrots.

Unknown

3 4 1

Ask not what you can do for your country, ask what's for lunch.

Orson Welles on reaching 300 pounds

3 4 2

Continental breakfasts are very sparse. My advice is to go right to lunch without pausing.

Miss Piggy

3 4 3

Miss Piggy is a boar.

Ed Lucaire

344

The key to a successful restaurant is dressing girls in degrading clothes.

Michael O'Donoghue

345

The food in Yugoslavia is either very good or very bad. One day they served us fried chains.

Mel Brooks

346

Good health makes the practice of virtue more difficult.
John Bunyan (1628–1688)

3 4 7

If you don't take care of your body, where will you live?

Unknown

3 4 8

Your medical tests are in. You're short, fat, and bald.

Ziggy (Tom Wilson)

3 4 9

How can I get sick? I've already had everything.

George Burns

3 5 0

When I told my doctor I couldn't afford an operation, he offered to touch up my X rays.

Henny Youngman

3 5 1

I quit therapy because my analyst was trying to help me behind my back.

Richard Lewis

3 5 2

The art of medicine, like that of war, is murderous and conjectural.

Voltaire (1694–1778)

353

Winston Churchill's habit of guzzling a quart or two a day of good cognac is what saved civilization from the Luftwaffe, Hegelian logic, Wagnerian love-deaths, and potato pancakes.

Charles McCabe (1915–1983)

354

I feel sorry for people who don't drink, because when they get up in the morning, they're not going to feel any better all day.

Frank Sinatra

355

I drink too much. Last time I gave a urine sample there was an olive in it.

Rodney Dangerfield

356

I never took hallucinogenic drugs because I never wanted my consciousness expanded one unnecessary iota.

Fran Lebowitz

357

Politics is a means of preventing people from taking part in what properly concerns them.

Paul Valéry (1871–1945)

358

Politics consists of choosing between the disastrous and the unpalatable.

John Kenneth Galbraith

359

Democracy is the name we give to the people when we need them.

Robert Pellevé, Marquis de Flers (1872–1927)

360

There has never been a good government.

Emma Goldman (1869–1940)

361

No more good must be attempted than the public can bear.

Thomas Jefferson (1743–1826)

362

Thomas Jefferson's slaves loved him so much they called him by a special name: Dad.

Mark Russell

363

When they asked George Washington for his ID, he just took out a quarter.

Steven Wright

364

George Bush is Gerald Ford without the pizzazz.

Pat Paulsen

365

A promising young man should go into politics so that he can go on promising for the rest of his life.

Robert Byrne

366

A politician is a man who approaches every problem with an open mouth.

Adlai Stevenson

367

A politician can appear to have his nose to the grindstone while straddling a fence and keeping both ears to the ground.

Unknown

368

My grandmother's brain was dead, but her heart was still beating. It was the first time we ever had a Democrat in the family.

Emo Philips

369

No matter what your religion, you should try to become a government program, for then you will have everlasting life.

U.S. Representative Lynn Martin

370

Most isms are wasms.

Philosophy professor Gerald Vision

371

We've upped our standards. Up yours.

Campaign slogan by Pat Paulsen

372

If I had known that my son was going to be president of Bolivia [in the 1940s], I would have taught him to read and write.

Enrique Penaranda's mother

373

Being head of state is an extremely thankless job.

Bokassa I, former emperor of the
Central African Republic, while on trial for
infanticide, cannibalism, and torture

374

If Roosevelt were alive today, he'd turn over in his grave.

Samuel Goldwyn (1882–1974)

375

When they circumcised Herbert Samuel, they threw away the wrong part.

David Lloyd George (1863–1945)
on a rival

376

Early today the senator called a spade a spade. He later issued a retraction.

Joe Mirachi

377

Voters want a fraud they can believe in.

Will Durst

378

A penny saved is a Congressional oversight.

Hal Lee Luyah

3 7 9

Are the people who run for president really the best in a country of 240 million? If so, something has happened to the gene pool.

Bob McKenzie

3 8 0

Nonviolence is a flop. The only bigger flop is violence.

Joan Baez

3 8 1

Nonviolence is fine as long as it works.

Malcolm X (1925–1965)

3 8 2

You're not famous until my mother has heard of you.

Jay Leno

3 8 3

The nice thing about being a celebrity is that, if you bore people, they think it's their fault.

Henry Kissinger

3 8 4

A celebrity is a person known to many people he is glad he doesn't know.

H. L. Mencken (1880–1956)

385

They want me on all the television shows now because I did so well on "Celebrity Assholes."

Steve Martin

386

People hate me because I am a multifaceted, talented, wealthy, internationally famous genius.

Jerry Lewis

387

In her last days, Gertrude Stein resembled a spoiled pear.

Gore Vidal

388

I don't like Diane Keaton anymore. She's had way too much therapy.

Patricia Wentz-Daly

389

It's sweeping the country like wildflowers.

Samuel Goldwyn (1882–1974)

390

Nominations in Most Boring Headline contest, sponsored by *The New Republic, 1986:*

> Worthwhile Canadian Initiative (*New York Times*)
> University of Rochester Decides to Keep Name
> (*New York Times*)
> Surprises Unlikely in Indiana (*Chicago Tribune*)
> Economist Dies (*Wisconsin State Journal*)

391

Every hero becomes a bore at last.

Ralph Waldo Emerson (1803–1882)

392

When I played pro football, I never set out to hurt anybody deliberately . . . unless it was, you know, important, like a league game or something.

Dick Butkus

393

Baseball is what we were, football is what we have become.

Mary McGrory

394

Go Braves! And take the Falcons with you.

Bumper sticker in Atlanta

395

Cal quarterback Joe Kapp used to call audibles that were just obscenities directed at the other team. I like that.

Stanford quarterback Greg Ennis

396

Yell for a losing football team:
Let's all jump and scream
For the lavender and cream.

Tom Batiuk

397

Baseball would be a better game if more third basemen got hit in the mouth by line drives.

Dan Jenkins

398

George Steinbrenner is the salt of the earth, and the Yankee players are open wounds.

Scott Osler

399

That's getting a little too close to home.

*Bob Feller on hearing that a foul ball
hit his mother*

400

I'm not going to buy my kids an encyclopedia. Let them walk to school like I did.

Another thing never said by Yogi Berra

401

Pro basketball has turned into Wrestlemania, which is why I like college basketball and high school basketball. Actually, it's why I like baseball.

Frank Layden

402

No comment.

*Doug Moe on hearing that he had been voted
the most quotable coach in the
National Basketball Association*

403

If you are caught on a golf course during a storm and are afraid of lightning, hold up a 1-iron. Not even God can hit a 1-iron.

Lee Trevino

404

Skiing combines outdoor fun with knocking down trees with your face.

Dave Barry

405

If you are going to try cross-country skiing, start with a small country.

From "Saturday Night Live"

406

Yell for a Virginia high school:

> We don't drink!
> We don't smoke!
> Norfolk!

Unknown

407

Fishing is a delusion entirely surrounded by liars in old clothes.

Don Marquis (1878–1937)

408

I bet on a horse at ten to one. It didn't come in until half-past five.

Henny Youngman

409

A good sport has to lose to prove it.

Unknown

410

As for bowling, how good can a thing be if it has to be done in an alley?

John Grigsby's ex-wife

411

When I feel athletic, I go to a sports bar.

Paul Clisura

4 1 2

Curiosity killed the cat, but for a while I was a suspect.

Steven Wright

4 1 3

It took me an hour to bury the cat, because it wouldn't stop moving.

From "The Monty Python Show"

4 1 4

Being a newspaper columnist is like being married to a nymphomaniac. It's great for the first two weeks.

Lewis Grizzard

4 1 5

As a novelist, I tell stories, and people give me money. Then financial planners tell me stories, and I give them money.

Martin Cruz Smith

4 1 6

The cure for writer's cramp is writer's block.

Inigo DeLeon

4 1 7

A painter can hang his pictures, but a writer can only hang himself.

Edward Dahlberg (1900–1977)

418

The multitude of books is a great evil. There is no limit to this fever for writing.

Martin Luther (1483–1546)

419

As she fell face down into the black muck of the mud-wrestling pit, her sweaty 300-pound opponent muttering soft curses in Latin on top of her, Sister Marie thought, "There is no doubt about it; the Pope has betrayed me."

Richard Savastio
Entry in San Jose State's bad writing contest, 1983

420

Desiree, the first female ape to go up in space, winked at me slyly and pouted her thick, rubbery lips unmistakably—the first of many such advances during what would prove to be the longest, most memorable space voyage of my career.

Martha Simpson
Entry in San Jose State's bad writing contest, 1985

421

Jake liked his women the way he liked his kiwi fruit; sweet yet tart, firm-fleshed yet yielding to the touch, and covered with short brown fuzzy hair.

Gretchen Schmidt
Entry in San Jose State's bad writing contest, 1989

422

Nice guys can't write.

Literary agent Knox Burger

423

If the doctor told me I had only six minutes to live, I'd type a little faster.

Isaac Asimov

424

Writing books is certainly a most unpleasant occupation. It is lonesome, unsanitary, and maddening. Many authors go crazy.

H. L. Mencken (1880–1956)

425

A blank page is God's way of showing you how hard it is to be God.

Unknown

426

Either a writer doesn't want to talk about his work, or he talks about it more than you want.

Anatole Broyard

4 2 7

In Ireland, a writer is looked upon as a failed conversationalist.

Unknown

4 2 8

To call Richard Brautigan's poetry doggerel is an insult
to the entire canine world.

Lazlo Coakley

4 2 9

I am here to live out loud.

Emile Zola (1840–1902)

430
I sound my barbaric yawp from the rooftops of the world.
Walt Whitman (1819–1892)

431
Nothing stinks like a pile of unpublished writing.
Sylvia Plath (1932–1963)

432
No passion in the world is equal to the passion to alter someone else's draft.
H. G. Wells (1866–1946)

433
Having your book turned into a movie is like seeing your oxen turned into bouillon cubes.
John LeCarré

434
Writing is a profession in which you have to keep proving your talent to people who have none.
Jules Renard (1864–1910)

435
The relationship of editor to author is knife to throat.
Unknown

436

If I had more time, I would write a shorter letter.

Blaise Pascal (1623–1662)

437

Reading this book is like waiting for the first shoe to drop.

Ralph Novak

438

A book must be an ice ax to break the frozen sea within us.

Franz Kafka (1883–1924)

439

The New York Times Book Review is alive with the sound of axes grinding.

Gore Vidal

440

JFK—The Man and the Airport

Somebody's suggested book title

441

Nine-tenths of all existing books are nonsense.

Benjamin Disraeli (1804–1881)

442

Books for general reading always smell bad; the odor of common people hangs about them.

Friedrich Nietzsche (1844–1900)

Nietzsche was stupid and abnormal.

Leo Tolstoy (1828–1910)

[Tolstoy's *War and Peace* and *Anna Karenina* are] loose, baggy monsters.

Henry James (1843–1916)

Henry James writes fiction as if it were a painful duty.

Oscar Wilde (1854–1900)

443

I hate books, for they only teach people to talk about what they don't understand.

Jean-Jacques Rousseau (1712–1778)

444

Books should be tried by a judge and jury as though they were crimes.

Samuel Butler (1835–1902)

445

Has the net effect of the invention of printing been good or bad? I haven't the slightest idea and neither has anyone else. As well ask whether it was a good or a bad plan to give over so much of the world's space to oceans.

H. L. Mencken (1880–1956)

446

Autobiography is a preemptive strike against biographers.

Barbara Grizzuti Harrison

447

I haven't read any of the autobiographies about me.

Liz Taylor

448

I always read the last page of a book first so that if I die before I finish I'll know how it turned out.

Nora Ephron

449

I'm thirty years old, but I read at the thirty-four-year-old level.

Dana Carvey

450

When you watch television, you never see people watching television. We love television because it brings us a world in which television does not exist.

Barbara Ehrenreich

451

Hear no evil, speak no evil, see no evil, and you'll never be a television anchorman.

Dan Rather

452

Imagine what it would be like if TV actually were good. It would be the end of everything we know.

Marvin Minsky

453
America is a mistake, a giant mistake.
Sigmund Freud (1856–1939)

454
Making duplicate copies and computer printouts of things no one wanted even one of in the first place is giving America a new sense of purpose.
Andy Rooney

455
Americans will put up with anything provided it doesn't block traffic.
Dan Rather

456
Tips for Americans traveling abroad:
    —Carry the Koran
    —Paint a red dot on your forehead
    —Wear sandals
    —Never ask how the Mets are doing.
Mark Russell

457
The shortest distance between two points is usually under repair.
Unknown

458

If all the cars in the United States were placed end to end, it would probably be Labor Day Weekend.

Doug Larson

459

Parking is such street sorrow.

Herb Caen

460

The guy who invented the first wheel was an idiot. The guy who invented the other three, *he* was a genius.

Sid Caesar

461

A hick town is one in which there is no place to go where you shouldn't be.

Alexander Woollcott (1887–1943)

462
All creative people should be required to leave California for three months every year.

Gloria Swanson (1899–1983)

463
In some parts of the world, people still pray in the streets. In this country they're called pedestrians.

Gloria Pitzer

464
Nebraska is proof that Hell is full, and the dead walk the earth.

Liz Winston

465
You can always tell a Texan, but not much.

Unknown

466

Texans are proof that the world was populated by aliens.

Cynthia Nelms

467

Canada is the vichyssoise of nations—it's cold, half French, and difficult to stir.

Stuart Keate

468

I moved to Florida because you don't have to shovel water.

James "The Amazing" Randi

469

In Buffalo, suicide is redundant.

From A Chorus Line

470

Why don't some people just shoot themselves in the head the day they are born?

Arkady Renko

471

In Green Bay, Wisconsin, ten bowling shirts are considered a great wardrobe.

Greg Koch

472

Not as bad as you might have imagined.
Motto suggested for New Jersey by Calvin Trillin

473

Preferable to Youngstown.
Motto suggested for Akron, Ohio, by Calvin Trillin

474

A person who speaks good English in New York sounds
like a foreigner.

Jackie Mason

475

New York is an exciting town where something is happening all the time, most of it unsolved.

Johnny Carson

476

An interesting thing about New York City is that the
subways run through the sewers.

Garrison Keillor

477

On a New York subway you get fined for spitting, but you can throw up for nothing.

Lewis Grizzard

478

New York City is filled with the same kind of people I left New Jersey to get away from.

Fran Lebowitz

479

On New Year's Eve, people in New Jersey stay up till midnight and watch their hopes drop.

Richard Lewis

480

If you want to be safe on the streets at night, carry a projector and slides of your last vacation.

Helen Mundis

481

The top TV shows in Russia are "Bowling for Food" and "Wheel of Torture."

Yakov Smirnoff

482

The Russians love Brooke Shields because her eyebrows remind them of Leonid Brezhnev.

Robin Williams

483

Art is about making something out of nothing and selling it.

Frank Zappa

484

I do not seek, I find.

Pablo Picasso (1881–1973)

485

A thing of beauty is a joy for a while.

Hal Lee Luyah

486

I am a critic—as essential to the theater as ants to a picnic.

Joseph Mankiewicz

487

Without music, life would be a mistake.

Friedrich Nietzsche (1844–1900)

488

I have played over the music of that scoundrel Brahms. What a giftless bastard!

Peter Ilyich Tchaikovsky (1840–1893)

489

If Beethoven had been killed in a plane crash at the age of twenty-two, it would have changed the history of music . . . and of aviation.

Tom Stoppard

490

Bach in an hour. Offenbach sooner.

Sign on music store door

491

I was involved in the Great Folk Music Scare back in the sixties, when it almost caught on.

Martin Mull

492

We aren't worried about posterity; we want it to sound good right now.

Duke Ellington (1899–1974)

493

SONG TITLES:

"I Can't Get Over a Man like You, So You'll Have to Answer the Phone."

Melody Anne

"You're the Only Thing That's Rising in the Sour Dough of Life."

Maxine Edwards

"If I Had to Do It All Over Again, I'd Do It All Over You."

Abe Burrows

"Don't Sit Under the Apple Tree with Anyone Else but Me."

Isaac Newton (1642–1727), perhaps?

"I Gave Her a Ring, and She Gave Me the Finger."

Unknown

"I Can't Fall Asleep Since You Sat on My Pillow Last Night."

David E. Ortman

494

If it weren't for the Japanese and Germans, we wouldn't have any good war movies.

Stanley Ralph Ross

495

Old soldiers never die, just young ones.

Graffito

496

War is the unfolding of miscalculations.

Barbara Tuchman (1912–1989)

497

The war situation has developed not necessarily to Japan's advantage.

Emperor Hirohito (1901–1989), after losing two cities to atom bombs

498

Violence never solved anything.
Genghis Khan (1162–1227), according to Bob Lee

499

A doctor could make a million dollars if he could figure out a way to bring a boy into the world without a trigger finger.

Arthur Miller

500

When a thing is funny, search it carefully for a hidden truth.

George Bernard Shaw (1856–1950)

501

It's hard to be funny when you have to be clean.
Mae West (1892–1980)

502

I never had a sense of humor. What started me in a theatrical direction was finding at a very early age that I had a talent. I could impersonate chickens. Buk buk buk bacagh.

Jonathan Miller

503

You don't stop laughing because you grow old; you grow old because you stop laughing.

Michael Pritchard

504

Old age comes at a bad time.

Sue Banducci

505

After a certain age, if you don't wake up aching in every joint, you are probably dead.

Tommy Mein

506

If you survive long enough, you're revered—rather like an old building.

Katharine Hepburn

507

You know you're getting old when you stoop to tie your shoes and wonder what else you can do while you're down there.

George Burns

508

Old age means realizing you will never own all the dogs you wanted to.

Joe Gores

509

Children are a great comfort in your old age—and they help you reach it faster, too.

Lionel Kauffman

510

My grandmother started walking five miles a day when she was sixty. She's ninety-seven now, and we don't know where the hell she is.

Ellen DeGeneris

511

When I was young, the Dead Sea was still alive.

George Burns

512

My health is good; it's my age that's bad.

Ray Acuff at eighty-three

513

An old man in love is like a flower in winter.

Portuguese proverb

514

My parents didn't want to move to Florida, but they turned sixty, and it was the law.

Jerry Seinfeld

5 1 5

Never ask old people how they are if you have anything else to do that day.

Joe Restivo

5 1 6

Death is not the end; there remains the litigation.

Ambrose Bierce (1842–1914)

5 1 7

If you don't go to other people's funerals, they won't go to yours.

Unknown

5 1 8

Death is nature's way of saying, "Your table is ready."

Robin Williams

5 1 9

Grave, n. A place in which the dead are laid to await the coming of the medical student.

Ambrose Bierce (1842–1914)

5 2 0

The old neighborhood has changed. Hurley Brothers Funeral Home is now called Death 'n' Things.

Elmore Leonard

521

No matter how rich you become, how famous or powerful, when you die the size of your funeral will still pretty much depend on the weather.

Michael Pritchard

522

Death sneaks up on you like a windshield sneaks up on a bug.

Unknown

523

The wages of sin are death, but by the time taxes are taken out, it's just sort of a tired feeling.

Paula Poundstone

524

Get out of here and leave me alone. Last words are for fools who haven't said enough already.

Last words of Karl Marx (1818–1883), allegedly

525

Errol Flynn died on a seventy-foot yacht with a seventeen-year-old girl. Walter's always wanted to go that way, but he's going to settle for a seventeen-footer and a seventy-year-old.

Mrs. Walter Cronkite

526

I don't want to achieve immortality by being inducted into baseball's Hall of Fame. I want to achieve immortality by not dying.

Leo Durocher at eighty-one

527

LAST WILL AND TESTAMENT:
I owe much, I have nothing, the rest I leave to the poor.

Rabelais (1494–1553)

528

Exercise daily. Eat wisely. Die anyway.

Unknown

PART THREE

One thing and another

529

I really didn't say everything I said.

Yogi Berra

530

Next to the originator of a great quote is the first quoter of it.

Ralph Waldo Emerson (1803–1882)

531

A committee is a group of important individuals who singly can do nothing but who can together agree that nothing can be done.

Fred Allen (1894–1956)

532

Diplomacy is the art of letting someone else have your way.

Unknown

533

Palm Springs University—more than one hundred degrees available.

Unknown

534

The trouble with England is that it's all pomp and no circumstance.

From the 1954 movie Beat the Devil

535

You can be sincere and still be stupid.

Unknown

536

I felt sorry for myself because I had no hands until I met a man who had no chips.

Kent G. Andersson

537

Make a bet every day, otherwise you might walk around lucky and never know it.

Jimmy Jones

538

I bear no grudges. I have a mind that retains nothing.

Bette Midler

539

Go to the zoo and enlist. Shave your neighbor's dog. Yo! Dump your spaghetti on that guy's head.

Inside the ears of crazy people with cartoonist Gary Larson

540

Two leaps per chasm is fatal.

Chinese proverb

541

People who sell macramé should be dyed a natural color and hung out to dry.

Calvin Trillin

542

The only thing standing between you and a watery grave is your wits, and that's not my idea of adequate protection.

From the movie Beat the Devil, *1954*

543

If the rich could hire people to die for them, the poor could make a wonderful living.

Jewish proverb

544

My karma ran over your dogma.

Unknown

545

Flying is hours and hours of boredom sprinkled with a few seconds of sheer terror.

Gregory "Pappy" Boyington

546

There is nothing worse than a "now" look with a "then" face.

Dave Falk

547

Prejudices save time.

Robert Byrne

548

The prime purpose of eloquence is to keep other people from talking.

Louis Vermeil

549

There are some things only intellectuals are crazy enough to believe.

George Orwell (1903–1950)

550

People performing mime in public should be subject to citizen's arrest on the theory that the normal First Amendment protection of free speech has in effect been waived by someone who has formally adopted a policy of not speaking.

Calvin Trillin

551

If you shoot at mimes, should you use a silencer?

Steven Wright

552

It is easier for a camel to pass through the eye of a needle if it is lightly greased.

John Nesvig

553

Time flies like an arrow.
Fruit flies like a banana.

Lisa Grossman

554

She had the Midas touch. Everything she touched
turned into a muffler.

Lisa Smerling

555

I've always found paranoia to be a perfectly defensible
position.

Pat Conroy

556

The early worm gets caught.

John Igo

557

Familiarity breeds contempt, but you can't breed without familiarity.

Maxim Kavolik

558

Familiarity breeds children.

Mark Twain (1835–1910)

559

Two heads are better than none.

Jean Green

560

The best car safety device is a rear-view mirror with a cop in it.

Dudley Moore

561

Leroy is a self-made man, which shows what happens when you don't follow directions.

Cartoon caption by Bill Hoest

562

If Noah had been truly wise
He would have swatted those two flies.

H. Castle

563

The fuchsia is the world's most carefully spelled flower.

Jimmy Barnes

564

I had a prejudice against the British until I discovered
that fifty percent of them were female.

Raymond Floyd

565

Washington Irving.
Answer to the question "Who was the first president,
Max?"

Steve Allen's Question Man

566

Any other last requests?
Answer to the question "Would you mind not smoking?"

Unknown

567

Wise men talk because they have something to say; fools talk because they have to say something.

Plato (427–347 B.C.)

Plato was a bore.

Friedrich Nietzsche (1844–1900)

568

Nietzsche is pietsche,
But Sartre is smartre.

Unknown

Nietzsche was stupid and abnormal.

Leo Tolstoy (1828–1910)

569

Help! I'm being held prisoner by my heredity and environment!

Dennis Allen

570

Drawing on my fine command of the English language, I said nothing.

Robert Benchley (1889–1945)

5 7 1

GREAT MOMENTS IN HISTORY:
> January 17, 1821: First recorded incident of a bird
> mistaking a civil servant for a statue.

Second Recorded Incident

572

The days of the digital watch are numbered.

Tom Stoppard

573

I have never seen a situation so dismal that a policeman couldn't make it worse.

Brendan Behan (1923–1964)

574

A clear conscience is often the sign of a bad memory.

Unknown

575

Praise does wonders for the sense of hearing.

Unknown

576

If I die, I forgive you; if I live, we'll see.

Spanish proverb

577

A pedestrian is a man whose son is home from college.

Unknown

578

Most conversations are simply monologues delivered in the presence of witnesses.

Margaret Millar

5 7 9
She's descended from a long line her mother listened to.
Gypsy Rose Lee (1914–1970)

5 8 0
Confusion is always the most honest response.
Marty Indik

5 8 1
I'm not confused, I'm just well-mixed.
Robert Frost (1874–1963)

5 8 2
Does the name Pavlov ring a bell?
Unknown

5 8 3
If at first you don't succeed, you're about average.
Unknown

5 8 4
Who's Bob?
What to reply to a person who says, "I'm so confused, Bob."
John Grimes

585

I was walking down the street wearing glasses when the prescription ran out.

Steven Wright

586

When I can no longer bear to think of the victims of broken homes, I begin to think of the victims of intact ones.

Peter De Vries

587

Have you always been a Negro or are you just trying to be fashionable?

From the television series "Julia"

588

If I had permission to do everything, I wouldn't want to do anything.

The one best thing Joe Palen ever said

589

Thou shalt not admit adultery.

Hal Lee Luyah

590

There's a deception to every rule.

Hal Lee Luyah

591

Easy Street is a blind alley.

Unknown

592

To disagree with three-fourths of the British public is one of the first requisites of sanity.

Oscar Wilde (1854–1900)

593

There are two kinds of complainers, men and women.

Unknown

594

There are two kinds of people, those who finish what they start and so on.

Robert Byrne

595

A hat should be taken off when you greet a lady and left off for the rest of your life. Nothing looks more stupid than a hat.

P. J. O'Rourke

596

Toys are made in heaven, batteries are made in hell.

Tom Robbins

597

I bought some batteries, but they weren't included.

Steven Wright

598

There's never enough time to do all the nothing you want.

Bill Watterson

599

Quote me if I'm wrong.

Unknown

600

The only thing I can't stand is discomfort.

Gloria Steinem

601

Oh, well, half of one, six dozen of the other.

Joe Garagiola

602

The trouble with dawn is that it comes too early in the day.

Susan Richman

603

When I think over what I have said, I envy dumb people.

Seneca (4 B.C.–A.D. 65)

604

What kills a skunk is the publicity it gives itself.

Abraham Lincoln (1809–1865)

605

If you have any problems at all, don't hesitate to shut up.

Robert Mankoff

606

Fear is that little darkroom where negatives are developed.

Michael Pritchard

607

Last night somebody broke into my apartment and replaced everything with exact duplicates. When I pointed it out to my roommate, he said, "Do I know you?"

Steven Wright

608

The town where I grew up has a zip code of E-I-E-I-O.

Martin Mull

609

They should put expiration dates on clothes so we would know when they go out of style.

Garry Shandling

610

Confidence is always overconfidence.

Robert Byrne

611

Lucy: Do you think anybody ever really changes?
Linus: I've changed a lot in the last year.
Lucy: I mean for the better.

Charles Schulz

612

The major concerns of Emily Litella:
1. Conservation of national race horses
2. Violins on television
3. Soviet jewelry
4. Endangered feces.

Gilda Radner (1946–1989)

613

Let a smile be your umbrella, because you're going to get soaked anyway.

Unknown

614

Gravity isn't easy, but it's the law.

Unknown

615

Queen Elizabeth is the whitest person in the world.

Bette Midler

616

Everybody is who he was in high school.

Calvin Trillin

617

I got kicked out of ballet class because I pulled a groin muscle, even though it wasn't mine.

Rita Rudner

618

Open your mouth only to change feet.

Stanley Ralph Ross

619

Gentiles are people who eat mayonnaise for no reason.

Robin Williams

620

Some guy hit my fender, and I said to him, "Be fruitful and multiply," but not in those words.

Woody Allen

621

The turn of the century will probably be made by a woman.

Unknown

622

Isn't Muamar Khadafy the sound a cow makes when sneezing?

Dave Barry

623

All Ireland is washed by the Gulf Stream, except my wife's family.

Brendan Behan (1923–1964)

624

Keep things as they are—vote for the Sado-Masochistic Party.

Unknown

625

He who lives far from neighbors may safely praise himself.

Erasmus (1466–1536)

626

Astrology is not an art, it is a disease.

Maimonides (1135–1204)

627

The closest anyone ever comes to perfection is on a job application form.

Unknown

628

Capital punishment is our society's recognition of the sanctity of human life.

Senator Orrin Hatch of Utah

629

So much work, so few women to do it.

Unknown

630

I'm not a Jew. I'm Jew*ish*. I don't go the whole hog.

Jonathan Miller

631

On Golden Blond.

Porn video title

632

I locked my keys in the car and had to break the windshield to get my wife out.

Red Skelton

633

Prostitution, like acting, is being ruined by amateurs.

Alexander Woollcott (1887–1943)

634

A good husband is healthy and absent.

Japanese proverb

635

WYMI—the all-philosophy radio station.

Mike Dugan

636

No man should plant more garden than his wife can hoe.

Old saying

637

If you have something of importance to say, for God's sake start at the end.

Sarah Jeannette Duncan

Sources, References, and Notes

Quotes are listed here only when there is something useful to add; the details given are all I have. Readers with fuller information are urged to write to me in care of Scribner, 1230 Avenue of the Americas, New York, New York 10020.

Quotation
Number

1. EB as quoted by Charles Roos in *The Rocky Mountain News*, August 31, 1986.

2. MD as quoted in *Rave* magazine, November 1986.

3. AE as quoted by Herb Caen in *The San Francisco Chronicle*, May 16, 1989.

4. WHA as quoted by Dear Abby in her column, May 16, 1988.

8. MR in the Introduction to his *The Best of Modern Humor*, Knopf, 1983.

10. LT and JW in *The Search for Intelligent Life in the Universe.*

12. Russian proverb quoted by R. W. Payne in *A Stress Analysis of a Strapless Evening Gown*, 1963.

14. RR as quoted by Alec Guinness in his autobiography, 1986.

15. Unknown, thanks to Rothwell D. Mason.

16. Unknown, as quoted in *The Hayward Daily Review*, February 18, 1986.

25. LW in a letter to RB.

27. Unknown, thanks to Marqua Lee Brunette.

30. KN on "Saturday Night Live."

32. EP, thanks to R. G. Fisher.

33. EW as quoted in *The San Francisco Chronicle*, April 8, 1989.

35. Unknown, thanks to Eliza Sunneland.

36. FK as quoted by Leah Garchick in *The San Francisco Chronicle*, August 21, 1988.

39. Osage saying thanks to Bob Lee.

40. KN as quoted by Herb Caen in *The San Francisco Chronicle*, August 10, 1985.

41. RWW as quoted in *The Journal of Irreproducible Results*, 1985.

42. AS in *The San Francisco Examiner.*

49. SR, thanks to C. Wesley Eicole, M. D.

51. LT and JW in *The Search for Intelligent Life in the Universe.*

53. SG as quoted by A. Scott Berg in *Goldwyn*, 1989.

54. Irish saying, thanks to Richard Meehan.
58. Unknown, thanks to Stephan Adams.
61. MF as quoted in *The Journal of Irreproducible Results*, 1985.
68. FW in *Down Among the Women*.
70. MW in the movie *Belle of the Nineties*, 1934.
75. BY, thanks to Robert C. Smith.
76. GU, thanks to Johnson Letellier.
78. JM in *The Chicago Sun-Times*, November 9, 1986.
81. RS in *The San Francisco Chronicle*, August 15, 1988.
88. DB is a syndicated columnist for *The Miami Herald*.
89. From TU's television show, May 5, 1989.
90. AH is a standup comedian.
92. PD as quoted by Milton Berle in *B.S. I Love You*, McGraw-Hill, 1988.
94. TS is a standup comedian.
95. SL, thanks to Emily Smith.
96. RB as quoted by Jon Carroll in *The San Francisco Chronicle*, April 1, 1986.
102. KB in a letter from the front, 1943.
103. JS, thanks to John Diones.
106. AL, thanks to John Grigsby.
109. WA in *The Lunatic's Tale*, 1986.
110. JBB is a syndicated columnist.
111. RR is a standup comedian.
112. DP in *A Telephone Call*.
113. JR is a standup comedian.
115. JT is a standup comedian.
117. MP writes for *The Providence Journal*.
134. Thanks to Dr. Win Bottom.
140. WA in the movie *Manhattan*, 1979.
142. JH in *Good as Gold*, 1979.
145. NS in *Brighton Beach Memoirs*, 1986.
146. WA in the movie *A Midsummer Night's Sex Comedy*, 1982.
147. From the show that aired October 7, 1987.
148. LB is a standup comedian.
150. LG in *Elvis Is Dead and I Don't Feel So Good Myself*, 1987.
152. Censors cut this MW line from *Every Day's a Holiday*, 1937.
153. JK in *People Will Talk*, 1986.
154. WD is a standup comedian.
155. KW in *Billy Liar on the Moon*, 1975.
158. From MG's cartoon strip "Life Is Hell."
161. AC is a standup comedian.
166. GG in *Playboy*, June 1989.
167. WA in *The Lunatic's Tale*, 1986.
177. Screenplay by Laurie Craig.
178. DB in *Florida* magazine.
179. DC is a standup comedian.

184. Q is a French writer quoted by Peter De Vries in *Into Your Tent I'll Creep, 1971.*

188. Unknown, thanks to Robert G. Smith.

192. RLS, thanks to Susan Trott.

194. From the television show "All in the Family."

195. SV is a standup comedian.

198. ML as quoted by Jeanne Wearing on KPOF, Denver, October 1986.

199. MJF as quoted by Leah Garchick in *The San Francisco Chronicle*, January 27, 1988.

200. BC in *Love and Marriage*, 1989.

201. RD in *Rave*, November 1986.

205. WA in *The Lunatic's Tale*, 1986.

207. SJ as quoted by Herb Caen in *The San Francisco Chronicle*, February 3, 1986.

208. TG as quoted by Herb Caen in *The San Francisco Chronicle*, February 3, 1986.

212. HC in *The San Francisco Chronicle*, June 13, 1986.

227. GK in a lecture at College of Marin (Kentfield, California), January 12, 1989.

229. EP as quoted by Guy Trebay in *The Village Voice*, January 7, 1985.

234. CL is a standup comedian.

239. FO'C as quoted by Mark Childress in *The New York Times Book Review*, May 21, 1989.

242. BH on "The Tonight Show," January 2, 1987.

243. RR is a standup comedian.

247. Unknown, thanks to Henry Crossfield.

248. RS's grandfather as quoted in RS's *Yes, My Darling Daughter,* 1976.

250. PK as quoted by J. Bryan, III in *Hodgepodge Two,* Atheneum, 1989.

251. Unknown, as quoted by Herb Caen in *The San Francisco Chronicle,* December 22, 1987.

258. Tribesman quoted by Margaret Mead in *Male and Female,* 1949.

264. CL is a standup comedian.

265. MS is a standup comedian.

268. CC, thanks to Bill McCollough.

270. TE as quoted by D. Fischer in *Historians' Fallacies,* 1970.

271. JM in *The Rocky Mountain News.*

272. PP is a standup comedian.

273. Unknown, as quoted by Ray Orrock in *The Hayward Daily Review*, February 28, 1986.

276. BA as quoted by Herb Caen in *The San Francisco Chronicle*, May 6, 1986.

277. MD, thanks to John Grigsby.

281. BL is a sports columnist for the *Philadelphia Inquirer.*

283. BC as quoted by Rob Morse in *The San Francisco Examiner*, June 1, 1986.

289. Unknown, thanks to Lee Simon.
290. GS as quoted by Herb Caen, *The San Francisco Chronicle*, December 22, 1987.
292. From TA's 1975 movie *Lies My Father Told Me*.
299. RSW in *The San Francisco Chronicle*, June 5, 1986.
305. DD, thanks to Marty Indik.
306. DM as quoted in *The New York Times Book Review*, December 29, 1985.
308. CM in *The San Francisco Examiner*, July 20, 1986.
310. JM in *The San Francisco Chronicle*, November 30, 1988.
313. NWJ in a letter to RB.
317. GN in *The San Francisco Chronicle*, May 18, 1989.
318. OW in *People*, March 6, 1989.
319. RQ, Cyra McFadden's former stepfather, as quoted in her *Rain or Shine*, 1986.
320. AW, thanks to Robert G. Smith.
322. JH is a standup comedian.
323. JH, thanks to Marty Indik.
325. Tribesman quoted by Jared Diamond in *Discover*, May 1987.
328. AC is a standup comedian.
330. AWB is a standup comedian.
333. JL as quoted by Herb Caen in *The San Francisco Chronicle*, March 3, 1986.
334. SJ as quoted by Herb Caen in *The San Francisco Chronicle*, July 10, 1988.
342. MP as quoted in *Miss Piggy's Guide to Life*, as told to Henry Beard, 1981.
343. EL to RB.
344. MO'D as quoted by Paul Slansky in *Playboy*, 1989.
345. MB as quoted in *Playboy*, 1975.
346. JB as quoted by Edward S. Gifford, Jr., in *He's My Boy*, 1962.
347. Unknown, thanks to Jim Eason.
358. JKG in *Ambassador's Journal*, 1969.
359. RP in *L'Habit Vert*, 1912.
368. EP as quoted by Guy Trebay in *The Village Voice*, January 7, 1985.
369. On Cable News Network, April 26, 1988.
370. GV, thanks to Stefan D. Koch, who was his student at Temple University.
372. As quoted by Carlos Fuentes in *The New York Times Book Review*, April 6, 1986.
373. As quoted by Dale McFeathers of the Scripps Howard News Service.
376. Cartoon caption by JM in *The New Yorker*, April 3, 1989.

379. BM is a television newsman in Oakland, California.

382. JL as quoted in *Esquire*, December 1986.

383. HK as quoted in *The Miami Herald*, January 3, 1987.

386. JL as quoted in *Esquire*, December 1986.

387. GV, thanks to Bill Weiss.

388. PW-D to RB.

389. SG as quoted in *The Moguls* by Norman Zierold, 1969.

392. DB, thanks to Johnson Letellier.

393. MM as quoted by Herb Caen in *The San Francisco Chronicle*, January 1, 1985.

395. GE as quoted by Jake Curtis in *The San Francisco Chronicle*, August 31, 1987.

396. TB in his cartoon strip "Funky Winkerbean."

397. DJ as quoted in *Boring Stuff* by Alan Caruba.

398. SO in *The Los Angeles Times*, November 1988.

399. From a column by Art Rosenbaum in *The San Francisco Chronicle*, January 20, 1988.

403. LT on "The Tonight Show," January 1985.

406. I remember this pep yell from the 1950s.

408. HY as quoted by Milton Berle in *B.S. I Love You*, 1988.

409. Unknown, thanks to Jason Olive.

411. PC as quoted by Herb Caen in *The San Francisco Chronicle*, July 11, 1988.

414. LG, thanks to Susan Richman.

415. MCS to RB.

416. ID as quoted by Herb Caen in *The San Francisco Chronicle*, August 15, 1988.

418. ML in *Table Talk*.

424. HLM at the 1940 convention of the American Booksellers Association.

425. Unknown, as quoted by Milton Berle in *B.S. I Love You*, 1988.

426. AB in *The New York Times Book Review*, May 21, 1989.

428. LC in a letter to *The San Francisco Chronicle*, February 9, 1988.

432. HGW as quoted by Macdonald Carey in *The Writers Guild of America News*, May 1986.

433. JL, thanks to Karl Fulves.

435. Unknown, thanks to Karl Fulves.

437. RN in *People* reviewing a book by Judith Michael.

438. FK in a letter written when he was twenty.

439. GV as quoted by David Show in *The Los Angeles Times*, December 12, 1985.

441. BD in *Lothair*, 1870.

442. FN in *Beyond Good and Evil*.

443. JJR in *Emile*.

444. SB in *Note Books*.

445. HLM at the 1940 convention of the American Booksellers Association.

446. BGH on the television program "Bookmark," April 2, 1989.

447. LT on "The Donahue Show," February 12, 1988.

448. A line from the movie *When Harry Met Sally*, 1989, screenplay by NE.

450. BE in *Mother Jones*.

451. DR as quoted in *The National Enquirer*, January 7, 1987.

452. MM as quoted in *The New York Times Book Review*, September 27, 1987.

455. DR, thanks to Bob Cudmore.

457. Unknown, as quoted by Ray Orrock in *The Hayward Daily Review*.

460. SC as quoted by Milton Berle in *B.S. I Love You*, 1988.

463. GP, thanks to John Grigsby.

465. Unknown, thanks to Jim Eason.

468. JR as quoted in *Money* magazine, September 1986.

470. AR is a character in *Gorky Park* (1981) and *Polar Star* (1989), novels by Martin Cruz Smith published by Random House.

471. GK made the remark after being traded by the Green Bay Packers to the Miami Dolphins.

475. JC on his 25th Anniversary Show, September 25, 1986.

476. From a lecture by GK at College of Marin (Kentfield, California), January 12, 1989.

478. FL as quoted in *Rave*, November 1986.

481. YS as quoted in *Rave*, November 1986.

483. FZ in *Money* magazine, September 1986.

486. From JM's 1950 screenplay for *All About Eve*, a movie based on a short story by Mary Orr.

490. As quoted by Joseph Gallagher in *The Baltimore Sun*, October 12, 1988.

495. Graffito, thanks to Stefan D. Koch.

497. H as quoted by John Toland in *The Rising Sun*; thanks to Robert Gordon.

498. GK, thanks to Bob Lee.

502. JM quoted in *The New Yorker*, April 17, 1989.

503. MP, thanks to Jim Eason.

504. SB as quoted by Herb Caen in *The San Francisco Chronicle*, April 9, 1989.

505. TM as quoted by Herb Caen in *The San Francisco Chronicle*, January 6, 1986.

510. ED is a standup comedian.

520. EL in *Glitz*.

522. Unknown, thanks to Stefan D. Koch.

524. KM, thanks to Jason Olive.

526. LD as quoted in *The San Francisco Chronicle*, July 27, 1989.

529. YB as quoted by George Will in *Newsweek*, April 14, 1986.

531. FA as quoted by J. Bryan, III in *Merry Gentlemen (and One Lady)*, 1985.

532. Unknown, thanks to Susan Richman.

534. Screenplay by Truman Capote and John Huston.

537. JJ is a horse trainer quoted by William Murray in *When the Fat Man Sings*, 1987.

540. Chinese proverb thanks to Michele Plunkett.

542. Screenplay by Truman Capote and John Huston.

545. GB shot down twenty-four Japanese planes in WWII.

546. DF as quoted by Herb Caen in *The San Francisco Chronicle*, December 6, 1987.

548. LV as quoted in *Forbes*, April 17, 1987.

549. GO as quoted by Alexander Bloom in *Prodigal Sons,* Oxford University Press, 1986.

550. CT in *The New Yorker*, May 15, 1989.

552. JN, thanks to Johnson Letellier.

554. LS, thanks to Kris Chotzinoff.

555. PC, from his novel *Prince of Tides*, 1986.

557. MK as quoted in *Perfect Pitch* by Nicolas Slonimsky, 1988.

559. JG, thanks to Susan Richman.

562. HC, thanks to John Grigsby.

563. JB as quoted by Herb Caen in *The San Francisco Chronicle*, August 9, 1988.

567. P, thanks to Bill McCollough.

569. DA in a letter to RB.

581. RF as quoted by Charles Roos in *The Rocky Mountain News*, September 26, 1986.

582. Unknown, thanks to Jason Olive.

587. Screenwriter: Alvin Sargent. Thanks to Jack Mingo.

591. Unknown, thanks to Jason Olive.

595. PJO'R in *Modern Manners*, 1988.

596. TR as quoted in *The San Francisco Examiner*, September 28, 1987. Thanks to Michael O. Stearns.

600. GS, thanks to Blair Chotzinoff.

611. From a "Peanuts" comic strip, March 28, 1989.

612. GR on "Saturday Night Live."

617. RR is a standup comedian.

621. The quote is sometimes credited to the late film star Alan Ladd.

622. DB as quoted by Herb Caen in *The San Francisco Chronicle*, April 22, 1986.

625. E in *In Praise of Folly*.

Index of Authors

Abeel, Bill, 276
Abel, Milt, 128
Acuff, Ray, 512
Aldiss, Brian, 221
Allan, Ted, 292
Allen, Dennis, 569
Allen, Fred, 531
Allen, Gracie, 217
Allen, Kelly, 34
Allen, Steve, 565
Allen, Woody, 64,
  109, 140, 146,
  167, 205, 620
Andersson, Kent
  G., 536
Anne, Melody, 493
Arapesh (tribal
  saying), 258
Asimov, Isaac, 423
Astor, Lady Nancy,
  285
Auden, W. H., 4
Baez, Joan, 380
Baker, Russell,
  338
Banducci, Sue,
  504
Barnes, Jimmy,
  563
Barr, Roseanne,
  77, 86, 91,
  202, 203, 211,
  213, 226, 312,
  335
Barry, Dave, 88,
  178, 233, 404,
  622
Barry, Lynda, 99
Batiuk, Tom, 396
Beard, Henry
  (Miss Piggy),
  342

Behan, Brendan,
  573, 623
Benchley, Robert,
  570
Berle, Milton, 141
Bernstein, Al, 238
Berra, Yogi, 400,
  529
Bierce, Ambrose,
  291, 516, 519
Blount, Roy, Jr.,
  96
Bokassa I, 373
Bombeck, Erma, 1,
  225, 316
Boosler, Elayne,
  17, 130, 132,
  139
Borge, Victor, 249
Bowie, Louise, 282
Boyington, Greg-
  ory, 545
Brecht, Bertolt,
  104
Briggs, Joe Bob,
  110
Brooks, Mel, 260,
  345
Broun, Heywood,
  218
Brown, A. Whit-
  ney, 330
Brown, John
  Mason, 235
Brown, Larry, 148
Broyard, Anatole,
  426
Bunker, Archie,
  194
Bunyan, John, 346
Burger, Knox, 102,
  422

Burnett, Ivy Comp-
  ton, 196
Burns, George,
  175, 349, 507,
  511
Burrows, Abe, 493
Bush, Barbara,
  180
Butkus, Dick, 392
Butler, Samuel,
  444
Byrne, Robert,
  107, 137, 365,
  547, 594, 610
Cabell, James
  Branch, 43
Caen, Herb, 212,
  459
Caesar, Sid, 460
Carson, Johnny,
  169, 475
Carvey, Dana, 449
Castle, H., 562
Cather, Willa, 63
Chamfort, Nicolas,
  38
Chopin, Dan, 179
Chreene, Tracy,
  after 107
Christ, Jesus, 9
Clancy, Tom, 156
Clay, Andrew
  Dice, 161
Clethan, Al, 328
Clisura, Paul, 411
Coakley, Lazlo,
  428
Cohn, Bruce, 283
Conroy, Pat, 555
Coolidge, Calvin,
  268

Cosby, Bill, 200, 230, 263

Crewe, Quentin, 244

Cronkite, Mrs. Walter, 525

Dahlberg, Edward, 417

Dangerfield, Rodney, 28, 165, 201, 355

Davis, Jim ("Garfield"), 314

DeGeneris, Ellen, 510

Delaney, Shelagh, 100

DeLeon, Inigo, 416

Dent, James, 309

De Vries, Peter, 586

Diamond, Jared, 325

Dietrich, Marlene, 2

Diller, Phyllis, 92

Disraeli, Benjamin, 441

Ditka, Mike, 277

Duck, Daffy, 305

Dugan, Mike, 635

Dumas, Alexandre, 185

Duncan, Sarah Jeannette, 637

Durocher, Leo, 526

Durst, Will, 67, 154, 377

Edison, Thomas, 270

Edwards, Maxine, 493

Ehrenreich, Barbara, 450

Einstein, Albert, 3

Eliot, T. S., 52

Ellington, Duke, 492

Emerson, Ralph Waldo, 391, 530

Ennis, Greg, 395

Ephron, Nora, 82, 448

Erasmus, 625

Evans, Edith, 87

Falk, Dave, 546

Feather, William, 252

Feiffer, Jules, 80

Feller, Bob, 399

Floyd, Raymond, 564

Fox, Michael J., 199

Franklin, Benjamin, 66

Freud, Sigmund, 176, 453

Friedman, Martin, 61

Frost, Robert, 581

Gabor, Zsa Zsa, 193

Galbraith, John Kenneth, 358

Garagiola, Joe, 601

George V, King, 231

Getty, J. Paul, 284

Golas, Thaddeus, 208

Goldman, Emma, 360

Goldwyn, Samuel, 53, 374, 389

Gores, Joe, 508

Gould, Tim, 266

Green, Jean, 559

Greenburg, Dan, 163

Greer, Germaine, 166

Grigsby, Mrs. John, 410

Grimes, John, 584

Grizzard, Lewis, 150, 187, 204, 414, 477

Groening, Matt, 158

Grossman, Lisa, 553

Hackett, Buddy, 242

Hardy, Jeremy, 323

Harms, Jeff, 322

Harrison, Barbara Grizzuti, 446

Hatch, Orrin, 628

Hawn, Goldie, 186

Heavey, Allan, 90

Heller, Joseph, 142

Hemingway, Ernest, 257

Hepburn, Katharine, 506

Hill, Benny, 245

Hirohito, Emperor, 497

Hoest, Bill, 324, 561

Hollander, Nicole ("Sylvia"), 73

Homer, 261

Igo, John, 556

Indik, Marty, 580

James, Henry, after 442

Jefferson, Thomas, 361

Jenkins, Dan, 397

Jim, Strange de, 207, 334

Johnson, Diane, 85

Jones, Jimmy, 537

Jones, N. Wylie, 313

Jong, Erica, 105

Kafka, Franz, 36, 438

Kauffman, Lionel, 509

Kavolik, Maxim, 557

Keate, Stuart, 467

Keillor, Garrison, 227, 476

Kerouac, Jack, 5

Khan, Genghis, 498

Kissinger, Henry, 383

Kobal, John, 153

Koch, Greg, 471

Koestler, Arthur, 11

Kreeft, Peter, 250

Kupcinet, Irv, 13

Ladman, Cathy, 234, 264

Landers, Ann, 106, 182

Lardner, Ring, 168

Larson, Doug, 458

Larson, Gary, 539

Layden, Frank, 401

Lebowitz, Fran, 23, 240, 356, 478

LeCarré, John, 433

Lee, Gypsy Rose, 101, 579

Lee, Susan, 95

Leno, Jay, 31, 133, 382

Leonard, Elmore, 520

Leonard, Joseph, 333

Levant, Oscar, 29, 97

Lewis, Jerry, 386

Lewis, Richard, 136, 138, 143, 214, 351, 479

Lincoln, Abraham, 604

Lloyd George, David, 375

Longworth, Alice Roosevelt, 216

Louis, Joe, 294

Lucaire, Ed, 343

Luther, Martin, 198, 418

Luyah, Hal Lee, 37, 157, 378, 485, 589, 590

Lyon, Bill, 281

MacDonald, Dwight, 306

MacNelly, Jeff, 271

Madonna, 174

Maimonides, 626

Malcolm X, 381

Mankiewicz, Joseph, 486

Mankoff, Robert, 605

Markey, Judy, 78

Marquis, Don, 232, 254, 407

Martin, Lynn, 369

Martin, Steve, 118, 385

Marx, Mrs. Heinrich, 295

Marx, Karl, 524

Mason, Jackie, 474

McCabe, Charles, 353

McClatchy, Jean 310

McFadden, Cyra, 308

McGee, Molly, 72

McGoorty, Danny, 160

McGrory, Mary, 393

McKenzie, Bob, 379

McKissack, Luke, 121

Mein, Tommy, 505

Mellon, Andrew, 126

Mencken, H. L., 384, 424, 445

Midler, Bette, 279, 538, 615

Millar, Margaret, 578

Miller, Arthur, 499

Miller, Jonathan, 502, 630

Milligan, Spike, 296

Minsky, Marvin, 452

Mirachi, Joe, 376

Moe, Doug, 402

Moore, Dudley, 560

Mortimer, John, 311

Mull, Martin, 491, 608

Mundis, Helen, 480

Nachman, Gerald, 317

Nation, Carry, 65

Nealon, Kevin, 30

Nelms, Cynthia, 22, 171, 190, 215, 466

Nesvig, John, 552

Newton, Isaac, 493

Nietzsche, Friedrich, 442, 487, after 567

Norris, Kathleen, 40

Novak, Ralph, 437

O'Connor, Flannery, 239

O'Donoghue,
Michael, 344
O'Rourke, P. J.,
595
Ortman, David E.,
493
Orwell, George,
549
Osage (tribal saying), 39
Osler, Scott, 398
Ovid, 56
Palen, Joe, 588
Parker, Dorothy,
69, 112, 302
Parker, Tom, 331
Pascal, Blaise, 436
Patinkin, Mark,
117
Paulsen, Pat, 364,
371
Péguy, Charles,
262
Pellevé, Robert,
Marquis de
Flers, 359
Penaranda,
Enrique
(mother of), 372
Philips, Emo, 32,
108, 229, 368
Phillips, Jeanne,
278
Picasso, Pablo,
484
Piggy, Miss (Henry
Beard), 342
Pitzer, Gloria, 463
Plath, Sylvia, 431
Plato, 567
Poundstone, Paula,
272, 303, 523
Priestley, J.B., 183
Pritchard,
Michael, 503,
521, 606
Proverb (Chinese),
540

Proverb (Irish), 54
Proverb (Japanese), 634
Proverb (Jewish),
543
Proverb (Portuguese), 513
Proverb (Russian),
12
Proverb (Spanish),
576
Prusick, A. L., 26
Python, Monty,
413
Qualley, Roy, 319
Quitard, 184
Rabelais, 527
Radner, Gilda, 612
Randi, James, 468
Rather, Dan, 451,
455
Renard, Jules, 434
Renko, Arkady,
470
Restivo, Joe, 515
Richardson,
Ralph, 14
Richler, Mordecai,
8
Richman, Susan
602
Rivers, Joan, 84,
124
Rivkin, Steven, 49
Robbins, Harold,
after 257
Robbins, Tom, 596
Rockefeller, John
D., 301
Rodgers, Joni, 113
Rodriguez, Chi
Chi, 315
Rogers, Will, 18,
93, 274
Rooney, Andy, 454
Rooney, Mickey,
197
Ross, Neila, 337

Ross, Stanley
Ralph, 19, 269,
494, 618
Rousseau, Jean-
Jacques, 443
Rubenstein,
Arthur, 21
Rubin, Bob, 129
Rudner, Rita, 111,
119, 243, 617
Russell, Bertrand,
20
Russell, Mark,
362, 456
Santayana, George,
24
Savastio, Richard,
419
Sayers, Dorothy,
162
Schmidt,
Gretchen, 421
Schoenstein,
Ralph (grandfather of), 248
Schulz, Charles
("Peanuts"),
47, 611
Scott, Howard, 275
Seinfeld, Jerry,
253, 514
Seneca, 603
Seuss, Dr., 222
Shandling, Garry,
120, 149, 159,
164, 170, 172,
609
Sharp, Tom, 94
Shaw, George
Bernard, 241,
500
Shazer, George de,
290
Sherman, Allan,
339
Simborg, Philip J.,
144, 298
Simon, Neil, 145

Simpson, Martha, 420

Sinatra, Frank, 354

Singer, Isaac Bashevis, 48

Skelton, Red, 191, 632

Smerling, Lisa, 554

Smirnoff, Yakov, 481

Smith, Margaret, 98, 265

Smith, Martin Cruz, 415

Snow, Carrie, 173

Spander, Art, 42

Spendlove, Scott, 237

Stark, Jim, 103

Stein, Gertrude, 6

Stein, Ruthie, 81

Steinem, Gloria, 71, 83, 600

Stevenson, Adlai, 366

Stevenson, Robert Louis, 192

Stoppard, Tom, 489, 572

Swanson, Gloria, 462

Talleyrand-Perigord, Charles Maurice de, 256

Taylor, Liz, 447

Tchaikovsky, Peter Ilyich, 488

Temple, Shirley, 246

Tenuta, Judy, 115, 116

Thomas, Joseph A., 307

Toffler, Alvin, 259

Tolstoy, Leo, after 442, after 568

Tomlin, Lily, 10, 45, 51

Trevino, Lee, 189, 403

Trillin, Calvin, 472, 473, 541, 550, 616

Tuchman, Barbara, 496

Twain, Mark, 55, 219, 558

Ullman, Tracey, 89

Upham, Gladys, 76

Valéry, Paul, 357

Van Doren, Mamie, 125

Vass, Susan, 195

Vermeil, Louis, 548

Vidal, Gore, 387, 439

Vision, Gerald, 370

Voltaire, 352

Wagner, Jane, 10, 45, 51

Walker, Laura, 25

Walters, Roy W., 41

Warren, Earl, 33

Waterhouse, Keith, 155

Watterson, Bill, 598

Weldon, Fay, 68

Welles, Orson, 341

Wells, H. G, 432

Wentz-Daly, Patricia, 388

West, Mae, 70, 114, 151, 152, 501

West, Rebecca, 74

White, E. B., 255

Whitehorn, Katherine, 300

Whitman, Walt, 430

Wieder, Robert S., 299

Wilde, Oscar, after 442, 592

Williams, Danny, 131

Williams, Robin, 482, 518, 619

Wilmot, John, Earl of Rochester, 224

Wilson, Tom ("Ziggy"), 46, 326, 348

Winfrey, Oprah, 318

Winston, Liz, 464

Woollcott, Alexander, 320, 461, 633

Wright, Steven, 60, 220, 228, 363, 412, 551, 585, 597, 607

Yeats, William Butler, 79

Young, Brigham, 75

Youngman, Henny, 304, 350, 408

Zappa, Frank, 483

Zellerbach, Merla, 327

Zola, Emile, 429

Index of Subjects and Key Words

Abortion, 30, 31
Abraham, 237
Abstinence, 102
Accomplice, 274
Additives, 333
Adopted, 60
Adultery, 589
Adults, 222
Age, old, 503–515
Aging, 546
Airport, 265
Akron, 473
Alimony, 298
Allowance, 238
Alzheimer's (disease), 10
Amateur, 259
Ambition, 45
America, 453–458
Analyst, 351
Anchorman, 451
Anchovy, 321
Animals, 107, 330
Anna Karenina, after 442
Answer, 6
Ants, 486
Apartment, 607
Ape, 420
Aphrodisiac, 155
Apple tree, 492
Arapesh, 258
Argument, 264
Art, 483
Asexual, 147
Astrology, 626
Athletic, 411
Atom bombs, 497
Attraction, 121
Audibles, 395
Author, after 257, 435

Autobiography, 446–447
Autograph, 246
Average, 61, 583
Aviation, 489
Ax, 438
Babies, 21–220
Baby, 89
Bach, Johann Sebastian, 490
Bad writing, 419–421
Bake, 324
Bald, 94, 348
Ballet class, 617
Banana, 553
Bangladesh, 312
Bank, 292
Bank account, 303
Banking, 171
Base, 88
Baseball, 88, 393, 397, 401
Basketball, 401
Batteries, 73, 596
Beach, 220
Beauty, 219
Bed, 84, 162–163, 172
Bed, vibrating, 153
Bedroom, 154
Beethoven, Ludwig van, 489
Beheaded, 232
Belief, 549
Bet, 537
Betting, 408
Bible, 8
Bibles, 193
Biographers, 446
Bird, 293

Birth, 24, 90, 124, 216, 624
Birth control, 128
Bisexual, 109
Bitch, 27
Bitter, 53
Blind, 188
Blind alley, 591
Blondes, 123–125, 631
Blood, 301
Bloomers, 160
Boar, 343
Bob, 584
Body, 347
Boil, 138
Bolivia, 372
Bonds, 126
Books, 418, 433, 441, 443–444
Bore, 383, 391
Boredom, 158, 545
Boss, 273
Bouillon cubes, 433
Bouquet, 92
Bowling, 410
Bowling shirts, 471
Boy, 104
Boyfriend, 119
Bracelet, charm, 316
Brahms, Johannes, 488
Brain, 368
Brautigan, Richard, 428
Braves, 394
Break up, 118
Breakfast, 113
Breakfast, continental, 342

Breed, 169, 557–558
Brezhnev, Leonid, 482
British, 564
British public, 592
Broken homes, 586
Buffalo, 469
Bulls, 169
Buried, 66
Burps, 203
Bus, 129
Bush, George, 364
Busload, 289
Butt, 267
Button, 179
California, 462
Camel, 552
Campaign slogan, 371
Canada, 467
Canadians, 269
Canine world, 428
Cannibals, 59, 329
Capital punishment, 628
Car, 67
Career, 71, 174, 271
Carrots, 340
Cars, 458
Cat, 412–413
Catholic wedding, 179
Cattle breeding, 169
Celebrity, 383
Chains, 185
Chains, fried, 345
Change, 611
Chasm, 540
Cheating, 118
Chickens, 502
Child, 79, 223, 228
Child raising, 224

Children, 111, 180, 221–224, 239, 243, 252, 258, 260, 509, 558
Chinese food, 326–327
Chips, 536
Christmas, 245, 250–251
Churches, 16
Churchill, Winston, 353
Cigar, 176
Cigar, exploding, 99
Cigar holder, 175
Circumcision, 375
Civil servant, 571
Clerk, 312
Cliff, 289
Clocks, 159
Clothes, 183, 609
Clothes, degrading, 344
Coach, 402
Cognac, 353
Cohabitation, 196
Collateral, 73
College, 577
Columnist, 414
Comfort, 79
Committee, 531
Common people, 442
Complainers, 593
Computer, 59
Condom, 129–134
Condom Week, 133
Confidence, 610
Confusion, 580
Conrad Hilton, 193
Conscience, 574
Consciousness, 356
Consequences, 305

Contempt, 80, 557
Conversationalist, 427
Conversations, 578
Corporation, 275
Corpses, 221
Corsets, 160
Country, 405
Cow, 76
Cows, 169
Creamed corn, 322
Creative people, 462
Credit cards, 304
Crime, 292
Criminal, 275
Critic, 486
Cronkite, Mrs. Walter, 525
Crucifixion, 251
Crumbs, 307
Curiosity, 412
Dad, 362
Dark, 123
Darkroom, 606
Darwin, 60
Dating, 111, 113–117, 120, 178
Dawn, 46, 602
Dead, 182
Dead Sea, 511
Death, 24, 516–528
Debt, 299
December, 248
Deception, 590
Degrading, 344
Degrees, 533
Deli, 199
Democracy, 359
Democrat, 368
Denominations, 16
Department store, 246
Desires, 109
Devils, 65
Die, 527, 543, 576
Diets, 313, 315, 317

Digging, 41
Digital watch, 572
Dinner, 240
Diplomacy, 532
Disappointment, 29
Discomfort, 600
Dishes, 84
Disillusionment, 42
Divorce, 111, 178, 189, 193
Doctor, 140, 350, 423, 499
Dog-eat-dog, 34
Doggerel, 428
Dogma, 544
Dogs, 107, 508
Dork, 78
Dough, 307
Draft, 432
Dreams, 203
Drink, 79, 308, 354
Drowning, 290
Drugs, 127, 356
Duck, 150
Duck feathers, 150
Dumb people, 603
Duplicates, 607
Dutch treat, 82
Duty, 162
Early worm, 556
Earth, 4, 7
Easy Street, 591
Eat, 311, 528
Eat and run, 337
Editing, 432
Editor, 435
Elbows, 92
Eloquence, 548
Elvis, 13
Empty, 143
Encyclopedia, 400
Enemy, 296
England, 534
English, 474
English language, 570

Environment, 569
Erogenous zones, 142
Essentials, 190
Eternity, 309
Evangelists (television), 19
Evil, 451
Evils, 122
Evolution, 60
Example, 241
Exercise, 528
Expiration dates, 609
Explosives, 50
Eyebrow, 321
Eye-opener, 188
Failure, 29, 277–278
Falcons, 394
Fame, 382
Familiarity, 557
Family, 253, 256
Family tree, 39
Fantasy, 143
Farming, 325
Fast food, 334
Fast forward, 179
Fat, 335, 348
Father, 80, 223, 231, 255, 261–262
Fattening, 320
Fear, 218, 230, 606
Feathers, 150
Feces, 612
Feet, 618
Female, 564
Feminism, 82
Fender, 620
Fetus, 31, 233
Fiction, 55, after 442
Fight, 206
Figure, 151
Financial planners, 415

First Amendment, 550
First base, 160
Fish, 323
Fishing, 407
Flies, 562
Florida, 468, 514
Flower, 513, 563
Flowers, 72
Fly ball, 88
Flying, 545
Flynn, Errol, 525
Folk music, 491
Food, 227, 308, 326
Food chain, 115
Fools, 567
Football, 110, 392, 396
Ford, Gerald, 364
Foreigner, 474
Foreskin, 375
Forgiveness, 576
Formula, 284
Fortress, 184
Fortune, 283
Fortune cookie, 326–327
Forty, 244
Foul ball, 399
Foundation, 306
Fox, 107
Fraud, 377
Free will, 37
Friction, 148
Friend, 229
Friends, 136, 296
Fruit flies, 553
Fruits, 314
Fry, 324
Fuchsia, 563
Fun, 252–253
Funeral, 521
Funeral home, 520
Funerals, 517, 521
Funny, 500–501
Future, 44
Gambling, 537

Garden, 636
Garters, 160
Gene pool, 379
Genius, 386
Gentiles, 248, 619
Gentlemen,
    125–126, 162
Geriatric ward,
    311
Germans, 494
Giant snail, 166
Gigolo, 81
Girdles, 160
Girl, 104
Girlfriend, 81
*Glass Menagerie,
    The*, 234
Glasses, 585
God, 1, 10–13,
    101, 112, 425
Golden Blond, 631
Government, 360
Government pro-
    gram, 369
Grandmother, 510
Grandmother's
    brain, 368
Grandparent, 254
Grapefruit, 315
Grave, 519
Gravity, 614
Greatness, 157
Green Bay, 471
Grindstone, 367
Groin, 617
Grudges, 538
Gulf Stream, 623
Gum, 108, 134
Hair, 94, 96
Haircut, 95
Hall of Fame, 526
Hands, 536
Hanukkah, 248
Happiness, 201
Happy, 182, 201
Harlots, 79
Hat, 595
Hate, 98
Head of state, 373

Headache, 165
Headlines, 390
Health, 346, 512
Hearing, 575
Heaven, 318
Hegel, 353
Hell, 26, 464
Hemingway,
    Ernest, after
    257
Heredity, 569
Hero, 391
Herring barrel,
    106
Hick town, 461
High explosives,
    50
High school, 616
Hilton, Conrad,
    193
History, 114
Hoe, 636
Holding company,
    274
Hole, 41
Hollywood, 31
Home, 399
Homicide, 323
Honesty, 56
Horny, 145
Horse, 293, 408
Horse racing, 18,
    408
Hospital, 218
House, 204
Housecleaning,
    84, 211
Housewife, 213
Housework, 84
Houston, 276
Humanitarians,
    329
Humankind, 52
Humor, 8, 502
Hunch, 51
Hungry, 326
Hurricane, 89
Husband, 163,
    194, 202, 634

Hydroelectric
    power, 132
Idiots, 74
Illegal, 320
Illusion, 167
Imaginary friend,
    229
Immoral, 320
Immortality, 526
Importance, 637
Inch, 77
Indifference, 5
Infant, 88
Infanticide, 373
Infidelity, 118
Ingredients, 333
Intellectuals, 549
Intercourse, 137,
    143
International
    House of Pan-
    cakes, 272
Intestines, 131
Ireland, 427, 623
Irving, Washing-
    ton, 565
Isms, 370
James, Henry,
    after 442
January, 340
Japan, 497
Japanese, 494
Jefferson, Thomas,
    362
Jehovah, 8
Jesus, 14–15, 17,
    112
Jew, 630
Jewish, 15, 245
Jewish woman,
    199
JFK, 440
Job application,
    627
Jobs, 90, 268, 269,
    271
Johnny Wadd, 148
Joy, 485

Judge and jury, 444
Justice, 263
Kansas, 322
Kapp, Joe, 395
Karma, 544
Keaton, Diane, 388
Kennedy, John Fitzgerald, 440
Keys, car, 632
Khadafy, Muamar, 622
Kids, 257
Kinky, 113, 149–150
Kissed, 180
Kiwi, 421
Knife, 435
Koran, 456
Lab assistants, 288
Labor Day weekend, 458
Laid, 139, 148
Last words, 524
Laugh, 9, 154
Laughing, 503
Lavender and cream, 396
Lawsuit, 291
Lawyers, 286–290
Leather, 32
Leroy, 561
Letter, 436
Lewis, Jerry, 386
Liars, 407
Liberals, 338
Lies, 57
Life, 21–25, 27, 30–31, 35, 47, 50, 239, 486
Life everlasting, 369
Lightning, 403
Listened, 268
Litella, Emily, 612
Litigation, 516
Live out loud, 429

Living, cost of, 40, 293
Living together, 196
Loneliness, 54
Lonesome, 97
Look, 168
Lose, 409
Loser, 281
Love, 99–101, 146, 159, 188, 287
Lovemaking, 167, 170
Lover, 158
Lucy and Linus, 611
Luftwaffe, 353
Lunatics, 74
Lunch, 341
Macramé, 541
Maiden name, 303
Man, 75–77, 87, 111, 122
Maps, 77
Marriage, 71, 119, 177–178, 180, 182–186, 192, 194, 197, 200, 205, 206
Marriage chains, 185
Married, 113, 156, 181
Marx, Karl, 295
Masturbation, 136, 137
Mayonnaise, 619
Meat, 323, 328, 331
Medical student, 519
Medicine, 352
Meek, 7
Memory, 574
Men, 65–69, 73–77, 79, 83, 86, 87, 105, 111, 113, 122, 191

Menace, 75
Mets, 456
Mexican, 15
Mexicans, 269
Midas, 554
Middle age, 252
Middle management 266
Milk Bone shorts, 34
Millionaire, 302
Mime, 550–551
Miracle, 200
Mirror, 172
Miscalculations, 496
Miss Piggy, 342–343
Missionaries, 18
Mistakes, 191
Mom, 212
Money, 178, 256, 294, 296–297, 300
Mongongo nuts, 325
Monogamous, 207, 208
Monogamy, 208, 209
Monologues, 578
Monotonous, 208
Month, 91
Mother, 70, 121, 214, 226
Mouth, 618
Mouth, open, 366
Moved, 158
Movie, 433
Mr. Right, 139
Muffler, 554
Mule, 93
Murder, 323
Music, 486–493
Mutual orgasms, 141
Nature, 64
Nebraska, 464
Necessity, 121

Negatives, 606
Negro, 587
Neighbors, 242, 625
Nerves, 294
New Jersey, 472, 478–479
New Year's Eve, 479
New York City, 474–478
New York Times Book Review, The, 439
Nice guys, 422
Nietzsche, Friedrich, after 442, 568, after 568
Noah, 562
Nonsense, 441
Nonviolence, 380–381
Norfolk, 406
Northern, 130
Nose, 219, 227
Novelist, 415
Number One, 28
Number Two, 28
Nuts, 314
Nymphomaniac, 414
Oat bin, 93
Object lesson, 241
Oceans, 445
Octopus, 338
Odds, 408
Offenbach, Jacques, 490
Oil, 284
Old age, 175, 311
Olive, 355
One-iron, 403
One-night stand, 161
Only child, 228
Operation, 350
Optical illusion, 167

Optimist, 43–44
Oral sex, 166
Orgasm, 140–141
Osage saying, 39
Outside, 202
Oxen, 433
Oysters, 164
Painter, 417
Palm Springs University, 533
Pantaloons, 160
Parade, 133
Paranoia, 555
Parenthood, 259
Parents, 230, 242, 254, 263, 264, 265, 282
Passion, 432
Patriotism, 341
Pavlov, Ivan, 582
Pear, 387
Pedestrian, 577
Pedestrians, 463
Penalty, 171, 285
Penny saved, 378
People, 98
People, kinds of, 594
Perfection, 627
Permission, 588
Personality, 129
Personals, 110
Perverted sex, 150
Pessimist, 43
Philosophy, 635
Physics lesson, 62
Piano, 216
Picnic, 486
Pig, 291, 310
Pigs, 107
Pigtails, 198
Pillow, 198
Plants, 330
Plastic surgeon, 92
Plastic surgery, 110, 304
Plato, 567
Playpen, 225
PMS (premenstrual syndrome), 91

Poetry, 428
Point, 154
Policeman, 274, 573
Politician, 366
Politics, 357–358
Pomp, 534
Pool shooting, 175
Poor, 182, 543
Pope, 419
Porn star, 148
Posterity, 492
Potato, baked, 318
Potato pancakes, 353
Power, 83
Praise, 575, 625
Pray, 463
Predictions, 49
Pregnant, 215
prejudices, 547
Prescription, 585
President, 565
Prettier, 122
Printing, 445
Printouts, 454
Problems, 50, 605
Projector and slides, 480
Promising young man, 365
Pro-nuclear, 98
Proof, 86
Prospector, 160
Prostitutes, 276
Prostitution, 633
Psychiatrist, 351
Puberty, 233
Public, 361
Publicity, 604
Punishment, 33
Puppies, 215
Pusher, 127
Quarter, 363
Quarterback, 395
Queen Elizabeth, 615
Quicksand, 228
Quotable, 402

Quote, 599
Quotes, 530
Race horses, 612
Radio station, 635
Rat, 324
Rats, 288
Reader, 448–449
Reality, 51–52
Rear-view mirror, 560
Reason, 235
Reasoning, 235–236
Reclining chair, 203
Record, 145
Religion, 369
Repair, 457
Reservoir, 132
Resignation, 63
Restaurant, 344
Revenge, 251
Rich, 182, 305, 521, 543
Ring, 492
River, 61
Rob, 292
Robbins, Harold, after 257
Robe, 149
Rock star, 177
Rooftops, 430
Roosevelt, Franklin, 374
Rope, 175
Roses, 245
Rules 85, 270, 590
Russia, 481
Rye, 339
Sacrifice, 237
Safety device, 560
Salami, 339
Samuel, Herbert, 375
Sandbox, 228
Sandwich, 339
Sanity, 592
Santa Claus, 246–247, 249

Sartre, Jean-Paul, 568
Sausage, 291
Scarface, 299
Sea, frozen, 438
Sears, 211
Secret, 190
Self-made man, 561
Senator, 376
Sewers, 476
Sex, 127, 135, 138, 143, 146, 155–156, 164, 166, 171, 175
Sexual performance, 164
Sheep, 12, 131
Sheep intestines, 131
Shepherd, 12
Shields, Brooke, 482
Shoe, 437
Shoes, 507
Shooting pool, 175
Short, 348
Shut up, 605
Sick, 21, 349
Silencer, 551
Sin, 20, 523
Sincerity, 535
Singles bars, 108
Singles jungle, 107
Six dozen, 601
Skiing, 404–405
Skunk, 107, 604
Sleeping, 144
Slides, 480
Slugs, 107
Smile, 613
Smoke, 99, 332
Smoking, 566
Snail, 166
Snakes, 107
Sneezing, 622
Snub, 285
Society, 13

Soldiers, 495
Somebody, 45
Son, 261–262
Song titles, 492
Sorry, 298
Sour, 53
Sour dough, 493
Southern California, 269
Soviet jewelry, 612
Space, 202
Spade, 376
Spaghetti, 539
Spirit, 192
Spite, 205
Spitting, 477
Sport, good, 409
Spouse, 190
Standards, 371
Starve, 336
State Farm, 141
Stein, Gertrude, 387
Steinbrenner, George, 398
Step-ins, 160
Stockings, 160
Stomach, 144
Stool, 108
Stork, 70
Strangers, 206
Straps, 32
Strife, 54
Stupidity, 3, 69, 535
Submerged, 62
Subways, 476
Succeed, 281
Success, 277–280, 282, 284–285, 583
Suicide, 116, 469
Sun, 39
Supreme being, 2
Surgeon, 92
Surrogate mother, 17
Swallow, 38
Swan, 210

Synonymous, 208
System, 244
Tabasco sauce, 195
Talent, 434
Talk, 217, 286
Tastes good, 319
Taxes, 523
Teenagers, 236
Telephone, 11, 62, 112, 492
Television, 385, 450, 452
Tempura, 73
Ten-foot pole, 152
Tennis ball machine, 149
Tension, 146
Terror, 545
Texan, 465–466
Thanksgiving, 250
Theories, 224
Therapy, 351, 388
Thinner, 312
Throat, 435
Throw up, 180, 477
Ticking, 117
Time, 553, 598
Toad, 38
Toast, 332
Tolstoy, Leo, after 442
Torture, 25, 373
Toys, 596
Traffic, 455
Tragedy, 289
Transom, 216
Traveling, 456
Trees, 63
Trigger finger, 499
Trout, 106
Truffles, 310
Truth, 55–58, 273, 500
Tupperware, 234
Turkey, 309

Turn of the century, 621
Twentieth century, 48
Two, 293
Two heads, 559
Type, 423
Ugly, 93
Umbrella, 613
United States, 458
Universe, 3
Unpublished writing, 431
Upper crust, 307
Urinate, 67
Urine sample, 355
Vacation, 220, 480
Vacuum cleaner, 211
Vatican 17, 200
Vegetarian, 328–329
Vegetarian restaurant, 331
Vibrating bed, 153
Violence, 380, 498
Violets, 245
Violins, 612
Virgin, 173
Virginia, 406
Virginity, 174
Virgins, 276
Virtue, 346
Visit, 249
Voice, 153
Voters, 377
Wadd, Johnny, 148
Waffle, 168
Wages, 523
Wagnerian love-death, 353.
War, 255, 352, 496
War and Peace, after 442
War movies, 494
Washington, George, 363
Wasms, 370

Wasserman, 103
Water, shoveling, 468
Wedding, 179
Weekends, 111
Weep, 9
West, Mae, 151–153
Whole hog, 630
Widowhood, 83
Wife, 72, 79, 141, 165, 194, 201
Wildflowers, 389
Will, 527
Windshield, 522, 632
Winter, 513
Wise men, 567
Withdrawal, 171
Wits, 542
Wolves, 107
Woman, 81, 85–88, 90–91, 114, 118, 130, 199, 629
Work, 272, 629
World, 36, 49
World War II, 353, 497
Wrestlemania, 401
Writer, 110
Writers, 424, 426
Writer's block, 416
Writer's cramp, 416
Writing, 418, 422–425, 433–434
Wrong, 194
X rays, 350
Yacht, 525
Yankees, 398
Yawp, 430
Youngstown, 473
Youth, 238
Yugoslavia, 345
Zip code, 608
Zones, 142
Zoo, 539